EDUCATION, POLITICS, AN

Series Editors:
Henry A. Giroux, McMaster University
Susan Searls Giroux, McMaster University

Within the last three decades, education as a political, moral, and ideological practice has become central to rethinking not only the role of public and higher education, but also the emergence of pedagogical sites outside of the schools—which include but are not limited to the Internet, television, film, magazines, and the media of print culture. Education as both a form of schooling and public pedagogy reaches into every aspect of political, economic, and social life. What is particularly important in this highly interdisciplinary and politically nuanced view of education are a number of issues that now connect learning to social change, the operations of democratic public life, and the formation of critically engaged individual and social agents. At the center of this series will be questions regarding what young people, adults, academics, artists, and cultural workers need to know to be able to live in an inclusive and just democracy and what it would mean to develop institutional capacities to reintroduce politics and public commitment into everyday life. Books in this series aim to play a vital role in rethinking the entire project of the related themes of politics, democratic struggles, and critical education within the global public sphere.

SERIES EDITORS:

Henry A. Giroux holds the Global TV Network Chair in English and Cultural Studies at McMaster University in Canada. He is on the editorial and advisory boards of numerous national and international scholarly journals. Professor Giroux was selected as a Kappa Delta Pi Laureate in 1998 and as the recipient of a Getty Research Institute Visiting Scholar Award in 1999. He was the recipient of the Hooker Distinguished Professor Award in 2001. He received an Honorary Doctorate of Letters from Memorial University of Newfoundland in 2005. His most recent books include *Take Back Higher Education* (coauthored with Susan Searls Giroux, 2006); *America on the Edge* (2006); *Beyond the Spectacle of Terrorism* (2006); *Stormy Weather: Katrina and the Politics of Disposability* (2006); *The University in Chains: Confronting the Military-Industrial-Academic Complex* (2007), and *Against the Terror of Neoliberalism: Politics Beyond the Age of Greed* (2008).

Susan Searls Giroux is associate professor of English and Cultural Studies at McMaster University. Her most recent books include *The Theory Toolbox* (coauthored with Jeff Nealon, 2004); *Take Back Higher Education* (coauthored with Henry A. Giroux, 2006); and *Between Race*

and Reason: Violence, Intellectual Responsibility, and the University to Come (2010). Professor Giroux is also the Managing Editor of *The Review of Education, Pedagogy, and Cultural Studies.*

Critical Pedagogy in Uncertain Times: Hope and Possibilities
Edited by Sheila L. Macrine

The Gift of Education: Public Education and Venture Philanthropy
Kenneth J. Saltman

Feminist Theory in Pursuit of the Public: Women and the "Re-Privatization" of Labor
Robin Truth Goodman

Hollywood's Exploited: Public Pedagogy, Corporate Movies, and Cultural Crisis
Edited by Benjamin Frymer, Tony Kashani, Anthony J. Nocella, II, and Richard Van Heertum; with a Foreword by Lawrence Grossberg

Education out of Bounds: Reimagining Cultural Studies for a Posthuman Age
Tyson E. Lewis and Richard Kahn

Academic Freedom in the Post-9/11 Era
Edited by Edward J. Carvalho and David B. Downing

Educating Youth for a World beyond Violence: A Pedagogy for Peace
H. Svi Shapiro

Rituals and Student Identity in Education: Ritual Critique for a New Pedagogy

Richard A. Quantz with Terry O'Connor and Peter Magolda
Citizen Youth: Culture, Activism, and Agency in a Neoliberal Era
Jacqueline Kennelly

Conflicts in Curriculum Theory: Challenging Hegemonic Epistemologies
João M. Paraskeva; Foreword by Donaldo Macedo

Sport, Spectacle, and NASCAR Nation: Consumption and the Cultural Politics of Neoliberalism
Joshua I. Newman and Michael D. Giardina

America According to Colbert: Satire as Public Pedagogy
Sophia A. McClennen

Immigration and the Challenge of Education: A Social Drama Analysis in South Central Los Angeles
Nathalia E. Jaramillo

Immigration and the Challenge of Education

A Social Drama Analysis in South Central Los Angeles

Nathalia E. Jaramillo

palgrave
macmillan

IMMIGRATION AND THE CHALLENGE OF EDUCATION
Copyright © Nathalia E. Jaramillo, 2012.

First published in 2012 by
PALGRAVE MACMILLAN®
in the United States—a division of St. Martin's Press LLC,
175 Fifth Avenue, New York, NY 10010.

Where this book is distributed in the UK, Europe and the rest of the world,
this is by Palgrave Macmillan, a division of Macmillan Publishers Limited,
registered in England, company number 785998, of Houndmills,
Basingstoke, Hampshire RG21 6XS.

Palgrave Macmillan is the global academic imprint of the above companies
and has companies and representatives throughout the world.

Palgrave® and Macmillan® are registered trademarks in the United States,
the United Kingdom, Europe and other countries.

HC ISBN 978–0–230–33826–5
PBK ISBN 978–0–230–33827–2

Library of Congress Cataloging-in-Publication Data

Jaramillo, Nathalia E.
    Immigration and the challenge of education : a social drama analysis in
south central Los Angeles / Nathalia E. Jaramillo.
        p. cm. —(Education, politics, and public life)
    Includes bibliographical references.
    ISBN 978–0–230–33826–5—
    ISBN 978–0–230–33827–2
        1. Children of immigrants—Education—California—Los Angeles—
Case studies. 2. Latin Americans—Education—California—Los Angeles—
Case studies. 3. Children of immigrants—California—Los Angeles—
Social conditions—Case studies. 4. Latin Americans—California—Los Angeles—
Social conditions—Case studies. 5. Community and school—California—
Los Angeles—Case studies. I. Title.

LC3746.5.C2J37 2012
371.826′912079494—dc23   2011024351

A catalogue record of the book is available from the British Library.

Design by Newgen Imaging Systems (P) Ltd., Chennai, India.

First edition: January 2012

10 9 8 7 6 5 4 3 2 1

Printed in the United States of America.

*To my mother, Gloria; my nana, Helena; and
to the memory of my father, Juan.*

CONTENTS

List of Illustrations   ix

Introduction: The Social Drama of Looking South   xi

Acknowledgments   xxxiii

1   Setting the Stage: The School-Community Borderland   1

2   The Pedagogy of the Burro   29

3   The Breach   47

4   Inner Theater: Social Drama as Shifting Consciousness   79

5   Antistructure: Counterpoints to Pedagogy of the Burro   97

6   Revolutionary Social Drama: Decolonial Pedagogical Processes   121

Notes   143

Bibliography   147

Index   157

ILLUSTRATIONS

FIGURES

1.1	Walking to school	13
5.1	Side gate entrance	106
6.1	Future pathways	140

TABLE

3.1	Seven Stages of Consciousness	67

INTRODUCTION: THE SOCIAL DRAMA OF LOOKING SOUTH

I began writing this book after a two-year appointment as a grant administrator in an elementary school designated by the state of California as "in need of improvement" and on a short leash to meet its "adequate yearly progress" benchmarks. At the time, California was far from bankrupt, reaping the benefits of an overinflated housing market and a consumer "bubble" dependent upon superfluous financial capital. The school principal asked me to administer state-level funds amounting to over 800,000 dollars to improve the academic achievement of a 2,000-student population. Within six months, I began working with the mothers of the community, channeling less than 3 percent of the monies toward activities geared for increased family participation in the school's governance and curricular activities. What transpired, however, had less to do with my efforts to bring the community into the school (I firmly believed, and still do, that participatory schooling structures can produce meaningful education) and more to do with the mothers' commitment to their children and to their developing social and political consciousness. *Immigration and the Challenge of Education: A Social Drama Analysis in South Central Los Angeles* chronicles these various school and community processes. It is simultaneously a commentary on the "challenges" that border crossing presents to institutional settings and community dynamics, as well as an anthropological and pedagogical look into how people achieve a change in consciousness with a change in activity. For the purposes of this book, I refer to the school as Mirasur, a Spanish alias whose English translation means "looking south." My observations and understandings of the school, the community, and the mothers' actions that unsettled the tempo and rituality of school life reveal what I refer to as the social drama of Mirasur (looking south).

Mirasur is located in the city formally called South Central Los Angeles, which is now referred to as "Central" Los Angeles instead.

Ever since the police beating of Rodney King on the city's streets that ultimately led to three days of rioting in 1992 (rioting that should be seen in the context of a larger uprising), the area has undergone a cosmetic makeover; removing "South" from its designation is intended to highlight a refurbished city—a restored space—with newer commercial shopping centers flecked against the aging liquor stores, markets, and tire repair shops that became victims to the spectacle of looting, fire, and protest during the upheaval. Behind the Starbucks-polished facades found at several major crossways lie an expansive network of families, public and religious institutions, and social artifacts of trans/intra-national migrations that challenge one-dimensional understandings of the city's significance for how we interact within evolving economies of cultural, ethnic, racial, and sexual markets of production and exchange. After becoming familiar with the school's institutional policies and curricular initiatives as well as the interactions among faculty and the wider community, it became increasingly evident that the city and its peoples' histories, dynamism, and conflicts uniquely shaped the everyday activities and relations that characterized school life. My work as an educator was often overshadowed by the clear displays of authoritarianism, violence, and discrimination against members of the school community, displays that referenced a much deeper historical account of how aggrieved groups and individuals came to relate to one another within the confines of Central Los Angeles. In my initial efforts to rescript the relationship between the school and the community, I attempted to reach out to the mothers of Mirasur, women whose diasporic treks from the barrios of Latin America to the neighborhoods of the City of Angels had brought them together in a hybrid city space. This city was a liminal space of singular intensities, at times toxic and dystopian but always rich with creative and transformative possibilities. Here the mothers wrestled with the imposition of new identities, resisting the coloniality of being the "Other" not only to their new "hosts" but to themselves and the histories, experiences, and collective memories that defined the core constructs of their agency.

LOOKING SOUTH

The social drama of Mirasur (looking south) is grounded in the historical, geopolitical, and epistemic relations between social actors in a community setting in South Central Los Angeles. A milieu, or setting, in the words of Ron Eyerman, "can provide or deprive the protagonists of a necessary symbolic arsenal" (2008, 22). The protagonists of the social drama of Mirasur are women of varying social statuses from the South who negotiate their lives in a social universe that is both symbolic and material. They are (among others) Mexicana, Guatelmalteca, Nicaraguense, and Hondurenses living in the United States with undisclosed immigration status. They represent a majority of the schoolchildren's families, who are also of "Southern" descent, from hybrid and mixed genealogies that can most certainly be traced outside the U.S. border. The women's voices, experiences, actions, and the ways in which their bodies express *inter and intra*-actions between and among school faculty and staff form the central tropes from which the social drama of Mirasur is narrated. Specifically, the main protagonist of this social drama is a woman by the name of Maria Lourdes Jimenez. This book chronicles Maria's movement(s) across time and space in the wider community and institutional setting of Mirasur. Through often competing social dramas—what I later refer to as the institutional drama of Mirasur and the intrapersonal drama of shifting consciousness—Maria and the mothers' actions and sociopolitical consciousness reveal much more beyond the institutional precincts of the school itself. Their struggles and activity constitute the major themes—mise-en-scéne—of this book and speak to wider debates over national identity, tradition, institutional authority and authoritarianism, history and memory, racism and sexism, and hope and possibility. The notion of "looking south" is very much an act of examining how we look south; that is, toward and with the subjects and the objects of our ethnographic gaze. It is as much about how we position ourselves in the act of looking, as it is the act of looking itself. In this way the social drama of "looking south" becomes a genealogy of the act of looking. I want to make the act of looking south a transgressive act, not the "looking south" of the dominant narratives of seeing that view the South as peripheral or epiphenomenal to the master histories of the North. Neither is this "looking south" an attempt to validate the humanity of those whose humanity has been questioned, even relegated to the status of Caliban in the islands of the colonial imagination. Such an act of looking in relation to the subject of the North would, as Lewis Gordon notes, "...be done at the price of a standard that affirms their subhumanity" (2008, 154). "Their," in this case, would be the peoples who reside south of the U.S. border. The looking south of Mirasur interrogates the dominant tropes and epistemes that condition how we examine and exert our agency within this modern world that prima facie separates us as people from either the North or the South, and nowhere in-between.

IMMIGRATION WOMB-POLITICS

At the time of this writing, immigration reform is being hotly debated and contested across the United States. The narco-trafficking industry in Mexico has exploded into an alarming state of unconstrained violence reminiscent of the drug wars of my native Colombia. The sheer proximity and intensification of violence across "la linea" have provided the "veil" for border states—specifically, Arizona, with other states soon to follow suit[1]—to institute strict policy measures that take the United States back to the heyday of Manifest Destiny. The isolated killing of an Arizonan rancher (allegedly by drug-trafficking immigrants) set the stage for a full-throttle assault against the millions of immigrants who work, live, and abide by civil codes and laws in the United States. In 2010, the passage of Arizona's SB1070, which has been stalled by the U.S. Department of Justice, would have required all state and local law enforcement agencies to verify the immigration status of individuals they suspect are in violation of federal immigration law (Su, 2010). Police would have become similar to dogcatchers; courts of law the equivalent of processing and detention centers for humans. Since the law's passing, an estimated 100,000 to 200,000 people have left Arizona (Robbins, 2011). Critics denounce the law for interfering with federal jurisdiction and they question law enforcement's authority and discretion in what would predictably lead to racial profiling on all public and privately held premises in the state. Proponents of the statute fault the federal government for its lax and ignoble efforts to curb the number of undocumented border crossers from *el sur*. For the popular majority, it has been all too easy, if not tempting, to reduce the immigration debate to a question of legality, safety, jurisdiction, or simply "law and justice." Such an analytical and rhetorical move, however, glosses over the complex layering of relations that underpin the ongoing discussions on U.S. immigration policy.

Since 2004, Arizona has implemented an array of legal measures intended to curb the hiring of undocumented workers and to limit their access to public services. This was preceded by similar measures in the days of Governor Pete Wilson of California, whose passage of Proposition 227 a decade earlier was subsequently rescinded by the courts. Discussions of immigrants as draining the pool of available social resources have obscured the debate. During the 1980s, then president Ronald Reagan admonished the "black welfare queen" that needed to be "put back to work." In Arizona and California, two states with a growing Latina/o majority (primarily from Mexico), the "aliens" will be put to work regardless, but they will not be able to bill the state for their "social wage." State authorities have ultimately recognized the economic interests of their respective communities—immigrants equal cheap commodities—supporting measures that allow them to "import healthy working age immigrants temporarily" (Wilson, 2008). Here, questions around the "production" of a labor force (i.e., their ability to work for production of services/goods) are separated from their "reproduction" (Wilson, 2008). Reproduction has dual meanings and consequences. On the one hand, states want to limit immigrants' access to social services that would reproduce their capacity to labor (i.e., health and education); on the other, they would also like to restrict immigrant women from reproducing a workforce, "anchor babies" that many state officials fear would undermine the principles of birthright citizenship in the United States.

In the mid-1990s, California governor Wilson requested that Congress amend the U.S. Constitution to deny citizenship to children born on U.S. soil to "illegals." In 2010, Arizona was primed to push through the state legislature what media pundits refer to as the "anchor baby" clause. Supporters argue that women from the South leave their families and homes behind and risk their lives in order to give birth to children in the United States, granting them "anchors" to stay and benefit from the (increasingly scarce) social services available in the country. For decades, thousands of wealthy women from Mexico have paid U.S.-based doctors to deliver their babies (Bledsoe, 2004). These doctors have proactively solicited these women, charging inordinate fees for performing the deliveries. This latter phenomenon is referred to as "birthright tourism" and the women are referred to as "maternity tourists" (Medina, 2011). The women come not only from Mexico, but from China, South Korea, and other nations as well (Medina, 2011). Giving birth to children in the United States has become a lucrative business adventure, with benefits extending to hotel chains that advertise month-long "baby stays" (Medina, 2011)—strollers and pacifiers included—and to the proprietors of makeshift maternity houses that provide illicit spaces for women to give birth. Questions around the commodification of birthing as well as attaching value to a child based on the location of his or her birth brings to the fore various questions about our global social order and the perceived dominance attached to claiming citizenship in the so-called West over the "rest," but it does not speak to the indurate logic surrounding efforts to repeal U.S. birthright citizenship. While the Pew Hispanic Center reports that a nominal 8 percent of the 4.3 million newborns in U.S. hospitals come from "illegal immigrant parents" (Dwyer, 2011), anchor baby legislation has unleashed a torrent of repressed angst directed toward working women from Mexico deemed "unfit" to mother U.S. citizens. Plans to introduce "anchor baby" legislation would result in the U.S.-born children of undocumented women being stripped of their citizenship (as provided by the 14th Amendment of the Constitution). Republicans of the U.S. Senate further support such measures with plans to call hearings to overturn the 14th Amendment. These senators denounce the constitution for encouraging "invasion by birth canal" (McGreal, 2010). Other representatives of the U.S. Congress have extended the discussion of "anchor babies" to questions of national security. Texas representative Louie Gohmert has been the most outspoken advocate of amending the constitution for related, albeit different, purposes. According to Gohmert, "anchor babies" can also become "terror babies," children born for the purpose of obtaining U.S. passports that can later be used for terrorism (Schulman, 2010). These mothers and children could, in the words of Gohmert, "be raised and coddled as future terrorists," and later, "twenty, thirty years down the road, they can be sent in to help destroy our way of life" (as cited in Schulman, 2010).

Echoes of such nationalist fears can be seen in earlier historical periods, including the building of internment camps on U.S. soil that housed legal Japanese immigrants during World War II, and the Cold War fears of Communist "sleeper agents" or subconsciously activated political assassins, best exemplified in John Frankenheimer's 1962 hit movie, *The Manchurian Candidate* (remade in 2004 by Jonathan Demme). And if we dig a bit deeper, the womb-politics of immigration reform can be felt in the colonial legal systems that affected women in the Americas during slavery, otherwise known as *partus sequitur ventrem*. This colonial law that originated from pre-imperial Rome established a child's free/slave status depending on the "condition of the mother" (Schweninger, 2009). *Partus sequitur ventrem* guaranteed that black slave populations would reproduce themselves naturally (Dorsey, 1996), stripped women of the opportunity to defend or claim rights for their children, and absolved men (especially white slave owners who fathered the babies of enslaved women) of their obligation to provide care for the children. Children born to enslaved women became property of the slave owner, decreasing his cost and dependency on acquiring external sources to expand or supplant his workforce. In both the "anchor baby" clauses of the twenty-first century and the colonial legacy of *partus sequitur ventrem*, the womb politics of citizenship status and birthright are embedded in legal and economic relations firmly rooted in kyriarchal[2] reason. The physical place where birth takes place carries little meaning in either of these cases, as it is women's bodies (and how they are signified geopolitically) that become the contested terrain for claiming or denying both citizenship and property rights.

Setting the backdrop and momentum for U.S. immigration policy initiatives are two parallel shifts in the demographic arena. The year 2006 marked the first time in 35 years that the average birthrate of women in the United States reached 2.1, the number experts claim is needed for the population to replace itself, what has been referred to as the "baby boomlet" (Huang, 2010). As noted by Priscilla Huang (2010), many in the public sphere received news of the "baby boomlet" with fear and discomfort. Claiming that undocumented women were to blame for the unexpected growth of the U.S. population, the political Right—including members of the Tea Party insurrectionist movement—began to canvas not only on behalf of immigration reform but also in favor of antiabortion lobbying (Huang, 2010). In his address to a College Republicans gathering, former house majority leader Tom Delay declared: "I contend [abortion] affects you in immigration. If we had those 40 million children that were killed over the last 30 years, we wouldn't need the illegal immigrants to fill the jobs that they are doing today" (as cited in Huang, 2010). These demographic shifts challenge the prevailing myth that the United States is a majority Protestant, Anglo-Saxon population. Coupled with the criminal attacks of September 11, 2001, the subsequent U.S. occupation of Iraq and Afghanistan, and the 2008 election of an African-American president, Barack Obama (whose birthright citizenship has also been questioned by the U.S. public and whom a growing number of U.S. citizens believe is a closet fundamentalist Muslim), the dominant white nomenclature has fixated on the reproductive capacities of women as the primary threat to the hegemony of the Protestant Anglospere. The uterus has literally become a battleground.

Clearly, this brief discussion on anti-immigrant legislative measures does not take into account the rights that nations have to control their border entry. I contend that "border control" is not the issue at stake in the above-mentioned polemics. Rather, the politics of Mexican immigration in the United States exposes some of the most virulent and undesirable qualities of the "American" structural unconscious: essentializing women in terms of their capacities to reproduce a labor force; reducing the birth of children to a manipulative quirk; stripping workers of an adequate "social wage"; treating human beings as human capital; mimicking the arguments of eugenicists past; rewriting the constitutional foundations of citizenship; and militarizing the border for fear of the big, bad, brown "other." Anti-immigrant groups such as the "restrictionists" (Doty, 2010) have parlayed the discussion around immigration reform into questions of national and societal[3] security, furthering the scope of an often violent, nationalist rhetoric and social practice. Roxanne Doty explains, "the perception of a threat to either national security or societal security or both depend upon the notion of an enemy; not a personal enemy, but a public enemy, whose very existence is disruptive to the social order" (2010). The rise of paramilitaries, the minutemen, and armed white supremacist militia at the border are an expression of a growing public resistance to engage in meaningful dialogue or debate about the intricacies of immigration, or simply about the changing nature of societies. The signs at rallies and posts on anti-immigrant websites communicate these sentiments clearly (acts that remind me of the colonial settlers depicted in J.M. Coetzee's novel, *Waiting for the Barbarians*): "JUST SAY NO TO WETBACK BREEDERS," "IF IT'S BROWN FLUSH IT DOWN," "TAKE AN ILLEGAL ALIEN DOWN" (Doty, 2010). These practices of exclusion, hatred, fear, Anglo-Saxon nationalism, and sexism can—and some would argue already have—become more intensely embedded in the wider social register. All of this, however, has not dissuaded members of the North American and European bourgeoisie from participating in what is called "reality tourism" or tourist "safaris" in crime-ridden enclaves of Mexican cities where they can enjoy the thrill of talking to real drug traffickers (Segura, 2010). One tourist agency also simulates the dangerous journey that people from Mexico and Central America undertake as they cross the U.S. border illegally. For only 15 dollars, tourists are taken on a nocturnal trek through a state park with guides posing as "polleros." Tourists are given the opportunity to wade through a river at night and hide in the bushes to escape the patrol lights of "la migra" (Segura, 2010). For those tourists who can't keep up, they are thrown in the back of a mock border patrol truck. The sensationalist voyeurism into Mexican immigration and drug trafficking, and the ethnocentric rants against immigration, pose a serious threat to the construction of a pluriversal society. They forcefully frame how social groups cohere and disassemble, and they affect in important ways how public officials are able to serve communities. And, of course, they profoundly affect the education of future generations of our youth.

The womb-politics of immigration reform are largely severed from questions surrounding the economic relations that bind Mexico and the United States. The Bracero program of 1942–1964 established a formal system of entry for Mexican workers into the United States in order to satisfy labor demands. The supply/demand relation between these two nations was inherently unequal, with Mexican *latifundistas*/landowners in the cotton and agricultural industry angered by losing "their" workers to the United States. In her historical account of illegal Mexico-U.S. immigration, Kelly Hernandez (2006) notes that landholders in Mexico's most productive and profitable zones of cotton farming demanded placement of the Mexican military along the border to prevent unsanctioned border crossings into the United States by Mexican cotton pickers. As migrating to the United States became more lucrative to Mexican workers, whether by the means allotted in the Bracero program or otherwise, Mexico began to formalize agreements with the United States that would quell the large-scale exodus of its workers. At the time, the United States also had to satiate the demands of its own labor industry, and it formally began to police the U.S.-Mexico Border. Operation Wetback of 1954 was an aggressive binational campaign that targeted Mexican nationals for interrogation, apprehension, and deportation (Hernandez, 2006). Collaborative efforts between the United States and Mexico eventually resulted in the forced deportation of over 1 million persons (primarily from Mexico). Trains removed between 600 and 1,000 migrants daily, followed by airlifts and removal by bus for those migrants who came from Mexico's northernmost states (Hernandez, 2006). As noted by Hernandez (2006), the costs of the large-scale transfer of deportees from the United States into Central Mexico were shared by both countries. Testimonies of the abuse and punishment of deportees have also been recorded on both sides of the border[4] (Hernandez, 2006). Operation Wetback linked U.S. and Mexican policing mechanisms and demonstrated the extent to which workers in the lowest strata of the economic hierarchy are denied their "rights" on either side of the border.

NATIVIST RISINGS

The hidden underside of the politics of immigration reform is characterized best by that which it represents: resurgence in U.S. nativist ideology that harkens back to the early 1920s. By nativism, I have (partly) in mind what James Banks refers to as "ethnic revitalization" (2004), the creation of a nation-state in which one group is dominant while all others are expected to forsake their traditions and language to assume citizenship in the "host" country. In ethnic revitalization, the focus is on the development of a national identity based on prevailing ideologies of power and material economic interests. Coupled with this, nativism as expressed through national myths and metaphors refers to what Daisy Machado characterizes as the "historical epic that is at the heart of (U.S.) self-identity" (2007, 92). National myths that often promulgate U.S. exceptionalism and triumphalism allow dominant groups to tell and create a blameless and noble history as a justification for the continued subordination of the "other." Nativism has distinctly American (U.S.) origins characterized by what George Sanchez (1997) refers to as a national identity that is "defensive in spirit"; a "habit of mind" that marks national anxieties and the "bounds of our tolerance"; and a virulent antiradicalism and racial nativism, strongly grounded in the Anglo-Saxon origins of the American nation (1997, 1019).

The womb-politics of immigration reform and the general backlash toward undocumented peoples from south of the border extend these notions and indicate that the United States is in a process of (re)nativising. And while nativism has often been discussed as a distinctly U.S. phenomenon, there are various examples of how the European nation-state, for example, has labored to secure its national identity in the face of Islam and in light of the increasing numbers of immigrants from African and Central Asian nations who have traveled to the "core" capitalist nations in pursuit of work and livelihood. A growing "Euroskepticism" (Berezin, 2009 as cited in Varsanyi, 2010) of the "other" has accompanied the restructuring of the European state apparatus—once considered a model of democratic empathy and opportunity—into an "increasingly disciplining, surveillance-oriented and militaristic institution that keeps the people in line with the project" (Varsanyi, 2010, 301). The "project" in this case has to do with the political and economic structuring that follows in the wake of neoliberal globalization: the privatization of the public sphere (in terms of social services) and the attendant logic of individualist, receive-what-you-earn/pay-as-you-go logic that pervades the restructuring of the welfare state into a singular corporate state. Instead of distributing social benefits predicated on a reciprocal ethos of meeting basic human necessities, the state becomes the arbiter of general human worth based on an idealized notion of "citizen." In this sense, nativism functions to provide the state with a rational appearance, or what Jacques Rancière (2010) adequately identifies as "state racism." State racism disguised as popular passion (otherwise read as a reasonable response to the problems presented by "immigrants") allows "discretionary state power to decide who belongs or doesn't belong to the class of those who have the 'rights' to occupy a rational space" (Rancière, 2010). The Western state, with its attendant modernist and triumphalist tropes, condones racial and ethnic antagonisms, while it occludes inherently social distinctions connected to its evolving material interests. This disconnect between race/ethnicity and class is fertile ground for nativism to emerge among and between social groups. To the general population, nativism simply becomes a question of protecting national identity and resources intended for those who can adjust to the racialized (and religious) constructs of citizenship. But to state-corporatists who lobby for draconian immigration policy reform and siphon taxpayers' money into the privatization of immigration detention centers, nativism becomes an extremely profitable ideology. In 2010, two of the largest corporations that own immigration detention centers, the Corrections Corporation of America and GEO Group, Inc., reported profits of 1.69 and 1.17 billion dollars, respectively (Detention Watch Network, 2011). In the same year, over 400,000 immigrants were reported detained in the United States, roughly half of which were kept in privately operated detention centers (Detention Watch Network, 2011). Nativist penal colonies are emerging in the United States, promulgating racism, intolerance, and a simplistic culture that reduces the complexity of social life to an ideological crusade for vanquishing the "obstacles" that undocumented workers seemingly pose to protecting the "American ideal and dream." The nativist risings of the twenty-first century are becoming increasingly mainstream, in many instances violent, and perhaps even chic. Figures in the United States alone suggest an increase in over 40 percent of nativist organized groups since 2008, a deliberate spike since the election of Barack Obama whose perceived "blackness" has undermined popular folklore around the construction of a postracial society. These groups take up arms and perceive their mission as defending the "Aryan man as the only sovereign over his land and life" (Ridgeway, 2011). The United States has also experienced the formalization of nativist political parties and legislative measures that under the pretense of due process become normalized into law. The ban on ethnic studies in Arizona's public schools is but one example (Medrano, 2010), in which programs that focus on the study of any one nonwhite racial group are seen as racially biased, separationist, and unworthy of public support, let alone violations of state law.[5]

The nativist risings of the twenty-first century are particularly subversive. While, for some, nativists' racist undertones may be painfully obvious, the movement itself is guised as antiracist.[6] Nativists appropriate the very language and terms that have historically been aligned with progressive sectors of society, such as equality and social justice. Banning the study of ethnic studies, for example, turns into a question of providing socially just views of whites. It so follows that popular news headlines pose the question, "Are Whites Racially Oppressed?" (Blake, 2011). In an astoundingly ironic move, nativism turns into a form of perceived social redress.

Even with the rigid and seemingly impermeable policies being put in place to "secure" U.S. borders and national identity, no one can decidedly predict the outcome of nativist risings at this time in history. We can think about the tendencies or laws in motion that underwrite human sociability, but ultimately the outcome depends upon numerous actions, not least of which include the redressive action of those directly engaged in writing social policy or enforcing legal statutes, and the protagonist action of those protesting on the steps of State Capitol buildings or next to the sprawling immigrant detention encampments in the desert (where, in counterprotest, Arizona Sheriff Joe Arpaio deafened inhabitants with the music of immigration activist Linda Ronstadt). Whatever unfolds will likely bring only temporary relief, as the demands for a cheap labor pool by the transnational labor market and the U.S. corporate structure show no immediate signs of weakening. To a large extent, what unfolds at the border, on radio airwaves, and in court chambers is nothing short of political theater.

Invoking the notion of theater is not intended to reduce or ignore the very real, toxic, and tangible effects of nativist anti-immigration efforts. I do, however, use the metaphor of "political theater" to connect the symbolism, rhetoric, and practices of anti-immigration to the historical and material processes that have led up to this historical moment.

IMMIGRATION REFORM AS POLITICAL THEATER

Establishing fear in the public, capitalizing on a singular act of violence (i.e., the abduction and killing of a rancher), and mobilizing both political and grassroots sectors of society to incorporate into the "movement" is a process with deep-rooted social and material origins. The processual forces of anti-immigration, national identity, racism, and sexism contribute in no small way to the totality of social relations in colonial-capitalist society. They expose, in rather alarming and seemingly unreal ways the extent to which people embody and perform territoriality and perceived social dominance/entitlement. The organizing metaphor of theater in this instance brings to mind the Orwellian odyssey *Touch of Evil* inspired in part by the Sleepy Lagoon Case of 1942. In Orson Welles' words, the Sleepy Lagoon went something like this:

> On the night of August 2, 1942, one Jose Diaz left a drinking party at the Sleepy Lagoon ranch near Los Angeles, and sometime in the course of that night he died. It seems clear that Diaz was drinking heavily and fell into a roadway and was run over by a car. Whether or not he was also in a brawl before he was run over is not clear. On January 13, fifteen American-born boys of Mexican descent and two boys born in Mexico stood up to hear the verdict of a Los Angeles court. Twelve of them were found guilty of having conspired to murder Diaz, five were convicted of assault. Their sentences ranged from a few months to life imprisonment...It wasn't only seventeen boys who were on trial. It was the whole Mexican people, and their children and their grandchildren. It was the whole of Latin America with its 130,000,000 people. It was the Good Neighbor Policy. It was the United Nations and all for which they fight...It began to be that kind of trial even before Jose Diaz met his death on August 2nd. The Los Angeles paper started it by building for a "crime wave" even before there was a crime. "MEXICAN GOON SQUADS" "ZOOT SUIT GANGS" "PACHUCO KILLERS" "JUVENILE GANG WAR LAID TO YOUTHS' DESIRE TO THRILL." Those were the curtain raisers, the headlines building for August 3rd.

In 1958, Welles costarred and directed *Touch of Evil*, a film noir that "emplots within its narrative the ideological contradictions and social antagonisms intrinsic to the U.S. social order" (Pease, 2001). With Charlton Heston, the iconoclastic American hero, playing Manuel Vargas (in brown face), a Mexican narcotics official married to a white American named Susan, Welles was able to subvert the system of representations that fit social groups into their proper niches. In so doing, as Donald Pease notes, "Welles underscored the historically specific social and political conditions that prevailed at the moment of the film's production...in the aftermath of the Second World War, when.... anxious white men interjected images of racialized otherness that had become the defining force in urban culture, in order thereafter to expel racial markedness from the field of visibility altogether" (2001, 5). The "mixed economy" (Bhabha as cited in Pease, 2001) of racism and sexism is enveloped at the level of intimate and political relations, undermining the sanctity of identity premised on U.S. exceptionalism and Mexican economic dependency.

Whether in the controlled imaginaries of a movie script or in the seemingly spontaneous acts of grassroots, paramilitary, and governmental forces, the notion of political theater in relation to U.S. immigration debates reflects animated responses to the perceived threat that immigrants pose to U.S. cultural authenticity or political authority in the public sphere. While the drama of everyday life is enacted mainly at the level of cultural representations, it is embedded in a wider political stage in which two main classes confront one another. The dominant class, what Steven Martinot (2010) describes as composed of "capital and white workers," and the subordinate class, or "racialized" workers. The economic and material dimensions of how people are socially positioned, in this case racially, give further meaning to how identity and cultural phenomenon are understood in the wider public register.

A similar theatrical backdrop was at play in the social drama of Mirasur, where a changing labor market over the past 20 years has shifted the population to an "immigrant" majority; where questions around language, culture, sex/gender, ethnicity, and national identity reinvoked themes from times past. What I wish to underscore about the events at Mirasur, however, is the way in which the mothers challenged the dominant theater of social life by defying the ideological, cultural, and gender roles assigned to them (from both the geographic

"South" and "North"). In so doing, they altered the processual form of the social drama of Mirasur and rendered other ways of incorporating themselves into the domains of nationhood, family, community, and school.

South Central Los Angeles is often eclipsed by its storied history of oppressive and tragic displays of human interactions. Within the popular imaginary, South Central Los Angeles represents an unsurpassable gulf between the rich and poor, black and white, and brown and black. Ignored is the history of its grassroots organizations, of its women, men, and children who labor and toil for a more dignified existence in communities that seemingly deprive them of the ability to do so. It would behoove residents and educators to remember the life and work of people such as Marian Wagstaff, who turned a local high school into a model of racial integration years before the infamous Brown v. Board of Education ruling or the civil rights protests of the 1960s (Woo, 2009). Or to recall the efforts of social activists such as Larry Aubry, whose race relations commentaries for the *Los Angeles Sentinel* inspire calls for justice (Newton, 2007), and Ruben Salazar, a former journalist of the *Los Angeles Times* whose brutal killing by a sherrif [7] after Salazar's reporting of the national Chicano moratorium against the Vietnam War incited the community to begin various organizations in his memory. These are the more popular, local vanguards of the community who are at times remembered and esteemed. Their stories are important, but mainstream depictions of their struggles often (if not always) systematically reduce social change and transformation to the determinations of a few isolated persons. This is part and parcel of the overriding logic of capitalist society: individualism trumps collective action, self-sacrifice surpasses the human right to participate and claim a role in the political organization of society. Books are dedicated to such notable persons, and, indeed, they abound in the educational literature. Children and youth in schools can find inspiration from the exceptional words and deeds of Martin Luther King, Rosa Parks, Cesar Chavez, Dolores Huerta, and other civil and social activists who have been inaugurated—and rightly so— into the humanitarian hall of fame. Missing from such narratives, however, is a contextualized study of the conditions and human networks that gave rise to the movements sparked by such luminaries. Acts geared toward social transformation cannot be understood on their own terms; they reflect relations that are largely left "invisible" from a solely phenomenological undertaking. In other words, no experience speaks for itself. Without a language and a broader social contextualization of experience, we miss the interconnectedness and relational characteristics that propel human existence. We absolve ourselves from responsibility in celebrating the acts of the few when we exclude the reciprocal causes and effects of our relationships to one another (and to the natural environment) within concrete, material conditions.

NOTES ON METHOD

The social drama of Mirasur is a contextualized look into the cultural and institutional mechanisms revealed in the mothers' actions to defend the education of their children and community. When I began working as a grant administrator, it was not my intention to write about experiences at Mirasur. I chose to focus on the school-community relationship as part of the scope of my work, and the idea of engaging in a systematic analysis was something that occurred after several years of working with the mothers. I was learning as I went along, as the common cliché goes. My contract term expired after two years and, to my knowledge, no system was in place to evaluate the benefits of improving school-community relations. My work would have been completed. I decided, however, to shift my role from grant administrator to a committed educator/social researcher when, on a very hot day in the early days of spring, I witnessed the mothers protesting on the front lawn of the school. They protested for several months and I was taken aback by the kind of reaction they solicited from the administration, teachers, local media, and the community. There was a performative element to the mothers' protest, and that too drew my attention. At that point, I began to systematically document my observations for the duration of my time at Mirasur, which spanned several more years. Once my contract ended, I continued to visit the mothers, as they worked ceaselessly to redefine their presence in the school's governance structure. This book is the culmination of both processes. It is part an auto-reflection of my time spent as an official employee of Mirasur as well as my observations, analyses, interviews, and collaborations with the mothers once I was no longer officially on the payroll.

I wavered for some time about the kind of methodology I would use to frame my observations, and I struggled with writing about a process where my roles as educator, a woman of color, a researcher, and writer continuously overlapped. I did not separate my pedagogical work from my labor as a social researcher. After all, social research is both pedagogical and political; we teach, inform, and shape conversations and practices with the words we pen on paper, and with the relationships we develop "on the ground." I also contended with the fact that I was emotionally vested in this project. I too experienced estrangement, fear, anger, resentment, hostility, care, love, and affection in relation to the events that transpired in both the school and wider community. And at times I also felt a certain, and perhaps inevitable, distance from the processes under way in Mirasur. This distance would reinscribe my own position as an educator and researcher in Mirasur.

My analysis of Mirasur is framed around two primary concepts, the late anthropologist Victor Turner's notion of social drama and the late Chicana feminist writer Gloria Anzaldúa's *paths of conocimiento (nepantla)*. For Turner, social drama was a way to understand the complex organization of social life in modern society and for giving an account to how ritual, like performance, is critical to the reproduction of culture. As communities become more diverse, "hybridized," and fragmented, Turner recognized the new and important ways to understand patterns of behavior and norms that establish coherence among social groups. Building upon his studies of ritual in traditional societies, Turner developed the concept of social drama to discuss how the ritual processes of transformation and reintegration were evident in modern industrial societies. Put simply, social dramas are a way to tell a story, "usually of human conflict by means of dialogue and action" (Turner, 1987, 27). Drama exemplifies a way of scrutinizing the quotidian world, viewing it as tragedy, comedy, or melodrama. Social dramas also depend upon the "social-structural, political, psychological, philosophical, and, sometimes, theological perspectives of the narrators" (Turner, 1987). Put another way, a social drama is "a spontaneous unit of social process and a fact of everyone's experience in every human society" mediated or addressed by strategies that social actors might normally employ. They are nonharmonic or disharmonic social processes arising in conflict situations (Turner, 1980). More specifically, Turner writes that social drama is "an eruption from the level surface of ongoing social life, with its interactions, transactions, reciprocities, and its customs making for regular, orderly sequences of behavior" (Turner, 1986, 196). In Turner's terminology, social dramas were "processually structured" (Turner, 1987, 34), extensions of ritual in traditional societies.

These notions of social drama appealed to me as I began to interrogate the norms and habitual routines of everyday life at Mirasur. I
wanted to understand in a deeper and more nuanced way how the faculty and the mothers came to define their relationship to one another,
and how the mothers were able to challenge and disrupt the everyday
sequence of events that established very clear boundaries and roles
between them and the school. In my initial attempts to narrate the
events of the social drama of Mirasur, I began to acknowledge other
competing narratives—those of the mothers, and in particular the
narratives of one specific woman, Maria Lourdes Jimenez. This led
me to question her "perspective" and her worldview more deeply,
as an immigrant woman from humble origins who transitioned into
a powerful advocate for her community. As she told me her story
(which she will tell you, the reader), I came to recognize the bane-
ful and enduring logic of colonization, patriarchy, sexism, and class
exploitation in her narrative. I needed to situate her experiences in a
language and conceptual register that privileged the historical speci-
ficity of a woman born and raised in an impoverished town in Mexico.
For Maria Lourdes Jimenez, the social drama of Mirasur was also a
personal testament to shifting consciousness. Given these reasons, I
have brought into conversation the indigenous and Chicana contributions of Anzaldúa and others on the topic of *nepantla*, a Nahuatl
(Aztec) term that illustrates the simultaneously disruptive and creative
processes of social transformation and survival.

Indigenous spiritual leaders under Spanish conquest in Mexico
used the term nepantla to convey their physical and spiritual responses
to colonization. First documented in the sixteenth century by Fray
Diego Duran (in an attempt to salvage the history of Mesoamerica's
indigenous populations), nepantla referenced the indigenous peoples'
liminal state of being—in-betweenness—as they confronted the forced
removal of their cultural heritage and spirituality by Christian mis-
sionaries. Since those first testimonies, nepantla has become a central
trope among literary critics and scholars for describing the conflictual
processes of living between nations and cultures. This is a point elaborated by Walter Mignolo (2000) when he writes:

> If nepantla comes from the history of Spanish colonization, its meta-
> phorical meaning can be extended to nineteenth-century British and
> French expansion to Asia and Africa, or to the borders reproduced by
> current global coloniality and the growing hegemony of the North

Atlantic. Nepantla, finally, and as the story of its emergence indicates, links the geohistorical with the epistemic with the subjective, knowledge with ethnicity, sexuality, gender and nationality in power relations. The "in-between" inscribed in Nepantla is not a happy place in the middle, but refers to a general question of knowledge and power. The kind of power relations inscribed in Nepantla are [sic] the power relations sealing together modernity and what is inherent to it, namely, coloniality.

For the purposes of the social drama of Mirasur, nepantla brings to the fore the specific conditions and worldviews of women living in transition, under conquest, and yet forging intercultural social relations. The focus here is on how Maria and the mothers developed their capacities and capabilities as protagonists in the education of their children.

In sum, the social drama of looking South is multifaceted and pluriversal. I have attempted to preserve the genuine meaning of the women's voices by including their transcripts in Spanish, with an English translation. I have also inserted myself as an actor in the unfolding social drama of Mirasur as I reflect upon and navigate my movement, not as a detached observer but as an active agent in the formulation of the breach of social relations that set the social drama of Mirasur in motion. I narrate primarily through field notes and diary entries that I generated throughout my tenure as a grant administrator. Here, I am appreciative of the insights offered by Mary Louise Pratt (1999), Victor Turner (1987), and others who describe the ethnographic processes of social inquiry as a form of narrative. While the presentation of this text does take form through the discursive elements of storytelling, the analyses of these narratives are grounded in the materiality of social life; more specifically, they reveal the dialectical relationship between agency and structure. The text is intentionally heterogeneous and multi-vocal; it is the by-product of women from varying backgrounds and dispositions, displaced from their countries of origin, who came into contact with each other in the vast metropolis known as the City of Angels.

ORGANIZATION OF THE BOOK

Chapter 1 traces the urban history, immigration patterns, and demographic shifts of the school-community borderland of South Central Los Angeles. This place and space that Jimenez and las madres first

encountered as young border crossers expose the tensions and contradictions of the City of Angels that was found at the bitter crossroads of increased poverty, violence, and racial/ethnic tensions. This
chapter sets the stage for the place-based and dramaturgical understandings of the Mirasur community. Here, I situate the social drama
in sociopolitical, economic, and geographical terms in an attempt to
highlight the conditions that gave rise to the ensuing discussions on
patriarchy, gendered consciousness, class exploitation, and intra/inter
racial rivalry. Chapter 2 reveals the social relations and interactions
between the mothers and school personnel. This chapter establishes
the context from which the *breach* (Chapter 3) of everyday routines
in Mirasur occurred. In chapter 3, the drama of protest is discussed
in acute detail, the climax, so to speak, of when the institutional
structure and its agents could not quell or appropriately respond to
the growing disenchantment and anger of the mothers protesting
on the street. Questions of how we go about documenting the difficult processes of political and ideological transformation in familiar communal settings, when one's consciousness and practice shift
from subjugated silences to protagonist clamor, is explored by means
of an imminent critique. Here, I examine the processes of developing
critical consciousness (Anzaldúa's paths of *conocimiento*) with a wide-
angle lens as I utilize some of Anzaldúa's theoretical constructs as a
heuristic device to enable me to capture meanings that lie at the edges
or fringes of most ethnographic texts.

Chapter 4, Inner Theater, focuses more centrally on la madre
Jimenez, in which she reveals important dimensions of her historical memory of coming to know herself as a woman, worker, wife,
and mother. This chapter is about how Jimenez came to see herself
through the eyes of others (i.e., her self-consciousness), but she also
expresses the contradictions of a woman who is subjugated by external
forces and who internally resists and participates in her own subjugation. I act as the interlocutor of Jimenez's text, and insert my reading
of her narrative, giving notice to the wider and more general processes
of exploitation, colonization, Christianization, and living as a border
crosser as a way of providing an integrative perspective for reading
her narrative. In chapter 5, I discuss the mothers' social organization
and participation in school life following the protest. The final chapter, Revolutionary Social Drama, brings the various elements of this
book together—consciousness, ritual, and social drama—and pro-
poses an alternative scheme for addressing the resulting tension that

is produced in the process of changing oneself, of re-narrating history from the standpoint of emancipation. Several of the ideas, concepts, and tropes from the social drama of Mirasur can be considered to fall within philosophical, sociological, pedagogical, and/or anthropological domains. While distinct academic boundaries exist both within and across these domains, such restrictions are often only recognized by those who speak, work, and write within the very institutional settings that created them. The knowledge, history, memory, and action that the women/mothers bring to this text cannot be compartmentalized into neat categories, and every effort has been made to demonstrate how their words and actions simultaneously address many sides of "being and becoming" in the realm of ideas, tradition, work, and community. In the conception of this written project, I had to consider what it would look like when I, as author and academician, engaged in an analysis of other people's lives, their community, their histories, and their memories; to put it succinctly, their social dramas. I did not want to reproduce what has been termed, in the anthropological sense, "epistemic violence," or in the sociological view, a brute "solipsism." So, in conclusion, I have attempted to breach boundaries, to speak in different languages, and to bring together various knowledge(s) and observations of the social world, which are often left unsaid.

ACKNOWLEDGMENTS

This book would not have been possible without the guiding support and affection of Maria Lourdes Jimenez and her family. While I have made every effort to present Maria's words and thoughts accurately, any errors in interpretation are solely my own. A special thanks to Carmen Jimenez for her photo journalism and assistance during the final stages of preparing this manuscript, and to Abel, *gracias por aceptarme con tanto cariño.*

There are many people who I have met over the years and who inspired me to continue working on this book. I am especially thankful to the women with whom I have shared several of the ideas of the manuscript and who provided me with critique and other ways of understanding and addressing women's shifting consciousness. To the women, activists, and educators from Venezuela, Mexico, and Colombia, I thank you for sharing your time with me and for teaching me about the various dimensions that frame (y)our social struggles. To my academic nepantlera/o/s and guides, I am eternally grateful for your mentorship and encouragement: Alicia Gaspar de Alba, Kris Gutierrez, Tyrone Howard, Donaldo Macedo, and Sheila Macrine. A warm thanks to Susan Searls Giroux and Henry Giroux.

I completed this manuscript in a small apartment overlooking one of the most historic university campuses in China. I would be remiss if I did not mention and offer thanks to my hosts—professors and students—from Wuhan University who provided me with time, space, resources, and friendly company during the final stages of preparing this manuscript. Special thanks are also due to the wonderful people at Java Roaster and Despair-Oh (BLASP) in Lafayette, Indiana; the coffee and your friendship went a long way. And to all of my friends and colleagues, both near and far, who have accompanied me on this journey, thanks for your love. Sandra Valle, Erik Malewski, and Heather Starr, I'm especially thinking of you.

The themes that animated the writing of this book were not simply academic endeavors, they were deeply personal and familial. As the old adage goes, the personal is political. My family has always comforted me with their love and faith, I appreciate them all. But a special nod is due to Veronica Helena Alvarez, my sister by default, and to my cousins, Angela Piedad Valencia, who helped with the Spanish portions of this text, and Angela Patricia Muñoz, the photographer of our family. My loving thanks to Peter McLaren for his unyielding support and companionship from beginning to end.

1

SETTING THE STAGE: THE
SCHOOL-COMMUNITY BORDERLAND

As I drove into the packed parking lot of Mirasur elementary, I looked past the signs that let me know exactly whose territory I had entered. F13 block letters, in black spray paint, at times legible and other times barely discernible, covered the walls and storefronts of the 99-cent store, la botanica, the indoor swap meet, liquor stores, the Western Union, and the ceramic and vinyl tile warehouse with merchandise offerings from south of the border. The limited knowledge that I had pulled together during my youth from Hollywood films such as Colors, Mi Vida Loca, Boyz n the Hood! and American Me about Los Angeles' barrios taught me that graffiti was an inner-city staple item, a semiotic marking that indexed territorial control, group membership, and the violence that Latina suburbanites like me attributed to it. The unfamiliar suddenly became more familiar, and the tensions and fears that make for intense movie dramas overcame me. Got off the freeway. Door locked? Yes. Windows rolled up? Yes. Deep breath.

When I pulled into the school's parking lot I encountered an old man with dark and leathery skin sitting on a plastic foldable chair and guarding the indebted belongings of the faculty and staff. He let me in. I nodded and proceeded to find a parking space in the overflowing and overpriced metal junkyard, with his help, of course. Otherwise I would have been forced to park on the street and that made me, to put it mildly, uncomfortable. After all, I was driving my brand new gas-guzzling, cruise-controlling, accident-prone, sport-edition Toyota 4-Runner. I was going to protect my stuff.

It wasn't the first time I found myself in a Los Angeles barrio. When my mother became a single woman in the mid-1980s she made her living selling everything from cemetery plots, lingerie, jewelry, and life insurance policies out of the trunk of her car to predominantly poor and working-class Latino/a/s in L.A. She was a traveling saleswoman, without a husband to come home to and unleash her day's frustrations. She traveled with me in tow instead. My mother is a gracious and caring woman who comes from humble beginnings but extravagant endings. She drove a Mercedes at the time, black or gray, or was it black-grayish? She had refused to downsize after her divorce. "Uno solamente puede mejorar en la vida, nunca ir para abajo/one can only improve in life, never go back down" were her words.

The month is October, which gives me reason to wear my floor-length black trench coat. My hair is pulled back, make-up not too inviting, blouse secured at the collar bone, and résumé is neatly pressed in my file folder. It is my first job interview since returning to Los Angeles from a two-year getaway on the East coast, where I received my master's degree and then practiced the skills that cost me thirty-thousand dollars plus interest at a nonprofit organization in Washington DC. Part of me dreads the thought of returning to an elementary school as a classroom teacher, and another part of me finds it liberating. Will I be subject to the all-too-common infantile treatment of teachers? Yes. Will I find some refuge in working with the children? I hoped so.

I didn't get the teaching job. The woman who exited the principal's office as I went in beat me to it. Her name was Natalie and I am Nathalia. Serendipitous.

The principal welcomed me into his office, nonetheless. He seemed taller than me, or was it that my chair was set lower than his? I felt as though he towered over me. I sat on the other side of his polished mahogany desk. He smiled. I handed over my résumé. He proceeded to gloss it over. "A graduate of Harvard," he asked. "Yes, I went to Harvard." I found it shocking to admit; I was never supposed to make it there.

Most of my life's learning had taken place in the kitchen with my Tia Chepa during the summer months I spent in Colombia or in a confessional with one of God's messengers back in the Catholic suburbs of Los Angeles. Chepa was a beautiful dark-haired woman labeled the ugly duckling of a family of eight, because her younger, taller, and thinner sister had already secured a permanent suitor. Her parents never allowed her to have a lover or an education or a job outside of the home; she had been chosen to watch over her male siblings and parents into their golden years. She kept a pack of cigarettes, a bottle of booze, and a sewing machine in the room set apart for hired help adjacent to the kitchen. In there she would tease my lips with the taste of anise-flavored eighty-proof liquor and my sense of smell with the addictive residue of burning *tobacco. We spent time staring through the glass-paned window to salute the man selling lotto tickets from the wooden case tied to his belly, greeting Chepa's male friend who infrequently passed by with sweets, or I would sit and watch her tailor the clothes of neighbors, family and friends. The latter was her only source of independent income. Chepa taught me how to be loyal to family; to love and desire to be loved; to long for freedom and experience joy in confinement; and how to be in the company of others and feel complete isolation. She also taught me how to awaken at midnight to satisfy my uncles' drunken appetite for a scrambled egg with rice, an arepa (a Colombian corn-cake), or my personal favorite, a steaming hot dog stuffed with cheese. My uncles would have spent the evening at a cantina, or in their private parking garage. Divorced by their wives and separated from their children, they would stumble into the kitchen with a joke to tell, or a memory to sob about. And whenever it was my father requesting a meal, I felt particularly saddened to see him grim faced with bloodshot eyes.*

As the principal stood up from his chair, I could tell he was barely taller than me. A man of Guatemalan descent, first U.S. generation, he was impressed enough with my credentials. "Well, I don't have a teaching job but I do have something else that can work for you," he said. My ears piqued and my eyes opened wider. Pause. He then explained that he had a grant that needed an administrator. Eight-hundred thousand dollars that needed administering. The money was intended to get the school on track, after decades of low test-scores, low teacher morale, low community involvement, low quality of just about everything. He assured me that the job would not be too demanding and that he had some ideas about how to spend a majority of the funds. New TV-DVD combos mounted in every classroom; white boards to replace chalkboards; tape recorders and English books on tape so that children could acquire English faster. He talked about some of the problems facing the school: poverty, gangs, lack of role models, lack of English-speaking role models, etc., etc. I asked him if I could think about it and he asked that I not take too long.

I phoned him the next day and accepted the job offer. Perfect, he replied.

MIRASUR ELEMENTARY

Mirasur Elementary is located on the 68-hundredth block of South Central Los Angeles, in between the neighborhoods of Florence, Huntington Park, and Compton. The very words South Central Los

Angeles evoke images of the Los Angeles uprising of 1992, along with the cross-coastal rivalry that pitted rap artists Tupac Shakur and Notorious B.I.G. against one another, culminating in both men's untimely deaths. But the neighborhood is now largely Latino/a, as industries have continued to exploit the cheap labor of immigrant workers, displacing many members of the African-American, working-class community. Now, a new wave of entrepreneurs try to make ends meet in the land of "great dreams," the American Dream, selling mangos, oranges, and *coco con chile* on main street corners or setting up swap-meet-style booths along the busy city streets. On the lawns of the neighborhood churches, girls with polished hair piled high atop their heads, and kept from springing free by fence-sized tiaras, mark their ritual transition into womanhood. Wrapped in chiffon dresses, elbow-length gloves, and perched unsteadily atop 3-inch heels, their sometimes permanently tattooed eyebrows playfully arched with excitement, they celebrate their *quinceañeras*/fifteenth birthdays with family and friends and with their baptismal godparents overseeing the procession into the dance halls. On Sunday the people of Mirasur go to church and on Saturday boys and girls dressed in ribbon-laced suits and white-ruffle dresses receive the holy sacraments of baptism and first communion. Photographers line up on church grounds prepared to snap portraits to add to the family collection and vendors offer some mementos for a small fee. A labyrinth of single-family homes, apartment units, duplexes, and motels with monthly rental charges of $199 partitions Mirasur into enclaves. Old unused railroad tracks cut through the neighborhood. West of the railroad tracks, families mostly live in the dilapidated apartment buildings and renovated motel rooms, while those on the east side live in predominantly single-family, semipermanent residences. In Mirasur, the poor can distinguish themselves from the poorer. The splitting of the community according to economic divisions manifests itself among the school-age population, as loyalties are forged with either side of the tracks.

Within a five-mile radius, a majority of the neighborhood children stumble through the educational pipeline, starting in Mirasur elementary with a population of 1,900 students, a middle school with close to 2,500 students, and a high school, taken over in 2010 by the state of California, with nearly 5,000 students in official attendance. Many students who are spread across these educational levels assume an identity directly linked to the fragmentation of neighborhoods. These divisions are reinforced by the broader politics of the local and California state school systems that are struggling to accommodate growth in already highly populated urban areas. School officials have attempted to allay overpopulated schools with a neighborhood tracking system, A, B, and C, which has a trickle-down effect on the type of resources and services offered to the families of different tracks. In the case of Mirasur, the fluent English-speakers are typically found on track A, the poorest of the poor on track C, and track B houses a combination of the two and all the "others." Ninety-eight percent of the school-age population identifies as Latina/o, 1.8 percent as African American, and 0.1 percent as white; 99 percent of students quality for free or reduced-price lunches. The elimination of bilingual education and an unyielding accountability system that further separates and quantifies students according to their anatomical "proficiencies" (language, reading ability, etc.) have resulted in a de facto intra-school segregation system. Teachers are distributed accordingly (the more "qualified" of the pack are typically assigned to the track with the most probable scenario for success) and classroom compositions reflect the inner dynamic of intra-community segregation.

A BRIEF HISTORY

During the early twentieth century, the migration of African Americans from the U.S. South to take up work in Southern California's wartime defense industries altered Central Los Angeles' racial/ethnic landscape, creating a majority African-American presence in the city. Marks of racial and class tension between the emerging black majority and white minority could be seen as early as 1948 when, at the cusp of racial integration efforts, black students were hung in effigy at one of the local high schools. It became clear from the beginning that the city would become one of the main symbols of racialized class tension across the United States. The Watts riots of 1965 became emblematic of struggles yet to come. A peoples' justified anger over increased joblessness, the intensification of poverty, the absence of basic services such as a viable medical facility, and acts of police repression in the city have (sub)consciously set a precedent for how subsequent generations would respond to existing racial and class antagonisms. Such schisms have far from been erased; rather, they continue to intensify, shifting form to the extent that changes in the workforce have followed pace with changes in the demographic constitution of the city.

The steady flow of peoples from Mexico and Central America into South Central Los Angeles as a low(er)-wage workforce has generated demographic shifts of seismic proportions, resulting in new tensions and forms of exploitation and violence. Families are provided with few social resources and networks to challenge the effects of poverty, as they become more and more excluded from the benefits associated with environmental amenities. Schools have failed at serving the population and have become notorious in the process; the industries that do remain continue to dump their toxins onto city streets, a practice that correlates with one of the highest incidences of child asthma across the country; and youth are constantly in the crosshairs of drug trafficking and turf wars. Some older generations of Mexican-origin groups may have earned enough income to move into nearby suburban developments, but for the most part the community of Mirasur and South Central Los Angeles proper has been affected by low-wage, predominantly immigrant labor and the changing racial/ethnic dynamics of communities as different generations of Latinos and African Americans come into contact with one another for the limited social opportunities of upward mobility.

Los Angeles has been named the "gang capital of America," an ominous distinction at best and one that has not deterred the business capital of America from the indiscriminate selling of their goods. Not only do firearms abound in South Central, but also do arms dealers for the U.S. government. Most recently, Botach Tactical, a company based in South Central that sells arms to the United States, is implicated in fraud charges for acquiring a 300-million weapons contract and producing for its clients decomposing ammunition generated by the early twentieth-century factories of Chairman Mao (Bullock, 2010). In addition, the corporate sector keeps up a strong presence in the community, as an increase in the working immigrant population has signaled a greater demand for consumption. Within one panoramic view of the sprawling neighborhood, many of the fat cats of enterprise—McDonald's, Burger King, Gigante Market, Office Depot, and Walmart—try to make *la gente del sur*/people from the south de los Estados Unidos de Mexico feel like they've never left home. Take a drive through the Mexican border cities of Chihuahua, Ensenada, Tijuana, Monterrey, Mexicali, Hermosillo, and Ciudad Juárez and you will find the same. The passage of the North American Free Trade Alliance (NAFTA) opened the floodgates for major retail centers to open their businesses south of the border. The feminization of the retail market, connected to low(er) wages (five dollars a day), allowed U.S.-based behemoths to keep their costs down. Distribution centers followed suit, and within a short period of time both U.S.-based distribution and retail centers had significantly impacted the shopping culture of Mexico. Mexican-based corporations that survived the impact subsequently began other joint ventures to stay afloat: for example, Gigante, Inc (soon to be Solaria, Inc) partnered with Office-Depot and Radio Shack. These businesses volley with each other, trying to satisfy the people's "need" for U.S. merchandise. Even in the remote southernmost towns such as Juchitan, Mexico, a former stronghold of Zapotec language, with identity and culture connected to a history of anticolonial efforts, Wal-Mart has found a home. To bridge the cultural divide, the obligatory Wal-Mart cheer is shouted in Zapotec, Gimme a W! is Dane Na Ti W! (Lyons, 2007). It is no wonder then that the savviest "coyotes" (a term used to designate somebody who charges large sums of money to carry "human cargo" across the border illegally) transporting peoples from Central America to the United States leave *la gente/*the people in the corporate cinedome in any one of these border cities on the Mexican side of *la linea*. The border crossers experience a profound shock once they realize that their trek to the land of milk and honey was a clever deception: it only appeared that they had arrived in the United States. This will soon change, as Wal-Mart's Mexican subsidiary, Wal-Mex, has begun opening supercenters in the impoverished region of Central America. But for those border crossers who were deceived, they learned a hard lesson when it came to U.S. capitalist expansionism: borders cross people, people don't cross borders.

Since the industrial revolution, Latin America has been a prime representative of *weak* capitalism, being situated along the periphery within an international capitalist system characterized by the super exploitation of its laborers. Latin America has structurally ended up transferring its human and natural value to the United States since the mid 1900s, and most recently to the giants of transnational capitalism (Dussel, 1995). The Bracero program of 1942–1964 and the elaborate network of employment agencies and labor recruiters stationed in border towns at the beginning of the twentieth century helped to give Los Angeles the notable distinction of having the largest Mexican population of any city in the United States (Sanchez, 1993).

The Mirasur community spans three populated city blocks, a fraction of the sprawling metropolis of Los Angeles, the official border city of the 1847 Treaty of Guadalupe Hidalgo. It is a city within a city whose history bears the marks of colonialism since the time "Yankee boosters and place promoters" began "sketching the outlines for a city of the future, a great modern metropolis rising on the site of a Spanish-Mexican pueblo" (Hise, 2004, 545). Immigrants have continued to flock to the town they once called their own and have been subject to the mechanisms of Americanization that have attempted to forcibly erase cultural heterogeneity as part of a larger project of homogenization designed to assimilate them into the precincts of the Anglo sphere. They have left their native villages and cities for Los Angeles, vacating the cobblestone towns of places such as Xicochimalco (Xico, Veracruz, whose waterfalls have been seen in movies such as *Romancing the Stone*), where a mural of the stoic general Hernán Cortés and the heart-shaped face of La Malinche remind visitors of their passing through on the August 19, 1519. Tracing the pathway of the Spanish-Indigenous pairing from Xalapa to Tenochtitlan with the image of a Christian cross overshadowing the majestic frame of an Aztec pyramid in a town formerly called *Fortaleza* (Strength) is both a montage and homage to *el mestizaje*, the mixture of bloodlines and cultures noted as the "pillar of Mexico today." Their mixed-blood cultural heritage will become further hybridized upon stepping on U.S. soil.

Anti-immigrant, and specifically anti-Mexican immigrant, sentiment has made its way into popular referendums and local politics in Los Angeles and California in general, unleashing a virulent social logic that is symptomatic of larger political-economic forces that classify rather than unify peoples who come together in this hybrid city space. As a result, many of the communities who occupy the urban landscape have been isolated as a distinct group, "aliens" of an already alien city, a colony with its own space (Hise, 2004). Layered against changing demographics propelled by demand in the labor force is a historical account of the ways in which Mexican-Americans and immigrants from Mexico have been incorporated into the institutional structures of public life. The Treaty of Guadalupe Hidalgo, which sanctioned both the racial identity and citizenship status of Mexican people, set the backdrop for successive interactions among Angelinos. As noted by Ariel Gross (2007),

> Mexican Americans occupy a unique position in the history of race in the United States, shaped heavily by formal, positive law. When Texas and California became part of the United States as a result of the Mexican-American War, thousands of people already living there, who had been Mexican, became U.S. citizens by the terms of the Treaty of Guadalupe Hidalgo. This Treaty guaranteed U.S. citizenship as well as rights to property, unless they declared their intent to remain Mexican

citizens within the year. Nevertheless, while a small elite of Mexican-American landholders who could prove that they were "Spanish" maintained white status, the majority of "Mexicans" were viewed and treated by Anglos as a separate race. (340–341)

Here, we can see how property status conflated with racial/ethnic status, further solidifying a hierarchical structure between "owners" and "workers" in terms of their preconceived racial identity. The politics of whiteness that comes to bear as social and legal policy in the United States for much of the early twentieth century resorted to physiognomic classifications to both marginalize and incorporate peoples of Mexican descent into the formal arrangements of society (Gross, 2007). Miscegenation rulings, the segregation of students in schools, and the constitution of juries to hear cases involving Mexican peoples relied on the arbitrary and delusive judgments of the "naked" eye: kinks in the hair, the angular facial markings of "Indian" blood, or darkness in the skin (Gross, 2007). For the most part, if "Indianness" or "negro-ness" could not be established, authorities classified Mexicans as white. From a social standpoint this was a limited arrangement, to the extent that public institutions relied on "other" information/characteristics to separate Mexican-Americans and adjudicate on behalf of the socially dominant whites. For Gross, these precedents established "cultural racism," the veiling of racial thinking in cultural terms (2007). In her words, "State officials in Texas and California—county attorneys, sheriffs, school board presidents—who clearly viewed Mexican Americans as an inferior race and treated them that way, learned over the course of the mid-twentieth century to explain their exclusion of Mexican Americans on the basis of language and culture rather than race" (2007, 341–342).

The segregation of U.S.-born children of Mexican descent from Caucasian U.S. citizens in schools was argued on the basis that their culture would deteriorate the quality of American schooling. To a large extent, however, the segregation of both U.S.-born and immigrant Mexican students was sanctioned by the Great Depression and the resulting anti-Mexican sentiment in immigration policy (Alvarez, 1986). In times of economic crisis, when the gaps between the wealthy and the poor widen, it becomes all too formidable and seemingly rational to target the most vulnerable sectors of society as the culprits of social and economic demise. The one case where school officials were unsuccessful in segregating children of Mexican descent was the highly regarded Lemon Grove Incident. Known for its booming agricultural industry and mining quarry, the area was transforming into an upper-middle-class community home to business owners and professionals. It was also home to Mexican families who worked in the mining and agricultural industry (Alvarez, 1986). In 1931 there were 75 Mexican students (primarily U.S.-born citizens) who went to school in the Lemon Grove district of San Diego. The school principal, under instructions of the school board, denied the children entrance into the school, directing them instead to a structure across the street that the children and their families eventually called La Caballeriza (the barn) (Alvarez, 1986). The families organized against the forced segregation of the children, sought legal counsel, and eventually won their court case against the school district. Legal counsel for the school district argued their case on the grounds that they were not intentionally segregating Mexican students, but that the children were in need of an "Americanization" school that could rectify their linguistic (and presumably, cultural) deficiencies (Alvarez, 1986). The judge, citing that the children were officially considered of the "Caucasian" race, ruled in favor of the families and dismantled the forced segregation of the students in the Lemon Grove District. More than a case of "race," the Lemon Grove incident was a testament to the collective power of families' protest.

Against this historical backdrop, Los Angeles and the Mirasur community in many ways function as a "counter-space" and "counter-weight" to that which the city's cultural and capitalist entrepreneurs imagined it to be (Hise, 2004). The Spanish-Mexican pueblo has disassembled into opposing fragments of wealth and poverty, English and Spanish, subordination and resistance. Over time, the result has been a parsing of individuals and groups in space "along lines defined by race—ethnicity; by income, status and class; by gender—whether elective or imposed, formal or informal, legal or extralegal" as the signature aspect of the "modern city under industrial capitalism" (Hise, 2004). The expropriation of peoples based principally on a logic specifically devised for social particularization in terms of racial characterizations (race conceived as an inherently natural object of categorization (Chang, 1985a, 1985b) acquires its facticity by means of the symbolic, material, and spatial configurations of human value: types of homes found from one block to the next are attributed to different racial groups, street signs separate groups by race, tagging on various walls or murals signals racialized turfs. These constitutive elements of the community shape larger ideologies and wear into the subjective identity formation of those who live in it, and also of those who live outside of the community.

Toward a "Border" Analysis of *School-Community*

The "borders" of Mirasur play out as a series of racial, cultural, gendered, and class antagonisms. The community has experienced displacement across multiple levels that tap into the core of how they identify and see themselves in a changing U.S. society. The notion of a border analysis gains more significance as it relates to not only people's movement from one place to another but to an entirely different way of being. Such histories of the hybridization of culture and social life have led numerous scholars to theorize the border not only in terms of a "physical" space but as a social construct itself (Sanchez, 1993). Historians, feminists, anthropologists, educators, and literary critics have often invoked the notion of "border" to reveal the disjuncture, tensions, and uncertainties that arise when people cross territorial and cultural borders (Giroux, 2005). The ways in which an individual's identity enters into agonistic conditions—sometimes leading to a shocking state when representation of citizenship hemorrhages with an excess of meanings, Americans who speak Spanish, who eat tamales, and/or burritos are nothing but beaners!—when confronted with the conditions of new social spaces, norms, and practices have led to varied interrogations and analyses that yield equally varied conclusions. Anthropologists have tended to focus on the "social patterns, interpretations, and expressions of people in contemporary life" (Alvarez, 1995, 462). Here the notions of "shifting" behavior and identity as they reveal adaptive patterns of those that have crossed the "border" are in focus. Identity, adaptation, and "hybridized behavior" become the main subjects of such analyses, illuminating the extent to which people can and do accommodate to social conditions for their economic and familial survival. Others interrogate the more subjective aspects of "living in-betweenness" (e.g., Saldivar, 1997; Mora, 2008). The psychosocial and affective dimensions where the history of migration and the memory of places lived converge to form a "border" consciousness have been the subject of numerous studies. Masculinity, patriarchy, sexual violence and exploitation, religious authority, sexuality, and connections to family and national identity also are included in the works of literary scholars whose focus has been on the linguistic aspects of identity. Such writings do not merely purge the author of her subconscious discontents but express the internal relations that are constitutive of reproduction of the subjective lineaments of everyday life: feeling love, shame, abandonment, exclusion, or, perhaps, acceptance. They reveal as much about their main protagonists (whether in the autobiographical exemplar of Gloria Anzaldúa's *Borderlands*, or in the fictional account of Carlos Fuentes' *Gringo Viejo* (Stephens, 2008)) as they do about the wider social order in which "interpenetration" (Stephens, 2008) takes place. These border narratives tell a story about human conflict, dialogue, and action; they also contribute to our understandings of how power, control, and exploitation circulate across time and space within capitalist society. They are, in their simplest terms, inquiries into the seemingly inevitable and often violent collisions between and among people, a characteristic feature of every known society, but one that takes on special characteristics in modern capitalist society in which people are compelled to produce value in order to survive.

The school-community borderland can be described as the space where institutional and state power and communities meet; it is the terrain where languages are built and vocabularies constructed as one power (institutional) attempts to communicate with other/s (communal power). The "colony" of the people is juxtaposed to the proprietary authority of the state. Schools are one of the first formal institutions with which border crossers will come into contact. They are the places where new sets of values and norms are introduced to the population and where dreams are met or failures secured. They are where the "border" identity of children, youth, and families will be formed to the extent that they will either be accepted or excluded from the formal arrangements of school life and life in the wider society. For many educators, the school-community borderland is a confusing abyss; they will study, judge, analyze, and try to diminish the appearance of difference between them (differences that are placed vertically on a scale of Americanness/non-Americanness and horizontally on a scale of insider/outsider) in an effort to provide new generations of youth with an education. It is this space in-between a school and community that I entered as a worker in Mirasur. Here is where the story begins.

The First Days on the Job

The first day on the job was relatively uneventful, sparing the fact that neither the principal nor any other administrator was prepared for my visit. I walked into the main office and noticed that the door leading to the principal's office was closed; the door leading to the office manager was also closed. Present before me was a 3-foot-high vinyl/plastic counter space, a faux barricade of sorts. Past it, three desks faced me, but two lacked occupants. I stared at the one with a living, breathing, sensuous body seated at it, but she was talking on the phone and seemed annoyed by my presence. Over time, I came to appreciate (or, better stated, respect) her expressive displays of impatience once I began to know her. Her name was Janelle. She had wit and an intoxicating love for her "baby girl" and teenage son. Her desk was covered with Lakers basketball memorabilia, and her pens, pencils, folders, and photos of loved ones were neatly secured in their respective places. That desk was her world, her space.

Institutional settings bear the personalized markings of their inhabitants. Every door leads to a setting that is uniquely mundane. Sometimes one finds clues about the individual's personal life: hobbies, desires, or signs of an obsession or neurosis. Other times, one finds nothing except for the framed portrait or plastered bust of a former leader. The traces found on walls and desks reveal the spoken silences of a given

Figure 1.1 Walking to school, photograph courtesy of Carmen Jimenez.

community: they mark boundaries, territories, so to speak. In this partially open office setting, with doors separating the public, faculty, and staff from the higher-ranked administrative officials, I recognized that I had approached *Janelle's* inner sanctum, and so I waited.

Anyone who has received even the most minimal training in teacher education knows that when you are a newcomer to a school it is in your best interest to befriend the secretarial staff. This is purely instrumentalist in reasoning, a pragmatic acknowledgment that your well-being will largely depend on how efficient and attentive they are to your needs. In other words, there is a reason to show your appreciation. They will ensure that your paycheck arrives on time, that you are enrolled for benefits, that your substitute is found when you can't make it to class, that your supplies get delivered to your classroom, and that you remain in the loop of any sudden surprises—lockdowns, earthquake drills, police visits, divorces, or new paramours forming. I did not mind, then, that Janelle rolled her eyes, took her time to end the call, and let out an exasperating sigh followed by a twang, "can I help you?"

I let Janelle know that I had arrived for my first day of work. "I don't know anything about that. Have a seat and hold on," she countered. After 10 minutes of phone calls and questioning other staff, a man approached me, introduced himself as the vice-principal, and invited me to his office across the hallway. Mr. Ramos had worked at the school for nearly a decade and was a recently minted vice-principal. I grew to know him as the second-in-command, the principal's protégé, and the man who carried an enormous amount of history and knowledge about the school and the Mirasur community in his memory reserves. Mr. Ramos initiated the conversation by excusing the man in charge:

> "Mr. Rodriguez had a regional principal's meeting today and he will not return until tomorrow."
>
> "OK," I replied.
>
> "Your office is going to be in the multipurpose room. Here is a copy of school's action plan for the grant you will be working on."

My story begins, then, in a specific relationship to Mirasur and the broader community, where I was given the position of grant administrator. I found it unsettling that the administration spent days after my arrival trying to come up with an appropriate title to characterize my work. They ultimately conceded on "Immediate Intervention for

Underperforming Schools Specialist," a title I found difficult to pronounce in a single breath and one that the teachers, staff, and families received rather ominously. Rumors spawned that I formed part of a special state accountability envoy. Popular folklore soon followed and the faculty branded me one of the principal's "preferred" workers (presumably for my storied ability to write grants at a moment's notice). I was 24 years old at the time and part of an ivy-league cohort who had received top-notch training in economics, qualitative research methods, and policy analysis to respond to the needs of impoverished communities and school settings. We were instructed on the methods of the World Bank and IMF in the so-called developing countries (what Eduardo Galeano more appropriately defines as the super-exploited), and we were expected to become the leaders, not the led, in such settings as Mirasur. Questions about how to reform educational services and settings in impoverished areas, where we would confront high poverty, child labor, single-led households, and civic strife framed our inquiries. For all intended purposes, I was tailor-made to do the job.

Having been under state surveillance for failing to meet its academic benchmarks, Mirasur had all the trappings of a school exiled into student failure. The administrative faculty was newly appointed; the old timers had been transferred elsewhere. A new curriculum was in place, coupled with school-site "coaches" in the core disciplines of reading and mathematics. This was to ensure that teachers followed the curricular mandates of prescripted lesson plans and weekly "fluency" tests, where children read as many words as they could, or computed as many mathematical equations as possible, per minute, to demonstrate their "fluency," and that "at-risk" children in the early grades received individualized attention to help them become more fluent. The state of California was also channeling a significant amount of money into the school, with the expectation that test results would gesture the school's gratitude for the additional resources. Indeed, the school welcomed and benefited from the additional resources, paring the school's infrastructure with the more elite and well-to-do elementary schools of the west side. I was familiar with all of these efforts, having spent a majority of my postbaccalaureate time as a classroom teacher, a doctoral student, or educational lobbyist in Washington, D.C. The reform efforts under way at Mirasur were neither new nor innovative. An elite guard of politicians, staffers, lobbyists, and special interest groups had worked on similar education reform efforts for decades, but to no avail.

The door that led to *my office space* was a portal into another universe, a social universe of daily gatherings and habitual actions hinting toward the general organization of Mirasur. Four women in addition to me worked in the large multipurpose room: the director of English language acquisition services, the director of Title I (federal program for the poor), and both of their support staff, teacher assistants who had been promoted to desk duty. Oversized storage bins and bookcases separated the room. On one side, the Title I staff occupied the room, sharing their space with two industrial-sized copy machines that teachers regularly used before, during, and after school hours as they rushed to make their instructional copies. On the other side was the English-language acquisition staff, coupled with a copy machine of their own, headphones and tape recorders for daily testing of children's language skills, dye cutouts for connecting the room's borders with the latest American holiday, workbooks, expired district policy notebooks, and other miscellaneous tchotchkes. And then there was me, somewhere in-between the worlds that each disciplinary staff occupied, and without reason to utilize any of the items in the room. During the first days of my job, I felt utterly useless: I didn't make copies and I didn't test children.

It had been a couple of years since I found myself immersed in a community of Spanish speakers and Latinas. Spanish is my mother tongue, but, even so, I was aware of how my tongue moved slower than usual when I spoke at Mirasur, stubbornly stopping at the roof of my mouth as I tried to roll my r's. My tongue felt weighted, barring the flow of air needed to mark me a native speaker. Speaking Spanish became a frustration, so I opted for a mix between Spanish and English, something my father and mother always advised against, out of fear that I would sound *Pocha*, or what translates into culturally *impure*.

Mr. Ramos showed me to my desk and introduced me to the English-language acquisition staff. "*¿De dónde eres*/Where are you from?," they asked. I always have difficulty answering that question. I know where I was born, North Hollywood, but I have never lived there. I know where I have moved to, but that includes at least six cities during my childhood and another six in my adult years. I also know that I feel connected to my Colombian roots, having spent a significant amount of my childhood visiting my family in Medellin, a city notoriously stereotyped as the home of *mulas*, drug lords, vengeful soccer players, and beauty queen assassins. So I keep it simple. I am from where I currently live. "*Yo vivo en Pasadena/*I live in Pasadena," I replied. "*¿Y que vas hacer aqui/*And what are you going to do here?" "*Voy a trabajar en el* grant, help in any way I can." "*Oh, que bueno/*Oh that is good." End of conversation.

Later that day I joined faculty for lunch in the cafeteria, knowing full well that becoming part of a school community included breaking bread with them. I initially thought that my greatest challenge would be to transcend the apparent hierarchy between a worker in an administrative office and a worker in a classroom. These are the micro-tensions that pepper every educational setting, the distinctions created between the "knowers" and the "doers" that accompany the fine division of labor in societies like ours.

Midway through the unpleasant pleasantries that often characterize first encounters over lunch, a woman asked if I knew where Mexico was and let out a gasp of disbelief when I responded in the affirmative, in Spanish. It wasn't the first time (nor would it be the last) for someone to express confusion over my race-culture-language-ethnic credentials, so I was neither offended nor shocked by her query or response, "*es que tu pareces gringa/*it's just that you look like a gringa." I felt like *una puerta en media manga/*a door in the middle of a grassy field.

I came to realize over the first few days at Mirasur that my self-definition and self-valuation would undergo a serious transformation as a result of my perceived social displacement. I was the new girl in town, and I most certainly looked like it. My skin is a light olive tone, and I am often mistaken for Greek, Persian, Arab, Israeli, Italian, Turkish, and any other Mediterranean "exotic" lineage. In the Mirasur community of 99 percent Latina/o/s primarily of Mexican and Central American descent, I looked, talked, and even walked with a difference. My body had adjusted to years of ear-pinching and under-the-table heel stabbing. My mother was considered a beauty in her family, having been born with pale skin, light brown-blondish hair, green eyes, and a perfectly symmetrical face that branded her my dark-skinned grandfather's favorite child of seven. As a young middle-class woman in her native Colombia, she often graced the window sills of aspiring photographers and politicians. She wore white dresses and matching satin gloves and stood frozen in time and space during annual Holy Week processions. She learned to stand upright, sit properly, smile gracefully, and wave apologetically to the performative mourners passing by her home, a lesson that she handed down to her only daughter.

My intention to relate with the faculty was overdetermined by the official and unofficial indexes of my ascribed identity as a Colombian-American, at times Spanish-speaking, always well-mannered and well-dressed, and an unforgivably childless woman with elite educational credentials. As I internally traced my lineage and the constitutive elements of my identity, I recognized how the postmodern subject's tendency to view place and space as the prime determinants of human relations can make even the most sedated observer dizzy with confusion. I was undergoing identity "shock" upon feeling that I did not belong, or could not become a part of, the racial/ethnic/linguistic community of Mirasur. I focused, then, on uncovering the relations that connect place and space, that animate the borderlands of identity formation and construction, and signify the categories of race, ethnicity, gender, and class, in the apparent diaspora of Mirasur. Performing the position of "gringa" or "not gringa" had less to do with my immediate sense perception (I felt odd both here and there) and more to do with how communities and the wider social order were both ideologically marked, and were in a process of marking themselves, historically, structurally, and materially (Hill Collins, 1999).

My first assignment as "specialist" was to purchase tape recorders and English books on tape presumably for children to learn English "better" and "faster" (learning through auditory osmosis), to find reasonably priced and mountable TV-VCR-DVD combos (learning through visual osmosis), whiteboards to replace chalkboards (learning through tactile osmosis), new storage bins, and a school marquee. I was in many ways a highly paid ordering clerk. This is not to suggest that the children of the school were not in need of material resources to enhance their learning environment or that the teachers would not benefit from the latest educational software and "toolkits," but my assignment did point toward recent trends in educational reform that have generated a culture of hyper-commodification in the learning industrial complex. Learning deficits have become the corporate sector's private cache. Catalogues abound in every teacher's mailbox, supplemental literacy and math kits guarantee results within weeks, DVDs are replacing real-time teachers, videos and CD-ROMs promise to shorten a teacher's already-dreaded teaching day, and in an era of heightened accountability and evaluation schemes, test-prep workbooks and take-home worksheets have a renewable energy tag of hundreds of millions of dollars a year. Less emphasis is placed on teaching and learning while more is placed on following the instructions located in the rectangular gray shaded box on the top left-hand corner of each standardized testing booklet. My orders came in verbal form and I followed them in due fashion and purchased every single item on the school improvement list.

Weeks after the purchasing frenzy subsided, I became more observant and better acquainted with aspects of the community that I had overlooked: the women who manned the school entrance from morning to early evening; the mother-volunteers who spent hours cutting paper, stapling worksheets together, and transferring them to the appropriate teacher's office; the steady stream of women and mothers—young ones and some who were more adult—who walked into Room One to check in with the Title I coordinator to ask about their day's "assignment"; the husband-and-wife street vendors who sold breakfast tamales and champurrado in the mornings; the unkempt children sent to the main office because they were classified as "dirty" or "misbehaved"; the police who frequented the school to interrogate students, families, and/or teachers who had been identified as victim or perpetrator in an act of violence.

*   *   *

The day is just like any other day. The morning bell has rung and teachers and staff are scurrying out of Room One to pick up their students. I'm sitting at my desk, sipping on a cup of coffee that the girls from the main office brew in the bathroom that is next to Janelle's space. I have been granted access to the girls' room after befriending Lucia, the social worker with long dark hair, slim build, and a few centimeters taller than me. People have come to know us as the twin towers.

A woman enters the room from the opposite side and approaches the copy machine. She stares at it for a minute or so until the Title I coordinator asks her if she needs help. After a few minutes she figures out how to use the machine and waits for the copies. Mr. Blanton, the vice principal, walks into the room. His eyes become fixed on the woman using the copy machine and his feet instinctually lead him towards her. He approaches her from behind and takes two steps to the front and right. She has no option than to face him as he violently shakes his index finger from side to side and yells, "Los TAs no deben de estar haciendo copias para los maestros despues de que suene la campana. Se les paga para que esten en las clases ayudando los niños! Los maestros ya saben esto/TAs (teaching assistants) are not supposed to make copies for teachers after the morning bell rings. You are paid to be in class helping the children! Teachers know this." The woman collects the copies, keeps her eyes fixed to the ground and silently walks away. She is Señora Maria Lourdes Jimenez, a mother volunteer.

Shifting Focus

Mirasur's action plan contained a host of thoughtful recommendations about how to remedy many of the school's failings. A committee comprised of an external evaluation team (retired principals and school superintendents), teachers, staff, and community representatives had designed intricate surveys and aggregated the results to help pave the path for the school's recovery. The items that I was asked to purchase—directly or indirectly—applied to several of the grievances indicated in the plan: the absence of materials, library, technology, books, and etceteras that would facilitate a more "robust" learning environment in an impoverished educational setting. These were not insignificant by any means. On the contrary, the ability for families, faculty, students, and staff to experience a sense of pride in their environment had an undisputable effect on their sense of place, purpose, and worth. The administration felt "worthy" in the sense that they could "see" and "measure" their everyday work based on the arrival and installation of new objects, the construction of a premier library, or the painting of a mural displaying some of the United States' most notable leaders and scientific accomplishments. The principal expressed the greatest sense of pride in the library. Two classrooms were joined into one, creating a large, warm, and inviting space. Stadium seating allowed children to sit and listen attentively to an enthusiastic storyteller, bookshelves housed thousands of grade-level appropriate books, globes decorated tabletops, and maps covered the walls. Mr. Rodriguez escorted every newcomer or visitor to see it. "There was no library here before," he would say. "Now we have the best, state-of-the-art facility." Visitors would typically respond with an emphatic set of oohs and aahs, followed by a request to take photos with the children reading or an offer to make a monetary or material donation. The faculty and staff presumably experienced a sense of value in feeling equipped with the material and resources to "do" their work; and families certainly appreciated the "care" given to their children's home away from home. In this sense, Jonathon Kozol's proclamation in *Savage Inequalities* that a lack of resources and materials, such as libraries, tend to communicate to the children that "In the eyes of this society, you are not much at all" (1991, 80–81) does not go unwarranted.

Not all items in the action plan referenced the need to purchase or update existing technology/material. Others stressed the importance of communication and support between the faculty and administration, the staff and faculty, and the community and faculty. In other words, the nexus of interpersonal relationships was also subject to inquiry, and measures were noted to facilitate and improve collaboration and support between the different factions of the school environment. Those items associated with staff "development" and teacher preparedness (i.e., quality) were out of my scope of designated duties, but the point made about enhancing the relationship and communication between the school and community was relatively within my reach. In addition to satisfying the request for a school marquee and automated messaging service to improve the unidirectional distribution of information—from school to the community—I decided to shift focus, to the spaces of personal interaction between the families and schools, to uncover the particular and material coordinates of authority and power that framed interactions such as those between Mr. Blanton and Señora Jimenez at the Xerox machine, and to interrogate the possibilities of, put very simply, doing things *differently*.

I introduce this brief history of the nature of my work and the situated observations I have expressed about the Mirasur community to show the complexity and the multiple sources of influence that play into the seemingly mundane acts—eating lunch, driving into a parking lot, drinking coffee, ordering supplies, monitoring staff—within an educational setting. From the perspective of its social actors, these daily actions and experiences take place naturally and unhesitatingly. Rarely does an opportunity present itself for actors to reflect critically upon the meanings conveyed or the institutional structures in place that configure the flow of information, the distribution of power and authority, and the systems of reward/punishment or inclusion/exclusion that frame social interactions. Or put differently, to inquire into the rules and discourses from which social action emerges (Turner, 1974). On the contrary, educators are often so concerned with education as a repository of curriculum content, access to resources, and the distribution of "quality" learning materials in our schools that even with the best intentions they fail to acknowledge the deep syntax of human sociability, the knotting of discourses to social relations that condition the production of knowledge, what we could call the "pedagogical unconscious.[1]" The pedagogical unconscious can be mapped by identifying the contradictory components that comprise the everyday ideology of the school—both the manifest and hidden components—and how pedagogical practices and the social relations that govern interactions between individuals conceal the very contradictions they conjoin. This is not to suggest that the latter takes precedence over the former, but it does indicate the need to examine how we have come to relate to one another and how our practices constitutively form our postindustrial, postmodern, and seemingly post-everything society.

LAS MADRES/THE MOTHERS

Maria Lourdes Jimenez is a mother of five, grandmother of three, wife, sister, *comadre*, and daughter, with a staunch character and inviting presence. Jimenez often wears her long brown-red-ash locks pulled back in a ponytail, a pragmatic look that accents her strong *mestiza* roots. She is no taller than 5'2" with a stocky build that hints at her considerable physical strength. She dresses casually—jeans, sweat pants, and T-shirts—but at times she would attend a school meeting in a bright red suit. Red is sometimes considered the color of fire and blood, charity, bravery, and courage. I, on the other hand, would often wear dark-colored slacks, sweaters, and overcoats. I wore black to be exact, *el color de luto*, the color of grief and sorrow.

Jimenez has an intoxicating smile and unforgettable cackle that incites inner warmth in passersby. She has a way of joining thoughts with words that result in poignant and thought-provoking messages, a trait that she stubbornly refuses to carry to paper. "*Mi letra es muy fea/*My writing is ugly," she claims. Her words, however, do not cede to social hierarchies. As she says, "*Pues, me gusta hablar. No sé escribir ni leer bien, pero hablar sí puedo y me tienen que escuchar/*I like to talk. I don't know how to write or read well, but I can speak and they need to listen to me."

I met Jimenez the evening that over 300 mothers and fathers, along with many of their kin, attended a meeting I had asked a not-for-profit community group to organize. The group had delivered an inspiring call to parents, asking them to participate in a 10-week seminar that would inform them of their rights and responsibilities in the education of their children. The topics to be covered included understanding the U.S. school system, establishing a supportive home-learning environment, promoting reading, and maintaining communication with a child's teacher. I was surprised by the level of interest in the community and unprepared to provide families with the childcare I had promised. The seminar took place in the early-evening hours in order to attract a large number of people after the formal workday had ended. It was six o'clock to be exact.

Earlier that week I had approached two women who were on the school's payroll as "support staff" and asked them to provide childcare for the parent institute. Señora Martha Villalobos had previously shared with me photos of her son in his school band outfit. Martha managed to catch me as I walked past the main entrance and toward my office. "*Pssst, pssst, Señorita Jaramillo, pasale por aqui un momentito por favor*/Miss Jaramillo, come over here for a minute please." I quickly recognized the cardboard box placed next to her personal belongings, the box with milk chocolate, chocolate-crispy, chocolate-almond bars stacked one on top of another, and the manila dollar-sized envelope for collected sales. "*No me compra un chocolate para la escuela de mi hijo*/Won't you buy a chocolate for my son's school?" I didn't ask how much, since, as long as I remembered, those chocolate bars had always sold for a dollar. Speaking to her put me back in time, thinking about the childhood anticipation that accompanied school fundraisers and the feeling of despair and disappointment at not reaching enough sales to qualify for a boombox or TV-VHS set.

Martha quickly introduced me to the son for whom she had solicited the purchase of chocolates. She had portrait-size, wallet-size, and keychain-size photos of him in fringed red, gold, and blue regalia and branding a shiny brass flute. "*Esta en la banda*/he is in the band," she boasted. She coiled the photos against her chest, exposed a coquettish smile, and slowly drew one photo out after the next, holding it several inches upward from her petite 5-foot frame. "*Mire mi hijo como esta de chulo*/Look at how handsome my son is." *Felicidades Señora Villalobos, esta muy chulo*/Congratulations Mrs. Villalobos, he is very handsome, I replied.

Martha's children had attended Mirasur and progressed through the educational pipeline into high school. Her son was her *prieto*, her youngest one. As I looked at Martha's face, it seemed that each line and crevice corresponded to the smiles and grimaces that accompanied decades of motherhood. She was the most senior member on payroll, officially on the books since 1974, a year before my birth.

Martha worked for three and a half hours Monday through Friday. She guarded the front entrance of the school and ensured that visitors signed their names on the sheet of paper she kept on a clipboard before they proceeded to the main office for a visitor's pass. She looked harmless, but she was a vicious guardian. "*Firmame por favor*/sign here please," she called out to the visitors who ignored her welcoming *buenos dias*/good morning. Occasionally she would be forced out of her chair to stop a wayward guest. On those occasions Martha leapt to her feet and traced the culprit's footsteps. Her short legs forced her to take three steps for every one of the visitor's, but she would eventually catch up and escort the visitor to the main office for their required pass. If they did not comply, she could rely on her whistle.

I asked her if she was interested in working at the childcare in the evenings while the parents attended the program. "*Pues si me paga*/Well if you pay me," she responded. *Si, le pagamos su salario regular por hora*/Yes, we will pay you by the hour. I let her know that I would ask her to sign some papers, but otherwise she should clock in and out using the time sheets in the main office. As I began to walk away, Martha let me know, "*oye, si necesita otra persona yo tengo una amiga que le gusta trabajar*/listen, if you need another person I have a friend who likes to work."

I approached Señora Guadalupe Mendez during her morning patrol of the playground. She was one of the five adults responsible for the 1300 children scattered across the asphalt, in between the temporary bungalows, on the dusty grass field, running in and out of the bathrooms, or sitting—patiently—on the lunch tables completing an overdue homework assignment. The morning was overcast and the last young person to approach her once the bell rang was her son, Michael. She bent down, kissed him on the forehead, and he scurried to his line.

Quiet. There was an overwhelming sense of growing quiet. I stood next to Guadalupe and we watched the teachers approach their lines one by one. To some the lines were not straight enough, others were judged too rowdy, and several of them were deemed just perfect: students with hands to their side or behind their back, heads forward, and silence. Complete silence. Those were the first lines to disperse to their classrooms. The principal availed himself to monitor the children this morning, so several of the teachers were making a concerted effort to get their lines more perfect, presumably an artifact of their classroom management skills. Guadalupe and I were fixated on their interactions and we could not help but laugh. A child in line five would not stop encircling his neighbor, a girl in line eleven had begun to cry, and the disheveled teacher from room 32 gave his students a frighteningly stern glare but escorted them regardless, as the students jumped, yelped, and skipped past the principal (some even attempted to give him a high-five) on their way to class.

Guadalupe agreed to work for childcare that following Monday. On the evening of the first meeting, we found ourselves as three ill-prepared women who could not provide care for the children, given the unprecedented level of attendance. As parents began to leave their children in our care, the sweat dripped from my brow and my facial muscles stiffened. I panicked. For as long as I remember, whenever I hold an infant my arms shake uncontrollably, and when they cry I seek assistance. I went to private Catholic schools and spent my pre- and postpubescent years reading scripture and enduring endless lectures about keeping my legs crossed until marriage. As part of religion, biology, and anatomy class, it was also required that we watch and listen to the trembling legs and unconscious cries of women undergoing abortions. And when a field trip was part of the curriculum, we could always count on identifying the "would-be" body parts of a floating mass of an aborted fetus in a glass jar. All I could think of as I tried to identify the limbs of the unsexed fetus, however, were the cold iced teas my Nana would serve me in similarly shaped antique glass fruit jars. I was warned throughout my childhood about the damning effects of childbirth outside wedlock, which in my case would have led to a nine-month long quarantine in a house of nuns somewhere in the floral hinterlands of rural Colombia. I learned early on to fear my body's essence, to sanctify prudence, and to reject corporeal indulgence. My body did not belong to me. It belonged to the church, to my family, and presumably to the man who would one day call me his wife. I lived on borrowed time and in borrowed flesh, paid by the death of a lone Nazarene for all eternity, so I've been told.

So that night when a mass of children awaited instructions on where to go and what to do, I was relieved at meeting Maria Jimenez. She detected my sense of despair, approached me, and offered her assistance. "*¿Necesitas ayuda, puedo cuidar los niños/*Do you need help? I can take care of the children." "*No señora, gracias, tu veniste para participar en el seminario/*No thank you, you came to participate in the seminar." "*No importa, me quedo para la segunda sección, deje que te ayude/*It does not matter, I will take the second session, let me help you." "*¿Tienes llaves?Abrís cinco salones y nos dividimos los niños, allí hacemos cualquier cosa con ellos/*Do you have keys? Open five classrooms and we divide the children there, we'll do something with them." And so I did. And so we did. For the next nine weeks, we took care of the children, every Tuesday night, from six to eight in the evening.

Maria Jimenez, however, has a different story to tell about our first encounter. She remembers meeting me in the large multipurpose room where I spent my time at work, secluded, tucked behind a desk in the far right-hand back corner. *Conocí una persona que me miró sobre los lentes. Pensé que era una persona grosera, y me dije quién es esta persona para mirarme así. Y allí empezó todo, Jaramillo. O ya perdí la cuenta, o no sé*/I met a person who looked at me over her glasses. I thought that it was a rude person. And I said, who is this person, how is she looking at me. That is where everything started Jaramillo. Or I have lost count, I don't know.

Although I, Maria Jimenez, and the group of women that I refer to as "las madres" came into contact in a setting that polarized us prima facie within our immediate social worlds as immediate outsiders—they from outside the school's structure, I from within—we attempted to supersede those distinctions and move into a space from where we could generate an understanding of our selves and contest the dominant social structures that framed what was to become *our* movement within the social drama of Mirasur. Here we managed to construct a psychosocial moratorium, a liminal space where—provisionally at least—we managed to dissolve cultural and social hierarchies and fashion a horizontal space for creating our own approaches to the transformation of the school. Together, we share with you the script that fills the remaining pages of this text.

In Mirasur, meaning was most immediately felt and lived through the text we carried in our bodies—the bodies of mestizas who displayed varying degrees of their "indigenousness" depending on how the observer chose to situate us based on our physiological characteristics. Meaning was also generated by the extent to which we had come to identify with and become a part of dominant U.S. society. Our immigration status, connection to our "home" countries, our bloodlines, language practices, traditions, and understandings of how we had been placed as women in this world served as the foundation from which the multiple social dramas of Mirasur were narrated. But as the following pages will make clear, such meaning about who we were and how we could come to relate to one another operated against a much broader cultural-political-economic landscape that was both historical and present in our everyday activity. Methodologically, then, the notion of two social dramas (the institutional and the personal) colliding, informing, and depending on one another speaks to the ways in which class relations, race, and ethnicity operate in the context of communities (the wider community of the United States and the local community of Mirasur). The abstract and the particular are the Hegelian threads that bring these social dramas together, demonstrating how intensely complex and intrinsically familiar are the operations of our social institutions and communities against the shared backdrop of capitalism, the history and ongoing experience of coloniality, patriarchy, and the ethnic/racial distinctions that frame human interactions. Here, too, the social drama of las madres, of motherhood, is intended not to reify the kind of heterosexual feminism (Nolacea-Harris, 2005) that has characterized much of the work surrounding the contribution of women's activism in Chicana, Mexican-American communities, but rather to signal the personal dimensions of being a *woman* and how that subjective position marks the integration of various spheres of social experience and history.

2

THE PEDAGOGY OF THE BURRO

PEDAGOGY OF THE BURRO[1]

"Friend Big-ears, what do you carry on your back?"

"I carry many cheeses for my master, friend Too-whay-deh," answered the Burro.

"Then give me one, friend, for I am hunger-dying."

No, said the Burro, I cannot give you one, for my master would blame me – since they are not mine but his, and a man of the pueblo waits for them.

Pueblo Indian folktale

*Un burro usted lo carga donde usted lo jala/*A donkey you carry wherever you pull it.

Maria Jimenez

I'm walking down the hallway and take notice of the hundreds of books stacked on the large rectangular tables at the front entrance. It does not surprise me to see Jimenez and las madres standing informally around the tables and working in what appeared to be a highly organized assembly line. I had grown accustomed to seeing las madres every morning, seated at the school entrance and oftentimes completing a task, or a so-called favor, for the school administration or teachers. "*Señoras, ¿tienen tiempo para hacerme un favor?/*Ladies, do you have time to do us a favor?," is how las madres were officially approached. Some of the mothers were paid staff and others were registered on the official school docket as volunteers. Some others were just passing by to break from the monotony of house duties, or to share a passing word or gossip with their comadres.

On this particular morning, I could see Jimenez taking the lead and orchestrating the mothers' actions. She picked up a book from one of the stacks on the table and passed it to another mother, Villalobos. Villalobos opened the book cover and stamped it with the school's name and address. The book is then returned to Jimenez and she stacks it on the red metal-framed dolly perched against the wall. Within minutes another mother joins the group, and another, and another. But with only two stamps available, Jimenez thanks the third mother and tells her there is nothing to be done at the moment. I stand and gaze as I watch the mothers' hands blacken with ink. They laugh, and Jimenez takes intermittent sips of coffee from her Styrofoam cup inscribed by ballpoint pen with the word, *Maria*. "*Oye, que estan haciendo*/Hey, what are you doing," I ask. La Señora Virginia tells me that the school just purchased new books for every classroom and that the principal asked if they could help by stamping them before they were distributed to the classrooms. This is to ensure "*que los niños cuando se los lleven a las casas, los regresen a la escuela. Es para que no se pierdan, no ves*/that when the children take the books home, that they return them to school. It is so that they don't get lost, you see." Stacks of books and cardboard boxes swarm the mothers. A custodial clerk approaches with another load and Jimenez asks him to wait until they make a delivery before he brings more books for them to stamp. "*Ya no nos caben mas*/We can't fit anymore." It is clear that with only two stamps at their disposal, they would spend hours, if not days, finishing their task. Looking toward the back door of the principal's office that leads into the main hallway, Jimenez utters, "*A ver si ese gabacho nos va traer otra estampilla para que trabajemos mas rapido*/Let's see if that *gabacho* is going to bring us another stamp so that we can work faster." She could not have timed her request with more precision, for within seconds the principal steps into the hallway shaking two over-sized ziplock plastic bags in the air, each one with a stamp and ink pad inside. He instructs las madres to use caution, "*Señoras, aqui tienen dos mas. Pero con cuidado me regrasan este es el mio*/Ladies, here are two more. But carefully return this one, it is mine." "*Ese viejo cansón*/ that old annoying man," Jimenez responds, under her breath.

Las madres then begin to load a class's set of books on the dolly; they had decided to distribute the books according to the corresponding grade level, beginning with the classrooms nearest to them. Mirasur was comprised of two permanent buildings, but over the years the school had outgrown its capacity. Portable trailers warehoused at least half of the schoolchildren, and the farthest container was approximately a five minute walk away. The thought of hauling hundreds of books such a distance added an air of agony to las madres' faces. Jimenez reads the women's expressions, *"empezemos arriba y después buscamos como hacer llegar los libros por alla/*let's begin upstairs and then we will figure out how to get the books over there."

Jimenez and las madres load several book sets on the dolly. A shaggy-haired instructor by the name of Mr. Sonnenkamp approaches them. The skin on his nose showed signs of decay after decades of sun exposure. He was one of the few pale-skinned instructors who also spoke fluent Spanish. His eyes opened wide and his cheeks turned a rosy pink. *"¿Que estan haciendo señoras?* /What are you doing ladies?," he asked, followed by a pause. *"Parecen burritas/* You look like little donkeys," "he continued. Mr. Sonnenkamp laughed and we chuckled. He walked away, las madres continued their work, and I returned to my desk.

Walking through the hallways of Mirasur or on the streets of this primarily Latina/o immigrant neighborhood, it is not uncommon to hear the word "burro" (donkey) directed to a child, a teenager, a man, and as the above scenario indicates, a woman and mother. Oftentimes the exchange goes something like this, *"ay, no seas burro; no seas menso*hey, don't act like a donkey, don't be a fool." The expression is commonplace, a way to both identify and be identified. Burro in the pejorative implies stupidity and obedience. It seems to slide off the tongue as simply as uttering "good morning" and "good night." Our own parent educators decried the ill effects of using "burro" as a way to motivate children and youth to work harder (the assumption is that when called a burro, the child will try not to act like a burro), and they pleaded with the families to refrain from its usage. Sitting in the classroom on a Tuesday night during our parent seminar, I listened to the instructor—a former student (and parent) himself—cheerfully giving a lesson on home discipline to the mothers and fathers in attendance. *"Oye, a quién aqui le gusta que lo llamen burro/*Hey, who in this room likes to be called a donkey?" he asked. *"Levanten las manos si gustan que los llamen burros/*Raise your hands if you like being called donkeys." The families laughed, much in the same way that we laughed when las madres were called burritas. That morning, Mr. Sonnenkamp's reference to las madres as burros brought forth a nervous laughter, the kind that attempts to conceal the effects of self-depreciation. Being called a "burra" was a description that for las madres held a double meaning. As a joke, it was not to be taken seriously, but at a deeper level it served to normalize and naturalize the hierarchy of Mirasur, drawing indirect attention to what las madres perceived as their lack of education, their lack of knowing, and, perhaps, their lack of feeling fully human. On a scale of human sociability, las madres were identified, in effect, at the lowest rank.

A few days later, Jimenez and *la madre* Ramirez officially joined the payroll to cover childcare for the parent institute. I invited them to my desk to fill out the paperwork. Jimenez protested, "*No se como hacer esto, soy burra para estas cosas*/I don't know how to do this, I'm a donkey when it comes to these things." Ramirez added, "*si, somos burras para esto, verdad Lourdes*/yes, we are donkeys for this, right Lourdes?"

Why call yourselves burras, I asked. To which Jimenez blatantly responded: "*Yo soy torpe. Torpe para escribir, torpe para saber como se hacen las cosas en esta escuela. Somos cobardes, torpes y egoistas con nosotras mismas*/I am a clumsy blunderer. A clumsy blunderer in writing, a clumsy blunderer in knowing how things are done in this school. We are cowards and selfish with ourselves."

Pero porque cobardes/but why cowards, I insisted? "*Porque no nos sabemos respetar ni defender*/Because we don't know how to respect or defend ourselves," Jimenez replied. For Jimenez, the idealized version of the burro as a mindless, docile, and complacent animal reflected an assessment of her own self-worth. And in my assessment, the metaphor of the burro captured the general tendency of faculty-community relations in Mirasur. I present this to you in the following reflections.

STAFF DEVELOPMENT

Every Tuesday we have one hour of "staff development" in the school auditorium. Staff development often translates to the principal and other administrative staff (literacy coaches, math coaches, special education personnel, psychologists, school attendance counselors, bilingual coordinators, Title I coordinators, computer coordinators) reviewing testing procedures, language classification protocols, classroom technical-support services and programs, classroom assignments, pupil attendance protocols, and so on. On this day, the school principal decided to go over "parent involvement protocols." I offer the following paraphrase of his remarks: "we've had a number of parent involvement programs at our school and we feel really good about parents getting involved. I'd like to ask all of you to treat the mothers who volunteer their time with respect. You know, they are good ladies who really want to help and feel needed. They like to have something to do. You can have them volunteer in your classes, help you with getting the take home reading booklets collated, and things like that. Think of them as free labor." One of the 80 or so teachers in the auditorium asked, "well how do we communicate with them so that they can manage their time effectively? It wouldn't be very fair if all of us asked them to help us." To which the principal responded, "they have a mailbox in the office, just put a little note in there when you need help and they will get to you." "Any more questions" he asked. "Okay, next item on the agenda is..."

The Mother Workers Wear Jackets

I am sitting next to Jimenez as she guards the side entrance gate. It's close to 8 in the morning. The principal walks by, "*¿Adonde esta tu chaqueta Señora Jimenez/*Where is your jacket Mrs. Jimenez?" Jimenez responds, "*Pues no la traigo. ¿Para que me la voy a poner?/* Well I don't have it with me. Why am I going to put it on?" He quips back, "*Para que yo te pueda encontrar mas facil señora/*So that I can find you more easily lady."

Thieves

Las madres and I are seated at tables in u-shaped formation in the parent center. We spent the morning writing a letter to the English as a Second Language (ESL) adult educator who had left a note on the chalkboard that read in bold lettering: **Parents, do not move my desk or take my Kleenex, items are my private property.** Las madres had invited the educator to teach families English twice each week in the parent center.

I asked las madres to tell me what to put in the letter. Jimenez responded, "*dile que la caja de Kleenex es de la escuela y que no somos ningunos ratones/*tell her that the box of Kleenex belongs to the school and that we aren't any thieves." Several minutes later the mother Gonzalez walked into the parent center. She had an exasperated look on her face, pursed lips and raised brows. We greeted her, "*buenos días Gonzalez/*good morning Gonzalez."

Gonzalez took a seat at the table and began, "*La señora de la administración me acaba de decir que me moviera de la puerta de la entrada donde yo estaba parada con mi hija porque iban a venir gente del distrito y teniamos que dar una buena impresión/*The woman of the administration just told me to move from the entrance where I was standing with my daughter because she said people were coming from the district and we had to give a good impression." "*Pues les voy a decir que tienen que estar mas preocupados por los maestros en la clase para hacer una buena impresión/*Well I am going to tell them that they should be more worried about the teachers in the class to make a good impression."

Ayyyyyyyyy, si las madres responded. Jimenez turned to her and asked, "*y le dijiste eso/*and did you say that to her?" Gonzalez responded, "*No. Me di la vuelta y me fui/*No. I turned around and left."

The message is clear: parents=thieves; mother's bodies=unfavorable.

IDIOTS DON'T TALK BACK

About an hour has passed since school was let out. I'm hanging out until the parent institute starts at 5 p.m. Jimenez walks into my office and asks me to speak with a mother who had just met with her son's second-grade teacher. We walked over to the cafeteria where the mother waited. "*Platicale de su problema, con confianza/*Tell her about your problem, with ease." The woman told me that she had met with her son's teacher because, "*Mi hijo me dijo que el maestro lo llamó tonto. A mi no me parece bien que un maestro le hable así a los niños. Le reclamé al maestro y se disculpó, dijo que hay veces se le sube la rabia, pero que eso pasa porque los niños no se portan bien. Cuando le dije que todavía no estaba de acuerdo, se enojó y me despidio/*My son told me that the teacher had called him stupid. I don't think its okay for a teacher to speak that way to the children. I asked the teacher about it and he excused himself, he said that sometimes his anger rises but that it happens because the children misbehave. When I told him I still wasn't in agreement he got mad and told me to leave."

PAPER GIRL

It is Monday morning. An overstock of *LA Times* newspapers from the previous Friday are on the front table of the main entrance. The bell rings, and students shuffle into line and walk to their classrooms. The office staff recognizes the bell as a signal to return to their work spaces. I make my way to Room One, passing the main entrance on my way. Jimenez is standing behind the stack of newspapers. She speaks to the mother Villalobos. The Principal walks by, a standard morning ritual as he makes sure that all teachers have met their student lines on time and that promptly is being wasted. Today he is in a cheerful mood, talkative, smiling at students and faculty as they pass him by.

He stops to greet the mothers. He glances at the newspapers. *"Oye, Señora Jimenez porque no sales al frente y vendes estos periodicos por 25 centavos. Asi le ayudas a tu esposo/*Hey Mrs. Jimenez, why don't you go outside and sell these newspapers for 25 cents. That way you earn extra income to help your husband." *"Porque no lo vende usted?/*Why don't you sell them," Jimenez responds. He walks away.

Strangling Misbehavior

I'm sitting in the computer lab working on a grant proposal for the school. A fourth-grade teacher walks in with a rowdy bunch of students, who look excited to play some "learning" games on the computer. The computer aide has the lowest voice I've ever heard, barely a whisper. He is a young man, and when he smiles his cheeks take the shape of dumplings. His smile is infectious. "Okay boys and girls, go to your stations.... quietly." The children are giggling and laughing, loudly rushing to the computers. "If you guys don't shut up I'm going to strangle you," the teacher screams. All of the blood in her body has rushed into her face. Silence. I close my document and leave the room.

Signing In

My mind is wandering this morning. I just returned from the main office with my cup of coffee. I'm trying to organize my thoughts about what I have to work on. I'm thinking that I will revisit the school's action plan to begin. Across the room I see several mothers walking in to sign the volunteer ledger. They do this every morning, but oftentimes I don't pay attention. Today I'm listening more attentively. They wait for instructions from the Title I coordinator about where to go. You, Josefina, go to the bathrooms in building X. You, Maria, go outside during recess. Do you, Lety, have anywhere to go today? Okay, let's see what work I have for you to do. What is the difference, I thought, between the day laborers that hang out in the parking lot of Home Depot, who have no say in where, when, or what work they will be doing, and the mothers? The difference, perhaps, is that the mothers do not receive wage compensation.

Kiwanis Visit

The library has recently been completed and the school is gaining press for its beautiful and well-stacked reading room. Word has also gotten around that we have one of the largest attendance rates for the parent institute: over 400 mothers and fathers. Four older-aged women from the Kiwanis club come by to visit the school and observe its progress. They enter the main office looking like a group of schoolgirls ready to go on a field trip. With painted eyebrows defying gravity, their brushed-on sparkles explode in their pores, like miniature suns in the galaxies, beneath their eyes. The women would like to know more about our parent program. The principal asks me to join the meeting and he also invites Mrs. Jimenez, Chepita Ramirez, and Rosalinda Gonzalez. We walk to the library together. I take a seat at one of the circular tables with the Kiwanis visitors and the principal. The mothers sit at one of the tables behind me. The visitors are impressed with the beautifully organized space of the library. We talk about the high quality bookcases, the freshly carpeted stadium seating, and the evolving catalog system. The conversation then moves to parent involvement. The principal begins, "those women, you know, they have learned quite a bit. We really value parent involvement and think it can make the school stronger." He shifts his body weight toward me and asks me to elaborate. I suggest that the mothers speak on their own behalf. I turn around and ask them to bring their seats to the table and to share their experiences. They join us. The visitors smile.

Photo Time

The Kiwanis visitors leave the library and I decide to stay and debrief with the mothers. A group of students walk in for their appointed library time. The librarian picks up a book from one of the shelves and prepares to read them a story out loud. The door opens again. A man wearing a three-piece suit quickly enters, accompanied by the school principal, vice principal, and a photographer. "Boys and girls this is Mr. Y, he is running for city council and will represent our school district." The principal asks the children to formally arrange themselves behind the candidate. He grabs a book and holds it in his hand. The photographer unleashes his Nikkon. After a perfunctory thank you, the political candidate exchanges a few words with the children. "How many of you like to read?" Some of the children raise their hands and wave them excitedly. "Reading is good for you," he assures them in a bland monotone. He leaves, and the photographer and school principal follow. Jimenez turns and looks at me and asks incredulously: ¿De eso sirven los politicos, solamente para tomarsen fotos con nuestros niños *y no hacen nada?*/Is that what politicians are for, only to take photos with our children and to do nothing else?

MARCANDO DIFERENCIAS/MARKING DIFFERENCES

I stopped by the parent center to help Jimenez organize the library. I asked her how she was doing. *Estoy muy mal Jaramillo, las cosas estan muy mal*/I'm doing really bad Jaramillo, things are really bad. Here is a brief summary of her story.

Her child's teacher asked her to help him with the talent show. Participating families were given two tickets for reserved seating at the front. Jimenez went to the auditorium half an hour before the show began to help the teacher. She had her children and grandchildren with her, three little guys in tow. The kids took a seat in the reserved section, held onto her bags, and waited while she worked. One of the teachers entered and asked, "and what are these children doing here?" "They are mine," she said. "All of them? Well, they need to go outside because there aren't privileges for anybody." So Jimenez grabbed her kids and walked them to the side of the room. The teacher then asked, "And these bags?" "They are mine," Jimenez said. The teacher responded, "Well, these bags can't be here, take them out. There are no privileges for anyone here, you are all the same." Jimenez took her children outside and waited in line.

THE PEDAGOGY OF THE BURRO AND SOCIAL DRAMA

My analysis of the social relations among the mothers of Mirasur follows Victor Turner's preoccupation with understanding and unveiling the processual and spontaneous aspects of human action and interaction within a variety of social contexts (Turner, 1974, 46). Concerned with the relations between persons in the "status-role" capacity and "between groups and subgroups as structural segments (Turner, 1974, 46)," Turner rejected strict structuralist or functionalist interpretations of social life; instead, he focused on understanding the "field" as a "social system" (Turner, 1974). This is an important distinction, especially in the case of Mirasur, where rules of custom and principles of action are relatively hidden. In other words, in Mirasur and in school settings in general, protocols and norms of behavior have been established to ensure the relatively seamless governance of a site. There is a time in the day when school will begin, and a time when it ends. There are a series of curricular handbooks, manuals, rubrics, and standards that guide teachers' instruction. Student desks are arranged in a number of given sequences intended to facilitate or limit communication among and between pupils. Families are officially incorporated in the school site as volunteers or through a formal parent organization. Underneath these formal arrangements and sequences, however, is a system that comprises sensuous human beings, who according to their broader social location relate to one another in specific ways. School life is determined by a series of social layers: from the isolated unit of a school site, to the larger totality of nation and global politics. In this instance, the "field" of Mirasur comprises "loosely integrated processes, with some patterned aspects, some persistence of form, but controlled by discrepant principles of action expressed in rules of custom that are often situationally incompatible with one another" (1987, 74). The "incompatibility" in the case of Mirasur would be revealed, as we will see in chapters that follow, once the mothers challenged their role as compliant burritas. It is for this reason that the social drama of Mirasur was conflictual and disruptive. On this note, consider Turner's further elaboration of social dramas:

> In the social drama latent conflicts become manifest, and kinship ties, whose significance is not obvious in genealogies, emerge into key importance. Through the social drama we are enabled to observe the crucial principles of the social structure in their operation, and their relative dominance at successive points in time. Manifestation, to revert to the "thrashing" metaphor, is the "grain" and "husk" of social life, the values and anti-values, the relationships of amity and enmity, which are revealed in the often passionate action of the social drama, and thus becomes part of a community's reflexive store, its knowledge of itself, stored in the bins of legal precedent, common knowledge, and even ritual symbolism. (1987, 92)

Turner devised the concept of social drama to study the dialectic of social transformation and continuity that transpires through a sequence of four processual acts and scenes—what Boje (2003) has described as a "postmodern theatrics." Turner (1986) remarks, "if daily living is a kind of theater, social drama is a kind of meta-theater, that is, a dramaturgical language about the language of ordinary role-playing and status-maintenance which constitutes communication in the quotidian social process" (181). Social dramas can be identified among groups that share values and interests and have a shared common history (Turner, 1980, 149). Turner has delineated four "acts" within the social drama. The first act is a rupture in social relations, or *breach*. The second act is a *crisis* that cannot be handled by normal strategies to amend social situations that cause conflict. This phase is commonly much more dynamic and forceful. In other words, it is a decisive and uncommon break from routine and mundane activity. The third act attempts to mediate the initial problem and is called *redress*. Here the social actor attempts to reestablish social arrangements. The final act can be manifested in two ways: *reintegration*, the return to the status quo, or *recognition of schism*, an alteration in the social arrangements (Turner 1980, 149). In both of the resolutions, there are symbolic displays in which the actors reveal their unity. Put differently, Elizabeth Bell writes that, "simply put, the social drama begins when a member of a community breaks a rule; sides are taken for or against the rule breaker; repairs—formal or informal—are enacted; and if the repairs work, the group returns to normal, but if the repairs fail, the group breaks apart" (2006). Citing Turner, Ron Eyerman brings to focus the "root paradigms" of a society that can be exposed during social dramas. Root paradigms are those "largely taken-for-granted frameworks of meaning that guide everyday social actions and aid actors in making sense of themselves and their world. Root paradigms, which include at their most fundamental level the founding myths of a collective, also demarcate the boundaries between those who are part of 'us' and those who are excluded" (2008, 22).

Social drama analysis attempts to make sense of collective action within the paradigm of modern, industrial societies. Social drama, then, is an expression of the habitual and ingrained acts that we carry into the public sphere; acts with historical and philosophical origins, forming our subjectivities and relationships to others with whom we come into contact. Social dramas are a way for us to analytically identify and make meaning of the performative, symbolic, and concrete acts of people who disrupt or transform the scripts that govern and establish the limits of human sociability.

The social drama of Mirasur is a way of expressing from below— from the registers of the immigrant women and mothers residing in the periphery of institutional power and authority—the disguises of social systems that have scripted their subordination. In Mirasur, the metaphor of the burro captures the general direction of the daily practices and discourses that established school-community relations. As burros, the mothers were reduced to a desubjectified ensemble of partial objects—arms to carry boxes of supplies, hands to sort papers, legs to run errands. In fact, they became limbs without organs—external markers of the larger social division of labor that separates mental work from manual work. The linguistic utterances between faculty and las madres come to signify the socially constitutive practice that helps to produce and reproduce social structures and social subjects (Joyce, 2001): the school structure incorporates las madres through their free labor, and, in turn, las madres are seen as adopting the form of burritas. The burro metaphor foregrounds the objective structures that exists seemingly independently of the consciousness and will of its participants, but that required their active participation to keep those structures in place. The embodiment of the burro metaphor is extra-discursive. Within each burro-body lies the history of the social conditions that created it. The very term burro calls forth its opposite: what it means to be human. The social relations of production that reify workers as things, in this case, as burros, produce both symbolic capital and surplus labor for the school administration.

Blurring the lines between human and nonhuman life may be considered foolish by some; a cognitive measure of self-depreciation and low self-esteem. Indeed, the very ways in which las madres referred to themselves as burras and permitted members of the faculty and administration to do the same revealed the extent to which they often devalued and underestimated their personhood. In many sociological or anthropological circles, the animalization of las madres' identity may signal a cultural deficit or bias, one that is inherent to immigrant women from Mexico, who very likely crossed the U.S./Mexico border under less than human conditions, steady and steadfast, like burras. Inevitably, in the process of auto-bestialization, las madres revealed the extent to which they had applied a "categorical sameness" (Bickford, 1997) to the human and animal domains, producing the "difference" that makes the categorization of "burra" possible. And yet this only becomes meaningful when las madres are positioned in contrast to another human group, in this case the faculty and administration of Mirasur. Appropriating animal characteristics in a process of self-dehumanization provided a screen against which the dehumanization of las madres by the teachers and administrators could be read.

The pedagogy of the burro is about actions and interactions; about the placement of individuals in the community of Mirasur along a continuum; and about the ethnic, racial, and gendered dimensions that apply to the organization of social life in Mirasur and the wider community. The burro is a metaphor whose meaning is not bound by symbolic conventions in the social drama. In other words, the burro metaphor does not gain its full meaning during a singular event or exchange. Metaphors link one domain of experience to another; they produce an ideological effect. One can attribute this effect to the fact that metaphors address both physical and social experience of various actors (Kirmayer, 1993). Metaphors help to select, emphasize, suppress, or organize features of social relations (Turner, 1974). It so follows that in the social drama of Mirasur the burro metaphor spans a range of experiences, places, and time.

The process of bestialization in social drama is not new in and of itself. There are countless examples of how humans appropriate the animal kingdom in the ritualistic form that social dramas in traditional societies were most concerned about. But in the case of Mirasur, the process of bestialization did not refer to a stage within a ceremonial process, or even a way in which to recuperate indigenous meanings and symbolic action into a productive (i.e., beneficial to self and community) capacity. Situated historically and politically, the process of bestialization harkens back past times and places that have marked social divisions across territories, women and men, the religious and nonreligious, colonizers and the colonized, and the ethnic/racial "other" against its light-skinned counterpart. The chronicles of colonial times specifically shed the tears of the men, women, and children who under the weight of imperialist expansionism and warfare were regarded and treated as anything but human. The Catholic Church played a significant role in writing such codices, imploring the seven sacraments and the cardinal rites of passage as a process of humanization (see, for example, Brandes, 1984). Most in the liturgical setting read any rejection of Christianity as a barbaric act, a willing move to remain in the animal kingdom that could in turn justify spiritual and physical violence. Calling humanity into question and emphasizing the animal-like qualities of the opponent provided much needed support for the grotesque spectacles of violence that ensued.

Karl Jacoby, for example, discusses animalizing the other in the context of the historical extermination of the Apache. Taking the history of ethnic genocide along the U.S.-Mexico border into account, Jacoby writes of how minimizing the humanity of "others" served to justify the settlers' "unequal conquest between humans and lesser humans" (Jacoby, 2008). However, if we are to understand the act of bestialization as both an occurrence of subordination and also one that can provide opposition to take place, then Jacoby's discussion of the bestial paradox is particularly apropos. In Jacoby's words,

> Euro-American efforts to lower their Apache foes to the status of animals nonetheless foundered upon an unresolved paradox. As much as the bestialization of the Apache helped justify settler efforts to exterminate them, what made the Apache such a threat in the first place was their all-too-human understanding of Anglo intentions—the very feature that allowed them to raid Euro-American settlements with such seeming ease. Moreover, reducing their opponents to mere animals risked diminishing settlers' ongoing struggle over the borderlands into little more than an unequal contest between humans and lesser animals. If only to elevate themselves, Euro-Americans needed to endow the Apache with a degree of humanity. (256)

The paradox that Jacoby highlights above in many ways characterizes the moment—the breach—that initiated las madres' intrapersonal social drama, their individual and collective pathways toward *conscientization*. It is that space, of acknowledging that las madres held the power to change, to speak and to act on behalf of their children and community that set the social drama in motion. The very context that conditioned las madres to be subservient and accepting of the deprecating acts of bestialization was the site where they began their transformation. This is the paradox of burra pedagogy, of understanding how the contradictions of social life play out in the dramaturgical setting of our interactions, subtle cues, and overt practices that situate people along an inhuman/human continuum. How we come to valorize individuals and communities based on how "human" they "act," "speak," or "look" discloses a wider historical and material optic for how we have come into being. Recasting the humanity of las madres was a difficult and extended process. It happened spontaneously and organically; an artifact of how memories of events past, neighborhoods abandoned, families disrupted, work completed, and borders crossed are reshaped in the course of developing another kind of literacy in the crosshairs of everyday experience.

RESISTANCE AND TRANSFORMATION

The pedagogy of the burro establishes a reference point for understanding how las madres saw themselves in relation to the school site, as well as how they were seen. But metaphors are also transformative, and while up to this point I have been discussing the metaphor of the burro in terms of its analogical constituents—of human labor, exploitation, and alienation—the flip side of the burro metaphor invokes the opposite distinction: about what it means to be human. The burro is a multivocal symbol, it signals a dialectical and metaphorical relationship—beast: human. Here, I am building upon Turner's assessment of the dialectical relation between structure and antistructure in social dramas, in which the latter signals an inversion of the former (but still retains an organizational form). In the case of las madres, the inversion of the metaphorical relationship of the burro took place in the way of a series of resistant acts—both symbolic and material—that began with a sudden breach of institutional norms and practices (in Turner's terms) and a fragmentation or rupture within themselves (in Anzaldúa's terminology). The pedagogy of the burro is foundational to the social drama of Mirasur in that it established the dramaturgical setting from which the subsequent traumas (and dramas) of this text are narrated. The burro metaphor reveals various levels and dimensions at work in the social drama of Mirasur that range from the institutional, communal, and personal lived experiences of las madres. In this way, the pedagogy of the burro sets the stage for understanding why las madres' transformation from "burritas" to conscientious agitators and defenders of the rights of their children caused such deep tensions and divisions in Mirasur and the broader community. It also reveals the inner, concomitant trauma of shifting consciousness that was dependent on las madres distancing themselves from the burro metaphor and rewriting themselves anew. The very feature that seemed to separate las madres from being part of the school community in a role that would have honored their participation was the very dimension that united them in their struggle to be treated with dignity and respect.

THE TURNER-ANZALDÚA CONNECTION

The processes of becoming "human" are best understood in relation to nepantla. The term *nepantla*, following the late Gloria Anzaldúa (1987, 1990, 2001, 2002), designates an intermediary material-spiritual-psychic space, where the formation of the agentive I (*yo soy*), released from the dominative structures that have historically kept the subaltern *sorda, ciega y muda*/deaf, blind and mute, connects with a process of developing knowledge(s) and forms of consciousness attentive of our pursuit for social transformation. As Anzaldúa writes,

Nepantla is the site of transformation, the place where different perspectives come into conflict and where you question the basic ideas, tenets, and ideas inherited from your family, your education, and your different cultures...Living between cultures results in "seeing double," first from the perspective of one culture, then from the perspective of another. Seeing from two or more perspectives simultaneously renders those cultures transparent. Removed from that culture's center, you glimpse the sea in which you've been immersed but to which you were oblivious, no longer seeing the world the way you were enculturated to see it. (2002, 548–549)

Anzaldúa's writings on nepantla—as process, liminality, and change (Keating, 2006, 7)—dealt with a different, yet related, social drama: the drama of the self(ves). Anazaldúa deplored rationalist epistemology (Levine, 2005) replete with its logocentrism, binary oppositions, and Eurocentric subjectivity grounded in the Eurocentric narrative of "I conquer, therefore I am" (Dussel, 1985). In contrast, Anzaldúa established an epistemology of synergestic consciousness that moved beyond modern constraints of reason and set forward a theory of the mapping of the "self" as a methodological tool (what she referred to as "mapping her own self-discovery's pathway" (Levine, 2005)). Anzaldúa wrote of the "geography of hybrid selves" (Levine, 2005, 183), an intersubjective and interdependent formulation that creates the basis for the "formation of alliances, solidarity movements, and contingent communities: temporary, fluid arrangements to empower the marginalized" (Levine, 2005, 183). Amala Levine (2005) elaborates further on Anzaldúa's conception of these "alliances, movements and communities" when she writes: "They are built across social, economic, cultural, racial/ethnic, or gender differences by those with a shared awareness as nos/otras, Anzaldúa's word for those who understand that 'to be human is to be in relationship,' not only because it is politically expedient but because of a shared vision of commonality" (183). Both Turner and Anzaldúa examined the "self" in relation to the social conditions and local contexts that gave rise to cultural, political, and social arrangements. They differ, however, in their identification of their unit of analysis. For Turner, the unit of analysis was the social drama that transpired among social actors; for Anzaldúa, the unit of analysis began with the volitional "I," the "mapping of self-discovery's pathways."

Bridging Turner's and Anzaldúa's philosophical, theoretical, and anthropological work creates a meta-frame from which to delineate the social drama of Mirasur as a way of uncovering the structural processes and social and cultural relations that configure the overall arrangement that characterized Jimenez's and las madres' relation to the school site. Here, a pairing needs to take place between an analysis that recognizes las madres as reproducing formal social arrangements within the larger social totality and the ruptures of experience that paralleled las madres' self-transformation (nepantla) within the contextually specific location of the Mirasur school community. The social drama of Mirasur is characterized by two overlapping processes: the institutional stage of the social drama ("the pedagogy of the burro") and las madres' collective drama (the "antistructure" of the pedagogy of the burro). Both forms of social drama are processual events, nested in each other, all affecting each other simultaneously in a furious dialectics of reciprocity. And although I am speaking about the social drama of Mirasur from the standpoint of las madres' performances in the school setting, my intention is to locate their performances in the material relations—institutional and social relations of power—that give shape to their metaphorical and processual meaning.

What, then, was the break in routine, the transgression of taken-for-granted norms that I am referring to as the social drama of Mirasur? For me, it began with a series of events and processes that were put in motion the day I decided to funnel a limited amount of funds into a 10-week-long workshop for parents. I began to forge new relationships, to see the women who worked in the school's hallways and entrances differently, and I took notice of the hidden presence of the working men and women who voiced their concerns about their children and their desire to become better acquainted with the school (symbol of hope) that would—ideally—become the conduit for satisfying their dreams for a better life and future for their children. My role and status began to shift, my alliances and loyalties came under question, and the normative routines of the school day were disrupted. Families began to visit the main office of the school and request their children's records, more parents began to schedule meetings with their child's teacher, and both the faculty and administration had to adjust to the new and increasing presence of mothers and fathers in the school day. I began to spend more time with the mothers in the school, and I willingly began to coordinate a series of efforts to increase their visibility and participation in the school's governance model. For me, a break was necessary in the day-to-day norms and practices of school-community relations. This "break" revealed the social drama of Mirasur that would have gone unnoticed, let alone uncontested, otherwise.

For the mothers, the break came on the day a first-grade male teacher was accused of hitting one of his students; a claim that resulted in a series of reactions, interrogations, protests, town hall meetings, and visits from the media, attorneys, school superintendents, and city council representatives. This "breach" in routine activated the mothers' consciousness, and their participation in the school began slowly, but incrementally, to change.

3

THE BREACH

"Breach is signalized by the public, overt breach or deliberate nonful-fillment of some crucial norm regulating the intercourse of the parties. In a social drama it is not a crime, though it may formally resemble one; it is, in reality, a symbolic trigger of confrontation or encounter. A dramatic breach may be made by an individual, certainly, but he [*sic*] always acts, or believes he [*sic*] acts, on behalf of other parties, whether they are aware of it or not. He [*sic*] sees himself as a representative, not as a lone hand"

Victor Turner, 1974, 38

LA PROTESTA DE LAS MUJERES SUMISAS/ THE PROTEST OF THE SUBMISSIVE WOMEN

At times they were five and at others ten, but never more than twenty. They marched in protest in circular formation, occupying the grassy area that led up to the main entrance of the school. A Los Angeles police unit drove by shortly after the mothers began protesting, and the women shouted louder. At the sign of authority, the mothers became more defiant. Their eyes squinted under the sun and their sweat crystallized into salted droplets in the creases under their brow. It was a hot day in spring. The morning dew had dissipated and the Pacific Ocean's mist had evaporated from the few shards of grass that surrounded the school's brick foundation. The mothers opened their mouths wide, taking in the air of dry heat. As their diaphragms expanded, the sound of their chants pierced through the school's concrete edifice. "*¿Que es lo que queremos? Justicia! ¿ Cuando lo queremos? Ahora! El pueblo unido jamas sera vencido!/*What is that we want? Justice! When do we want it? Now! United people will never be overcome!" The mothers' voice became louder as a teacher or staff member walked into the school building or as they caught a glimpse of the principal peeking through the front door to examine the chaos unraveling on *his* property.

No one anticipated the mothers' protest. Word had spread that the mothers were upset and were organizing against the principal, but when we saw them on the school's front doorsteps—as agitators rather than the docile workers that typically greeted us in the mornings—it was shocking. I knew that the principal's removal of a first-grade teacher angered the mothers, but I did not understand why they would sacrifice their time and energy to protest on the teacher's behalf. Those of us with administrative duties had limited knowledge of the case, pending a legal investigation. We knew that a first-grade child alleged that her teacher had hit her across the face and bruised her cheek. We examined her face the day she walked into the office to report her injuries, and we assumed that another educator had lost his senses, again. The administration followed protocol, alerting the police department and calling in the city's social service workers. The following day, the teacher was placed on leave and the administration proceeded to interview the mother volunteers and students in the teacher's classroom to verify the claim. Maria Jimenez was one of the volunteers and she denied the child's allegations. Her daughter was one of the child's classmates interviewed by the administration. Without Jimenez's consent or presence, her daughter "signed" an affidavit verifying the abuse. This coercive act enraged Jimenez and propelled her to denounce the administration's actions. To those of us working from an insider position, the administration followed protocol, ensuring the safety of the children. Events were unfolding "normally." But to Jimenez and the mothers, the administration did not honor their young children's rights. This was a sufficient breach in the eyes of the mothers—an act that followed months of dissatisfaction with the school administration—to mobilize and voice their discontent in the form of a protest (the first time the mothers had ever participated in an act of civil disobedience).

On the first day of the protest, I stood with the principal and the administrative staff in the main office, peering through the barred windows that partially obstructed our view. I felt more comfortable watching the mothers from the inside. I could stare at them for longer periods of time, feeling less ashamed about transferring their every move to memory. Jimenez incited the mothers to chant and invited women and men who passed by to join their movement. Together with

Jimenez were other familiar faces, Chepita, Leticia, and Rosalinda. Chepita stood closest to Jimenez, occasionally speaking into her ear. Chepita's son watched from across the street. He was a gangbanger who had been shot several months prior and was paralyzed from the waist down. Chepita never spoke about what happened to him, but it was common knowledge. He sat in a wheelchair next to his *carnales* and lent a curious eye to the mothers. Leticia had recently given birth to her second daughter. She wrapped her in a heavy cloth and draped the baby against her chest. Undeterred by the baby's sleep, Leticia chanted loudly on point. Exuding an air of utmost seriousness was Rosalinda. She rarely smiled, and the expression on her face made me think of only one emotion, anger. After ten or so minutes, the mothers took a break. They smiled and laughed, huddling together. They seemed proud of their efforts and enthusiastically discussed the aims of their protest with people who stopped and inquired about its purpose. A colleague whispered to me, "*esas señoras, como son de atrevidas/*those women, they are so daring," and the principal shook his head in disbelief, threw his hands up in the air, and marched straight back into his office. He picked up the phone, dialed his district office supervisor, and kicked the door shut. The secretarial staff laughed and joked about how it wasn't wise to piss off a group of women, and I thought silently to myself "*estas madres tienen huevos/*these women have balls."

The mothers marched in defiance, their faces bright and alive, not their typically tired or weary selves. To the staff, they were unfamiliar women in familiar bodies. Their pudgy frames and dark skin belonged to the women who delivered books, made photocopies, and cut paper, but now they looked, sounded, and moved differently. "Poor women, they don't know what they're talking about. They haven't seen the evidence. They just look for an excuse to feel important." "Those women are crazy." To some members of the community, they were brazen women out of place, profane bodies in need of *una buena sonada/*a good spanking. Several of the men and women that drove by yelled at them, "*Bola de viejas chismosas/*Group of gossipy women." In the midst of this institutional and social resistance, the mothers clenched handwritten shields and passed out leaflets detailing their protest. For over four months they protested.

As the days passed, the group changed in size and the mothers became more insolent. New women joined the protest relieving those who went home to cook lunch for their husbands or prepare for the afternoon's home activities. The protesting group would gain in size for one hour and then shrink to three or five women the next hour. Several of the mothers brought their young children and instructed them to chant for the principal's removal. "*Mijo, ¿que es lo que queremos? Que se salga el buey!*/Son, what is that we want? That the bull leave!" *Los chiquillos*/The children marched with them held by the hand, or in a stroller, or resting against their breasts. They took breaks and drank coffee purchased from the corner store or poured coffee brewed at home from one of the thermoses. As days turned into weeks, the mothers could be seen sitting on green foldable chairs brought from home. They greeted all who passed by and answered questions for those who dared ask: "*Estamos aqui por el bien de nuestros hijos, queremos justicia en la escuela*/We are here for the good of our children, we want justice in the school."

About two weeks had passed since the mothers began protesting. Jimenez walked into my office and told me that they were planning a visit to the superintendent's office. "*Ya tenemos la dirección de la oficina y sabemos como llegar por bus*/We have the address of the office and we know how to get there by bus." Chepita's husband had offered to drive them to the bus stop. I did not try to encourage or dissuade Jimenez. Part of me did not approve of their protest, therefore, I responded with silence. I did ask, however, about their expectations. "*Mire, Jaramillo, en esta escuela pasan muchas cosas que no estan bien. Una mama me mostro una carta del médico despues de que un maestro le pego a su hijo y no han hecho nada. La mama tiene evidencia, y hablo con el director, pero el maestro sigue dando sus clases*/Look Jaramillo, in this school a lot of things are not right. One mother showed me a letter from her doctor after a teacher hit her son and this school didn't do anything. The mother has evidence and she spoke to the principal, but the teacher is still in the classroom." The protest suddenly became larger than the case of an individual teacher and the questioning of children that the mothers opined was in violation of their rights. The drama of Mirasur was quickly unraveling. The mothers' presence on the front lawn became a site where families and, eventually, faculty began to air their grievances. Teachers started taking sides, some organized on behalf of the displaced teacher and others against. Union representatives solicited the mothers' support for causes unrelated to violence against children in the school. A mole within the ranks of teacher assistants substantiated the claim of another teacher's physical abuse of a child. The following morning, the mothers left promptly and went to the school district's central office.

When Jimenez returned and told me about their visit, I tried to imagine the experience: five women traveling by bus wearing their finest clothes, approaching the district office and requesting a visit with the highest authority of the school district. When they arrived at the district headquarters—a tall building in the heart of downtown Los Angeles—they were instructed to meet one of the superintendent's subordinates. Unbeknownst to Jimenez, he was the school principal's former colleague. They were both men in their mid-50s, of Latino heritage, and had worked their way up the political and economic ranks of the school system together. They were *compadres*.

It was the first time that Jimenez and the mothers rode an elevator. She talked about the physical sensation she experienced when the elevator settled on the top floor. Her insides had taken a sudden leap with gravity. "*Pense que nos ibamos ir pa'abajo/*I thought we were going to drop back down." A secretary escorted them to one of the conference rooms, where the mothers had a 180-degree view of Los Angeles. "*Las cosas se ven tan distintas desde arriba/*Everything looks so different from above," Jimenez surmised. "*Al principio me dio miedo, pero despues no/*At first I was scared, but then no." The mothers quickly overcame their fear of heights and prepared for what would turn into a short and animated visit with the assistant superintendent. "*El entro y nosdijoque lasuperinten-dente no estabadisponisble, queteniamosquepedirunacita con ella/*He walked in and he told us that the superintendent was not available, that we needed to schedule an appointment to talk to her." I quietly agreed. Jimenez continued, "*Estaba bravo el señor, diciendo que nosotros estabamos haciendo problemas en la escuela. Y que no importaba lo que haciamos, porque el maestro que sacaron no iba volver y las cosas no iban a cambiar/*The man was angry, saying that we were causing problems in the school. He said it didn't matter what we did, because the teacher had been expelled and he was not going to return. He told us that things were not going to change." I asked her how she felt. "*Como unaniñaque la estanregañando/*like a little girl who was being scolded," she replied. "*No importa/*It doesn't matter," Jimenez continued. "*Nosotros vamos a llamar a los medios de comunicación para que nos pongan atención/*We are going to call the news media so that people will pay attention." And they did. They phoned the local media and invited them to the protest the following day.

FROM BREACH TO CRISIS TO REDRESSIVE ACTION

In the weeks that followed, business went along as "usual" within the school site. From 8 a.m. to 3 p.m., school faculty continued their routine practices and las madres remained steadfast on the school lawn, thus widening the breach and extending the protest into a crisis state. The liminal characteristics that Turner writes about in social drama were making themselves evident as the protest escalated. The more or less stable processes of due course and negotiating grievances in the school site had been interrupted. The mothers refused to wear the masks of little "mules" and they claimed to reveal the true state of affairs in the school site. Something wasn't right in the school's practices, and the mothers were not going to stay silent. They refused to follow protocol, exert patience, or simply ignore the injustices they had identified among the faculty and administration. From the perspective of Turner's social drama analysis, las madres initiated a crisis, assumed a "menacing stance," and dared "the representatives of order to grapple with it" (1974, 39). This was, in effect, las madres' intent. Chanting, marching, and brandishing signs that called for justice and the school principal's removal were all symbolic codes of contestation— their meaning was generally understood. As the breach widened, and the crisis escalated, las madres motioned toward *redressive action*. The principal paced the hallways, and on occasion he stepped outside to exchange a few words with the mothers. But for the most part the mothers and the administration had reached a stalemate. Either the mothers would tire and end the protest, or something else needed to take place for resolution.

Jimenez walked into my office one morning. "*Sabes que*/do you know what," she said, "*vamos a tener un foro con todos los padres y va venir la superintendente*/we are going to have a parent forum and the superintendent is going to come." Oh, I replied, and what are you going to talk about? "*Pues de todo los chingasos que están haciendo en esta escuela y del maestro que esta abusando de los niños en su salón*/ well, of all the shit that is happening in this school and of the teacher who is abusing children in his classroom." I suggested that she write down a list of items and try to organize the list of concerns that she was going to discuss. "*Yo no se escribir bien Jaramillo, deje que con la palabra vamos a decir bien las cosas*/I don't know how to write well Jaramillo, just let us use the spoken word to say things right." Jimenez continued, "*Ya llamamos los medios de comunicación, y Lety* *me ayudo con el flyer. Esta tarde vamos casa por casa para invitar los padres/*We already called the newsmedia and Lety helped me make a flyer. This afternoon we are going door to door to invite the parents to attend."

Several days later, the mothers held the forum. Anticipation had been building for days, as those of us from the inside did not know what to expect from the mothers. We saw the news van belonging to the Spanish media channel parked in front of the auditorium and we could detect a slight nervousness from the school principal, from his seeming inability to stand in any one place for more than a few seconds. I sat toward the back of the newly remodeled school auditorium as a sea of brown faces filled the empty seats around me. I looked at the projector hanging from the center of the ceiling, one of the prized possessions we had purchased with the monies allocated for school improvement. Just a few months earlier, this same auditorium had housed the mothers and fathers who had graduated from the parent institute. Now, it was filled to capacity with many women and men, many of whom I recognized. Las madres stood at the front, with microphone in hand. Maria Jimenez wore her staple red suit, and she commanded the stage. The school principal and his two bosses, the local superintendent and her assistant superintendent, accompanied the mothers. The administrators also dressed in suits. Jimenez' voice crackled but she remained steadfast. The first item on the agenda was the alleged abuse of children in a special education classroom. Jimenez stood and requested that the mother of the child describe what happened. The allegations were severe. This child, the mother claimed, had been thrown against a wall. Other children had been tied to their chairs with duck tape for not following the teacher's directions. The mother waived a letter in her hand that she reported came from her doctor documenting the child's injuries. She talked about approaching the principal with her complaint, but that nothing had resulted from the meeting. The mothers wanted to know why an investigation had been initiated into one teacher's behavior but not that of another. The discussion became racialized. One teacher was Latino and the other was white. People became visibly angry, and they made concrete demands. "*Nosotros queremos cambio. No podemos dejar que abusen de nuestros hijos. ¿Cuando van a sacar el maestro? ¿Que va pasar?/*We cannot allow them to abuse our children. When are they going to dismiss the teacher? What is going to happen?" The superintendent assured the women and men that an investigation had been initiated. The following day, the school district reassigned the teacher to another school.

That moment in the auditorium was a time for the mothers and fathers to express their grievances about a particular incident, but it also exceeded those concerns. The mothers' protest opened a space and created an opportunity for the broader community to intervene protagonistically in the schools' practices. This breach of everyday events and subsequent crisis stripped the families of their docility and humility. Emotion filled the room as anger and resentment took hold. Jimenez asked the audience to voice their other concerns in front of the superintendent and her second in command, *"bueno, ahora les ofrecemos la oportunidad para que ustedes hablen, hablen de las preocupaciónes que tienen*/okay, now we are going to offer you the opportunity to speak, speak of the concerns that you have." One by one, a mother or father took to the microphone, "Our bathrooms are dirty," "The water from the drinking fountain is brown." "There isn't enough vigilance before and after school." "The cafeteria isn't orderly." "There's a hole in the side gate that students can crawl out of, I saw some boys doing it the other day." "Vacation time is too long and teachers don't send enough homework home." "*Señoras, señores, por favor, uno por uno*/Ladies and gentlemen, please, one at a time." the principal pleaded. The colleagues seated next to me shook their heads and remarked, "the parents are too disorganized," "they aren't being very clear," "they always talk about the cafeteria and bathrooms," "they never say anything new," "this is too chaotic."

In their disorder and perceived irrationality, the mothers had wielded the power of their collective unity. In contrast, members of the school administration and faculty wielded their power to disregard and to downplay las madres' and the community's concerns. Two antagonistic camps emerged: the families on one end, and the faculty/administration on another. Las madres were perceived as making irrational demands, when, in effect, their demands were exceedingly rational. Ultimately, the water could have been tested to ensure the children's health and safety, and a letter could have been sent home to verify the results. A technician could have been called to repair the gate adjacent to the kindergarten classrooms, to make sure that children did not disappear during the school day. Cafeteria workers could have been summoned in a meeting, and disciplinary procedures could have been reviewed. And it would only be in the interest of the school administration to work collaboratively with the teachers to devise a plan for keeping the students on track during their extended vacation time. Already, the children's school year had been shortened by 20 or so days, by virtue of the year-round school calendar. The families had demanded basic rights and privileges: proper food, water, and shelter. The critics who observed las madres' revolutionized form in the auditorium characterized their activity as "chaotic" and their concerns as "ordinary" and "repetitive." The mothers had defied ordinary practices of the school day, and the dominant structure of the school was presented with an option: either to acknowledge the community's concerns, or to deny and negate their claims.

It was the performative, or, more precisely, the ritualistic, "form" of the protest and town hall meeting that most challenged the administration. It was not a linear petition for change, or a content-based criticism that simply itemized the mothers' demands. The "form" was not static but processual, and it brought about a condition of liminality that challenged the entire symbolic economy of Mirasur. As McLaren (1982) argues, while liminality is the seedbed of creativity, it could also engender violence, as various social groups not only challenge preexisting systems of control and authority but the very idea of control and authority itself. In Mirasur, the mothers expressed rage during the townhall meeting because they recognized that any system of control and authority associated with the school served an entirely different set of interests than theirs, or that of their children. The violence that this recognition brought about among the mothers was not directed intrapersonally at just the administration or the teachers but rather at the entire symbolic universe of the school. Violence can be read in many different ways, and while the town hall meeting did not necessarily end "violently" in terms of physical injury, it did demonstrate both the creative possibilities and volatility of civil discord. In this sense, the coming together of the school's administrative *structure* with the *antistructure* of the community led to a third, overlapping liminal space in the auditorium. In the most potent sense, these acts could be called rituals of recognition. In other words, these acts symbolized las madres' recognition of their own power as representatives of their community and their social class. In this liminal state they were transformed into speaking on behalf of all members of their community. But this recognition, as such, could only take place through the process of demonstration; that is, only by demonstrating the power of their community through rituals of protest could they create the liminal state necessary to come to recognize their power as such. These acts of protest were rituals of initiation. The mothers became living symbols of struggle and in doing so they initiated a new relationship between themselves and the administration, not in terms of actually leveling the structural hierarchies that separated them, but virtually, in terms of the willingness to negotiate around such structures. Neither faculty nor community members were able to resolve the imminent crisis unfolding between them, because both "camps" were in a processual state of coming to know and understand the newly revealed form of one group to another. Put differently, the mothers and members of the community were in a process of coming to see themselves and one another as capable and entitled to make demands on the school administration. In turn, the administration revealed its inability and discomfort in relating to the mothers' new form. It was impossible for the administration to return to its previous tactics of intimidation and control, for the simple reason that power was diffused among 200 men and women in the auditorium and a handful of representatives of the media who held the ultimate authority in making public this "private affair." The *limen* (threshold) of events in the auditorium could be considered an extended pause, where the mothers and the community attempted to transcend the dictum and hierarchical arrangements of school life. Here, Turner's insights into the limen as a "realm of pure possibility" (1967, 97) connects to the faculty's resistance to the community's actions. Limen is a dynamic state of interchange and flux. In an organizational setting such as Mirasur, limen is greeted with such skepticism because it undermines the spoken and unspoken rules of constraint that typically separate people into their proper niches.

For several days I could not stop thinking about las madres' town hall meeting. I wished that I had added some of my own observations: there is a second-grade teacher in the bungalows who calls his students morons. There is a gaping hole in the ground at the front of the school and it exposes children and families to physical risk. There is a fourth-grade teacher upstairs who turns the lights off after the lunch break and takes a nap at her desk while students watch a movie. Students are segregated and tracked according to their English language proficiency and most of them don't transition into mainstream classes—I know this because I write the reports. The parents don't have a parent center. There is a fourth-grade female student who allowed the boys in her class to "touch her privates" in exchange for play-money distributed as part of a classroom management scheme—the teacher laughed it off, the boys were told to take their money back, and the girl was given one or two counseling sessions. I'm concerned about all of these things and more.

The protest and the community meeting kept the social drama of Mirasur in motion. The protest marked a breach, and it escalated into a crisis and "redress" that took place in the school auditorium. Although the events were related, the meeting in the auditorium initiated another processual stream in the social drama of Mirasur. The "never-before-seen community members" who were in attendance and voicing their concerns set off a distinct course of "breach, crisis, and redress" in the social drama of Mirasur. Instead of five, ten, or 15 women marching on the front lawn, there were now over 200 women (primarily) and men confronting and contesting the school's practices. The crisis became more amplified, and therefore the modes of resolution became more pronounced: Jimenez and las madres took to the stage and beckoned people from their community to join them—and they did. Here, it is important to recognize that while the town hall meeting was a consequence (an attempt for redressive action) of the protest, each event in its own particular way initiated a "mini-drama" within the overall social drama of Mirasur. In other words, the social drama of Mirasur became the "meta-theatre" in which short- or long-term events reflected some or all of the phases of social drama analysis. Put another way, the pedagogy of the burro was undergoing a splintering effect.

The "breach" dimension of the protest had transformed the identity of las madres within the school setting. Jimenez became aware of this change of status.

*Después de la protesta nos dimos cuenta cómo cambió la actitud de las personas adentro de la escuela con nosotras. El director ya me llamaba revolucionaria, decía que nos hicimos famosas. El trato ya era mejor, pienso yo, porque ellos se dieron cuenta que nos podíamos defender. Pienso yo que ellos son miedosos, miedosos de su propia imagen, la cual nosotras les hicimos ver/*After the protest we became aware of how people's attitudes changed in the school. The principal would call me a revolutionary, he said that we became famous. The treatment was better I think because they became aware that we could defend ourselves. I think they are scared, scared of their own image, the image that we made them see.

In the process of asserting their identity and presumably assuming a new performative role (that of revolutionary), lasmadres recognized that social actors within Mirasur and the broader community, in time, began to alter their relationship with them.

The initial "breach" of the protest triggered an ongoing processual cycle of "breach, crisis-redress, and reintegration" within the social drama of Mirasur. Jimenez and las madres renewed their presence once the protest ended, but, in this case, on their own terms. They continued assisting teachers with their tasks, but, as Jimenez notes, *"ya nadie se pone de voluntaria sin chequiar con migo. Me preguntan que si creo que es justo el trabajo que piden de ellas/* now no one signs up to volunteer without checking with me first. They ask me if I think its fair the work that they are being asked to do." Indeed, Jimenez and las madres reintegrated physically into the school site, but remained in liminality, betwixt and between, in a continual space of crisis as they continued to respond to the needs of their community.

It took me some time to fully comprehend the significance of the protest for Jimenez and the mothers, as an event that marked a personal sense of rupture that resulted from presenting themselves in radically different form to the community. It also took me some time to uncover the extent to which the protest marked an extensive period of breach, crisis, and redress in the social drama of Mirasur. My understanding began with hearing about the process directly from Jimenez.

Jimenez: Habían sacado el maestro de mi hija del salón de primer grado. Yo no sentí que era justo, porque además yo trabajaba con él, y nunca lo vi hacer nada malo; pero no sé, no me quería meter en broncas. Pero después le hicieron preguntas a mi hija sin yo estar presente, y le hicieron firmar una declaración. Yo no sentí que eso era correcto, yo tuve que responder por ella. Y además Jaramillo, había muchos otros problemas en la escuela, mucha más evidencia contra otro maestro, quien si estaba abusando de los niños. Una de las asistentes de clase se nos arrimó y nos dijo que el maestro había agarrado un morenito del cuello y lo aventó. Empezamos a investigar y nos encontramos con una mamá quien había traído una carta del médico comprobando que fue maltratada por el mismo maestro, pero no hicieron nada por ella. Estamos de acuerdo, que si un maestro hace un delito sea castigado. Pero de lo que nos dimos cuenta en la escuela, es que no se estaban haciendo las cosas con justicia. Para nosotras las acciones de la escuela eran racistas. Un maestro era Latino y el otro maestro Anglosajon; pero solamente se le estaba juzgando al Latino y ni si quiera empezaron

una investigación del otro, cuando teníamos evidencia de los padres.
Entonces, ¿ahora que? Uno que hace? Y lo pensé mucho. Hablé con mi
viejo, y el me preguntó: ¿crees tu que es justo lo que están haciendo? No,
le dije. Pues métete entonces. Y allí fue como empezó todo.

They had removed my daughter's first-grade teacher from the classroom. I did not feel that it was just, especially because I worked with
the teacher and never saw him do anything wrong, but I don't know,
I didn't want to get into problems. But afterward they questioned
my daughter, without me present, and they had her sign a declara-
tion. I felt that wasn't right and I needed to respond for her. And on
top of that, there were many problems in the school, there was much
more evidence against another teacher who was abusing the children.
A teaching assistant approached us and told us that she saw her teacher
grab a black boy by the neck and throw him against the wall. We
started to investigate and we came across a mother who brought a letter from her doctor proving that her daughter was mistreated by the
teacher, but they did nothing for her. We were in agreement that if a
teacher commits a crime then he be punished. But what we observed
in the school was that they weren't doing things right. For us, the
school's actions were racist. One teacher was a Latino, and the other
an Anglo-Saxon, but they were only judging the Latino, they didn't
even start an investigation of the other even when parents had evidence. So what? What do you do? I spoke with my old man, he asked
me if I thought the school's actions were just. No I told him. So get
involved he said. And that's how everything happened.

*Jaramillo: ¿Pero como te involucraste en la marcha?/*But how did you
become involved in the protest?
Jimenez: Pues no se, una mama se me arrimo y me dijo que teniamos que
hacer algo. Que nos teniamos que poner afuera. Entonces yo le dije que
bueno. Pero yo se que mucha gente no estaba de acuerdo, ni siquiera
usted Jaramillo. Usted salio una vez y nos dio una mirada bien fea,
*yo dije, que gacha/*Well I don't know, a mother approached me and
said that we had to do something. That we had to put ourselves outside. So I told her okay. But I know that a lot of people were not in
agreement, not even you Jaramillo. You came out once and gave us
a dirty look. I thought to myself, what an ass.
Jaramillo: Es cierto Jimenez, yo no estaba de acuerdo en ese tiempo/
That's right Jimenez, I did not agree with you at that time.
Jimenez: Mire, cuando estuvimos afuera fue una experiencia difícil,
porque recibíamos insultos de la gente. Nos decían "bolas de viejas chis-
mosas que no tienen quehacer en sus casas." Unos señores nos decían:
"sus maridos deben de ser unos mandilones que no se las llevan por las

*greñas a sus casas." Nos decían groserías. A veces sentí miedo. Cuando
me tocó poner los cartelones en la entrada de la escuela, qué miedo que
me dio. A mí se me movió todo el cuerpo, no podía creer que yo lo estaba
haciendo. Y de repente pasó una patrulla y le dije a mi hija: aléjate
de aquí. Solamente les dije a las demás: me llevan unos cigarritos de
pérdida si me sacan de aquí. Pero no, la patrulla pasó y no dijeron
nada. Yo colgué esa manta, pero que terror que sentí haciéndolo. En
esa bendita huelga el director salía y me preguntaba que dirá tu esposo
con verte aquí afuera. Yo le pude decir que mi esposo sabe lo que estoy
haciendo, que el no diría nada. Nosotros tuvimos un cambio en la
casa. Fue importante porque mi esposo no se opuso. Ese fue el primer
paso, porque no sentí oposición en mi casa, y eso es que él no era ese tipo
de hombre para que la vieja estuviera allí afuera.*

*Fue cuando empecé a salir mi verdadero yo dentro de mí. Yo era alguien
que no conocía. Empecé a reconocer dos personas en mí. Una era la sumisa, la humillada, la que era mártir. Yo siempre tuve mi autoestima en
el suelo, me decía que el que tenía dinero era el que tenía el poder. No es
bonito ser un mártir, es una vergüenza. Porque el mártir se destruye. Yo
me decía, es que yo no fui a la escuela, es que yo no sé ingles. Ahora digo
no, no soy mártir. Eso es lo que le digo a los papás. Que no es bonito ser
mártir, es mejor ser luchador.*

*Mire lo que pasa. Uno se siente con un poquito de más fuerza. Sentí
que la gente empezó a sentir rencor por mí, cuando salían a humillar-
nos. Pero les dije a los padres, no llegamos a ser 100, ni 50. Ni siquiera
llegamos a ser 30, pero queremos justicia. No estábamos organizadas ni
preparadas. No sabíamos cómo se tenían que hacer las cosas. Nosotras
llegábamos a lo bruto. Pero ya cuando uno veía que estaban tomando
atención, nos dimos cuento que sí teníamos poder. Después de la segunda
semana se me quitó el miedo. Me movilizaba en la noche. Me comunicaba
con las madres por teléfono.*

*Cuando reconocimos nuestro poder, los insultos ya no nos interesaban.
Un señor llegó, se acercó y nos dijo que éramos baba de perico. Pues ni
le escuchamos. Al rato sí nos preguntamos: ¿que estamos haciendo? Y el
director salía con sus chistes baratos, pero insultándolo a uno. Como la vez
que me dijo que yo estaba quedando tan negrita: "usted está agarrando
un color como..." Pues sí, parezco negra, le dije; pero el color se me va
quitar, tu reputación no. Yo ya no era la mujer sumisa. Y después de eso
la gente me empezó a buscar. Se venían conmigo, pero yo ni siquiera sabia
lo que estaba haciendo.*

When we were outside it was a very difficult experience for us because
people would insult us. They would say to us, groups of gossipy women
who don't have enough chores to do in their homes. Some men would
say to us "your husbands are a bunch of wimps for not taking you back
home." They would say bad things to us. At times I felt scared. When

it was my turn to hang the posters at the school's front entrance, I felt so scared. My whole body shook, I couldn't believe that I was doing it. Next thing you know a police car passes by and I told my daughter, move from here. I only told the others to bring me some cigarettes in case they take me from here. But the policemen went by and didn't say anything. I hung the posters, but what fear I felt doing it. In that damn protest the principal would walk out and ask me what my husband would think if he saw me outside. I was able to tell him that my husband knew what I was doing. There was a change in our home. It was important because my husband didn't go against me. That was the first step for me, because I did not feel opposition in my home, and I knew that he was not the type of man to have his woman outside.

That is when I began to come out from within myself. I was someone who I did not know. I began to recognize two persons inside me. One was the submissive woman, the humiliated woman, the martyr. I always had my self-esteem on the ground, I would tell myself that the one who has money is the one who has power. It is not good to be a martyr, it is shameful. That is what I now tell the parents. That it is not good to be a martyr, it is better to be a fighter.

Look at what happened to me. I began to feel that I had a bit more, with strength. I felt that people began to resent me, when they would come out and humiliate us. But I would tell the parents, we don't need to be 100, or 50. We weren't even 30, but we wanted justice. We weren't organized and we were not prepared. We did not know how things were supposed to be done. We approached stupidity. But when we began to see that people paid attention to us, we started to notice that we had power. After the second week I no longer had fear. I would mobilize at night. I would communicate with mothers over the telephone.

When we recognized our power, the insults no longer interested us. One man approached us and told us that we were nothing but talk. Well, we didn't even listen to him. At times we would ask ourselves, "what are we doing?" And the director, he would come out with his cheap jokes insulting us. Like the time he told me that I was becoming dark, black, he said, you are getting a color like ... well yes, I look black I said. But I told him, the color of my skin will go away, but your reputation will not. I was no longer a submissive woman. And after that, people started seeking me. They would come to me, but I didn't even know what I was doing.

BREACHING SOCIAL RELATIONS: INTERSTICES OF RUPTURE AND FRAGMENTATION

When Jimenez and lasmadres altered their role of domestic housewives in the protest, a role presumed not to encompass an activist voice, they were ridiculed and insulted by some members of the wider community and of the school site. At this point, a gendered and racialized process of naming surfaced, where women were devalued and were made less for moving away from their prescribed and proscribed roles and their labor as housewives. Here, their activity came to be regarded as a form of petty drudgery carried out by a group of gossipy women. In the latter case, the administrator's clearly prejudiced and racialized views (as a Latino male) were revealed in his attempt to deride Jimenez for "becoming dark skinned."

Racial distinctions have their own particular social characterization, and the logic behind classifying the "other" according to variations in skin color varies from place to place (Chang, 1985a). In the context of las madres, we see how skin color serves as a proxy of value in a place where most members of the community (including the school principal) have more to share with respect to the tone of their skin, but where, nonetheless, the reification of race (as a "thing" that you can just as easily put on or take off) signals social status among the status-less. Race, when coupled with lasmadres' conceived status as poor, immigrant women, relegated to housework, makes the "joke's" underlying message very clear. When the women engage in civic activity, it substantially reduces their perceived social value.

The gendering and racializing of discourse that Jimenez rearticulates expose deeply entrenched racism and sexism that can only be fully grasped or understood when seen in relation to the material relations in which discourses are embedded. Her descriptions of the community's response to las madres' revolutionized form compel us to consider how sexist and racist ideologies expose both the economy of injustice in which people labor and the relations of power and domination (Guillaumin, 1995) that permeate culture and community. This is not just a one-way or top-down typology of generating meaning from the oppressor to the oppressed; rather, it is an expression of congealed power and domination *within* the borderland of community and culture. Viewed from this perspective, we can see that when men and women within the community lash out against Jimenez and las madres for rupturing the codes of patriarchal social control, it is partly an attempt to contain their own discomfort. In observing from a distance las madres' revolutionized form, community members became self-conscious and uneasy about their own roles in the environment they claimed their own. I refer to this as a "politics of discomfort." Las madres forcibly displaced subjects from the social positions that they inhabited. They threatened masculinity by marching proudly on the street instead of crouching on the kitchen floor, and questioned institutional power when they rose up from its bottom ranks.

Many people in the community tried verbally to lash las madres back into precincts of domestication where they looked familiar and nested. Yet, a numbered few overcame their discomfort, and some even came to support lasmadres' protest. Regardless of the number in favor or in opposition, the protest marked for Jimenez and lasmadres a crossing point—a liminal portal—into the terrain of counter-memory (Lipsitz, 1990) as they began to make uncomfortably visible the hidden histories excluded from the dominant narratives that shaped their existence. During la protesta, a new presence of the body emerges among lasmadres, as previous codes in which their bodies were written became unchained. La protesta served as a form of re-signifying the body, re-fleshing the inert, subjugated body, and remaking or re-signifying its passivity into a protagonist form of agency. Voice boxes that had only numbingly echoed the utterances of the master were suddenly speaking fluently in tongues of fire, in languages never before spoken by lasmadres. La protesta marked for Jimenez, in the words of Gloria Anzaldúa (2002), the first phase of developing conocimiento/consciousness. It was an event that separated Jimenez from the realities of her past, allowing her to "see" through her culture and to breach the social relations that had contained her presence in the world. As Jimenez recounts, *"pues fíjase, si no hubiera pasado esa protesta, si yo no me hubiera hechado ese problema encima, yo no estuviera aqui/*well look, if the protest had not happened, if I had not taken that problem on, I would not be here." "Here" for Jimenez was not only a physical space but a place of understanding. A perspective from where she could make assessments and judgments. It was essentially an ethical space in which commitments are made or affirmed, one that critical educators argue precedes epistemological spaces that come with learning new languages of analysis. La protesta allowed Jimenez to examine the ways she had constructed knowledge and how it had constructed her. In Anzaldúa's conception, la protesta signaled the "earthquake" that "jerks you from the familiar and safe" and "catapults you into nepantla." In nepantla, the second phase of conocimiento/consciousness, counter-memory is activated.

Jimenez risked self-isolation and shame as lasmadres confronted, clashed, and collided against all that was deemed natural and even commonsensical in their social world: that they were poor immigrant women, of little self-worth, with no voice or role, other than to keep their homes and children tidy, *y los deseos de sus esposos atendidos/*and the desires of their husbands met. In Anzaldúa's terms, las madres "hicieron caras." In *la protesta de las mujeres sumisas/*the protest of the submissive women, las madres made defiant, scornful, and determined faces. *Caras/*faces shift and change, they provide a protective layering—both physically and semiotically, by means of gestures and looks—for the most vulnerable surface of the body (Anzaldúa, 1990). The masks are "steeped with self-hatred and other internalized oppressions," but in the space between the masks, in the "interface," lies the possibility from where one can crack the masks. Anzaldúa (1990) asserts that "making faces" has the added connotation of "making gestos subversives, political subversive gestures, the piercing look that questions and challenges" (xv). "*Entrabamos a la escuela después con la cara de revolucionaria, como el (el director) nos decia, nos hicimos famosas/*We later entered the school with the face of a revolutionary, like he (the principal) would tell us, we became famous." Las madres learned to recognize the art of "making faces." In Jimenez's words, "*Yo siempre tuve la máscara de hipocresía puesta/*I always had the mask of hypocrisy on. *Con la máscara puesta aprendí/*With the mask" on I learned. *A sonreir cuando tenia que llorar/*To smile when I needed to cry. *Ahora ya se cuando no me tengo que poner ninguna máscara/*Now I know when I don't have to put on any mask." Jimenez was on the path of discovering the interface from where she could crack the alabaster masks she wore, masks that she had made and masks that had made her.

La protesta de la mujer sumisa symbolizes a process of uncovering the interfaces that were kept hidden from, to borrow a phrase from Marx, Jimenez's "species-being." In la protesta, the masks started to lose their coating. When the political actions of the mothers began to reveal the masks of subversion that underlay the masks of submission, a battle of words and blank stares erupted, as members of the community and the school attempted to *ponerlas (las madres) en silencio/*place them (las madres) in silence. Nevertheless, in a short amount of time, Jimenez and lasmadres managed to form a formidable nexus of solidarity. Jimenez reflects,

Lo que más que sirvió (en la protesta) fue que hicimos una amistad y nos pusimos a apoyar. En cierto modo era tímida y desconfiada, pero ya con el tiempo no le di importancia a eso. Y como que sentía, ay, yo soy la Jiménez, porque después empezó que era yo la que tenía que estar metida. No sé por qué me dejaron a mí. Yo no sabía. La señora Valencia siempre me puso a mí adelante. Sabiendo ella más que yo; siempre decía encárguese con María. No sabía si agarrar o no la responsabilidad, y me preguntaba a mi misma: ¿por qué darme a mi la responsabilidad? Y ya todos los papás eran conmigo. Fíjese, ahora digo que éramos nada, pero éramos un millón a la misma vez. Eran amas de casa que sintieron que la causa era injusta y estaban allí. Fue cuando yo empecé a decirme, vaya, soy grande. Empecé a enfrentarme con el director. Bueno, no sé cómo lo hicimos esa vez con 200 personas en el auditorio. Y lo hicimos nosotras. Fue cuando empezamos a sentir que sí teníamos poder. What was most helpful (in the protest) for us is that we built a friendship and we started to support each other. In a certain way I was shy and lacked confidence but with time I no longer cared about those things. And how it felt to say, hey, I am the woman Jimenez. Because after they began to say that I was the one who needed to be involved. I don't know why they chose me. The lady Valencia always put me in front. And she knew more than me but she always told people to take things up with María. I didn't know if I should take the responsibility and I would ask myself, why give me the responsibility? And then all the parents were with me. Look, now I say that we were nothing and we were a million at the same time. They were housewives, felt that the cause was unjust and they were there. That is when I began to say, look, I am big. I began to confront the director. Well, and I say it, I don't know how we did it that time with 200 people in the auditorium. And we did it and that is when we began to see that we did have power.

A sense of solidarity among the protesting mothers, and the support that Jimenez received from other members of the community, contributed to her changing identity formation. Jimenez continued,

Fue cuando empecé a salir yo dentro de mí. Yo era alguien que no conocía Empecé a reconocer dos personas en mi. Una era la sumisa, la humillada, la que era mártir. Que fue el cambio en mí. Los padres me apoyaron. Ellos me pusieron donde estoy. Digamos que yo antes era Lourdes, y en la protesta nació María. Ahora soy María Jiménez. That is when I began to come out from within myself. I was someone who I did not know. I began to recognize two persons inside me. One was the submissive woman, the humiliated woman, the martyr. What was the change in me, I don't know, the parents supported me. They put me where I am.

Let's say that I was Lourdes before and in the protest Maria was born.
I am now Maria Jimenez.

Jimenez's narration of la protesta brought forth a memory of the very
processes that led to her movement into the unknown, unanticipated,
and liminal spaces of transformation. It was an organic movement
that hinged on the seeming unpredictability of circumstances: the
removal of a classroom teacher, the inappropriate method of questioning a six-year-old, and the spontaneous will of lasmadres to organize
a four-month-long protest on the school's front lawn. Maria began to
formally recast the etchings of her formation as *la mujer sumisa/*the
submissive woman. In the protest, Jimenez and las madres came to
recognize their own oppression as *mujeres* and the oppression of their
community. They took risks and engaged in self-isolation. But their
self-imposed risk and isolation allowed them to move into divergent
worlds to develop innovative and potentially transformative practices.
Jimenez and las madres were in a process of becoming visionary cultural workers, who would make possible new forms of community and
social action.

THE SEVEN STAGES OF KNOWING

Jimenez's reflection on the protest is as much a source from which
to articulate localized and different understandings of the dominant
social structure of the school and society as it is a path that Gloria
Anzaldúa calls "conocimiento." In Anzaldúa's terminology, the path
of conocimiento crosses over seven stages of developing consciousness
(see table 3.1). The first is the rupture, or fragmentation of the self,
the "earthquake" that jolts the subject into the unknown and liminal
spaces of nepantla (phase two). In nepantla, the formerly coherent self
begins to implode from within, questioning and seeing through the
self-imposed and cultural scripts that have historically tamed her mind
and tongue; she opens herself to full awareness of the present conditions that have moved her from a space of comfort into discomfort and
into liminality. In neither the "here" nor the "there" cleavages of liminal time and place, the subject begins to change her interpretation of
reality, what Anzaldúa defines as the "coatlicue" state (phase three),
of *deconocimiento/*unknowing, where the body/mind is lost in a state
of chaos, trying to find a path back to the comforting narratives that
kept her intact. From deconocimiento, she begins to negotiate with

Table 3.1 Seven Stages of Consciousness

Seven Stages of Conocimiento	
Rupture, fragmentation	Breaching the walls you've built around yourself, shifting into the cracks between the worlds that have shaped you
Nepantla	Seeing double through opposing social worlds, opening by yourself the space/time between transitions
Coatlicue state	The state of unknowing, reclaiming body consciousness in the midst of personal chaos and transition
Crossing and conversion	Seeing your identity in transition, reinterpreting your past and reshaping your present
New personal and collective stories	Rewriting stories of the self, reframing your story, exploring aspects of reality that lead to a new synthesis of the self-society relation
Clash of realities	Nepantleras emerge, positioning themselves in the existing social order from a new identity position
Acting out the vision, spiritual activism	Honoring people's otherness, practicing empathy and enacting change in the social world you inhabit

herself, with the woman she once knew and the one she was becoming. This is the fourth stage of conocimiento, where, Anzaldúa notes, "reactions to past events change" and experiences are remembered in a "new arrangement." On the path to conocimiento she stretches beyond herself to write new stories of her self-formation (phase five). The "clash of realities" (phase six) between the narratives she knows and the ones she is rewriting pushes her over to the seventh and final stage of Anzaldúa's assessment of conocimiento: acting out the vision or spiritual activism. The "knowing/knower" that emerges from this path is imbued with a new sense of self and others; from this knowledge construction, she gains a new presence in the world, her vision is sharper, her words are more direct, and she gains the ability to act in the social world more from choice than from an external directive (Anzaldúa, 2002).

In retelling the events that constitute la protesta, Jimenez is engaged in the act of testimony. Here, I am following the definition of testimony provided by Felman and Laub when they write, "the testimony is the process by which the narrator reclaims his position as a witness: reconstitutes the internal 'thou' and thus the possibility of a witness or a listener inside himself. Repossessing one's life story through giving testimony is itself a form of action, of change, which has to actually pass through in order to continue and complete the process of survival after literation" (1992, 86). While Felman and Laub write about the act of testimony in relation to their work with holocaust survivors, their insights into the act of giving testimony is instructive in exploring dimensions of Jimenez's narrative account.

Jimenez's recollection of her formation in la protesta is an act of giving testimony. In describing the ideas, events, and institutions (Mirasur, the police, the news media) that intervened in her breaking through the retaining walls of a domestic housewife, Jimenez is enacting the position of standing witness to her formation. Her mindful and bodily recollection of la protesta establishes the conditions for her to claim the position of witness to her history. It is in the active processes of testifying from inside her "otherness" (as Lourdes) that she finds the voice to emerge as "María." Lourdes becomes the subject of María's testimony; she is the woman-subject that María introduces to me as *la mujer sumisa*/the submissive woman, and to lasmadres when she recounts the way in which she and lasmadres have remained devalued and voiceless. Jimenez sets in motion and in dialogue the women that she witnesses within— María and Lourdes. Giving testimony of her formation as María and Lourdes is part of her course into shifting consciousness. It is in the act of giving testimony, of telling, retelling, creating, and re-creating herself in relation to the events that inform her subjective position within the community that Jimenez crosses boundaries and relinquishes her sense of martyrdom. She crisscrosses the seven stages of conocimiento (Anzaldúa, 2002; see table 3.1) as she begins to live the knowledge that she has gained of herself in embodied ways, "*ya no me agacho la cabeza*/I no longer put my head down," stretching beyond the limits of cultural restrictions, "*ya los insultos no me importaban*/insults no longer mattered to me." A new synthesis is created between the woman she knew (Lourdes) and the woman she was becoming (María) "*fue cuando nacio María Jimenez, murio Lourdes. Yo me sorprendo de mi*/it was when Maria Jimenez was born, Lourdes died. I am surprised at myself."

The protest signaled a breach of normative relations on several levels. It was a discernible break from the school's routine practices (of a protest taking place on the front lawn), but it further triggered a host of other reactions based on the fact that it was women—mothers, burritas—who were taking up sticks and poster boards in symbolic acts of defiance against the school's authority. Las madres were not only contesting and breaking from the school's normative stance, they were also in a process of breaching the public roles that they had assumed in the wider community. Their actions sparked (1) a break from normative practices for addressing conflict (i.e., submitting a letter of grievance to the district office) and (2) an interruption of the "burrita" labor process (tied to their class-gender position). Simultaneously, the protest breached certain norms and practices of the community. The protesting madres (1) violated patriarchal norms and practices (they were on the street instead of in the kitchen) and (2) cracked through the complicit codes of behavior that had characterized school-community interactions. In sum, la protesta marked a "breach" from normative rule-oriented codes and scripts as well as a real-time break from patriarchal class relations that had characterized relations of the school-community borderland.

The pedagogy of the burro was being inverted, dismantled, and transformed, and social actors within the social drama of Mirasur—both faculty and community members alike—relied on their authoritative stances to resolve the crisis initiated by lasmadres. Resolution, however, translated into an attempt to silence the women and not into an effort to address their concerns. Social actors inside and outside the school setting tried to force lasmadres back into the "burro" form that they were accustomed to seeing. As Jimenez recounted, "When we were outside it was a very difficult experience for us because people would insult us. They would say to us, groups of gossipy women who don't have enough chores to do in their homes. Some men would say to us 'your husbands are a bunch of whimps for not taking you back home.' They would say bad things to us." The protest was a "genesis"—a putting of women into discourse—and called into question the underlying system of beliefs that had characterized their performance in the community and school site.

REFLECTING ON THE SOCIAL DRAMA FROM WITHIN

My examination of the social drama of Mirasur stemmed from the performative register that I assumed as an administrator (and later researcher) embedded within the general architecture of the school site. But in coming to know Jimenez and lasmadres more intimately, I decided to disengage from the normative and regulative models of practice that I as a pedagogue and researcher was accustomed to assuming. I was experiencing a breach in numerous dimensions, coeval in time and space. In turn, I examined the social drama of Mirasur from the threshold spaces of liminality that resulted from my engagement/disengagement with the normative rules, procedures, and practices of the school (as an administrator-actor), in addition to the ruptures I experienced from within (as a woman and pedagogue).

LA PROTESTA REVISITED: BREACHING RELATIONS

Las madres' protest took place several weeks after we had met and begun working as child-care providers for the parent institute. Jimenez walked into my office one morning and inquired about the school's actions to dismiss her daughter's first-grade teacher.

> *Jimenez: ¿Crees tu que es justo lo que esta haciendo la escuela?*/Do you think it's fair what the school is doing?
> *Jaramillo: Pues no se Jimenez, creo que es necesario que investiguen lo que paso*/I don't know, I think it's necessary for them to look into what happened.
> *Jimenez: ¿Sabes tu que hicieron que mi hija firmara una declaración sin yo estar presente?*/Did you know they made my daughter sign a declaration without me being present?
> *Jaramillo: No Jimenez, eso es contra la ley, ellos no pueden hacer eso*/No, that is against the law, they can't do that.
> *Jimenez: ¿Pues que hago?*/Well what do I do?
> *Jaramillo: ¿Ya hablaste con el director?*/Have you spoken to the principal?
> *Jimenez: ¿Que me va a decir ese gabacho?*/What is that white man going to say?
> *Jaramillo: Vaya con el Jimenez, pregunte porque le tomaron una declaración*/Go to him, ask him why they took her declaration.

Several days later, Jimenez and las madres organized the protest. I approached Jimenez shortly thereafter.

> *Jaramillo: Jimenez porque no regresas a la escuela. No has visto toda la evidencia, yo vi las fotos, deje que la corte se encarge del maestro/*

Jimenez, why don't you return to the school. You haven't seen all the evidence, I saw the pictures, let the court take care of the teacher.

*Jimenez: No Jaramillo, eso no lo puedo hacer. Aquí estoy y aquí me voy a quedar. Yo nunca vi que hiciera nada el maestro, yo estaba allí todos los días. ¿ Cómo quieres que yo no defienda mi hija? Tu sabes que lo que hicieron no es correcto. La escuela no es justa/*I can't do that. I am here and this is where I am going to stay. I never saw the teacher do anything, I was there every day. How could you expect me not to defend my daughter? You know that what they did isn't right. The school is not just.

After that encounter, Jimenez stopped speaking to me for weeks, and during the infrequent times that we did exchange a few words, she was uncharacteristically cold and reticent. She greeted me with an abrupt and direct, "*Buenos días Jaramillo, ¿ vas a necesitar cuidado de niños hoy?/*Good morning Jaramillo, are you going to need child-care today?" *Y eso fue todo.* That was it.

We met our commitments with the parent institute but did not speak to one another aside from the required formalities of organizing child-care and ensuring that the institute staff and families had the necessary materials to proceed with their classes. We no longer shared a workspace, or a cup of coffee, or talked about our weekends, or schooled each other about our histories. The times that I attempted to approach Jimenez and initiate a conversation, she ignored my efforts. Her silence forced me to reconsider what I had done to cause it, and in so doing, the abstract border between us became concrete. I was the person from the other side of the tracks, the foreigner, the alien, the one who selectively sees and hears whatever she chooses and who avoids contact when conditions within her institutional nest destabilize her rank or authority on knowledge. Jimenez's silence had jolted me out of position: I could assume neither an authoritative stance nor a position of solidarity with her. Without Jimenez (my "member check" so to speak) I was unable to see through the cracks of the school-community borderland. She was my bridge into a community that I did not occupy. Her eyes saw what I did not see during school hours and her body felt what I could not feel 40 miles away in the comfort of my Pasadena home. She pushed me into a state of paralysis in denying me the ability to learn and work with her. Jimenez approached me several weeks later:

Jimenez: *¿Ya oyó lo que paso?*/Have you heard yet what happened?
Jaramillo: *¿Que paso?*/What happened?
Jimenez: *El juez perdonó los cargos contra el maestro*/The judge dropped
   the charges against the teacher.
Jaramillo: *¿De veras?* Really?
Jimenez: *Si, ¿ ya me crees?*/Yes, do you believe me now?

Jimenez intuitively recognized my deference to court justice and she sensed that I waited for a higher legal authority to cast judgment on the teacher's fate, which would, in turn, either legitimate or delegitimate her activity during la protesta (from my standpoint). The issue at hand between me and Jimenez had little, however, to do with the teacher's legal status. The interactions that transpired between us had more to do with the different positions that we occupied and power that we exercised within the social drama of Mirasur, and the ways in which we performed our respective roles within the institutional setting. I had resisted any attempt to engage or understand Jimenez's and las madres' embodied understanding of the relations of power and domination that shaped their participation in and observation of practices within the school setting. The embodied activity (marching, chanting, organizing on the front lawn) that lasmadres assumed during la protesta signaled to me (and to a majority of the staff) a breach of crucial norms that had been established within the school site—of following due process and conferring judgment to the legal authority. In Turner's terms, las madres had breached crucial norms that regulated activity between the community and the school, and it had made me uneasy.

It takes a deliberate, focused, and sustained effort to critically self-reflect upon the social, cultural, and institutional practices that are reproduced in the dominant social order and status quo culture. The social drama of Mirasur is infused with power relations established through the hierarchical structure between and within faculty, students, and the community. The power of the social drama of Mirasur is hegemonic in that it does not simply dominate actors, it incorporates them. Social drama actors are agents and strategic improvisers who respond dispositionally to various situations. People are governed by social rules insofar as it is in their interest to do so. In retrospect, it was in my best interest to incorporate Jimenez back into the social rules of the social drama of Mirasur so that I could continue working with her. But Jimenez had a different view of the social rules with which she should or should not comply.

Our different points of view, and the ways in which power relations had incorporated us into the school setting is what established the breach of social norms between and among us.

Power relations and their attendant institutional structures sustain and reproduce hegemonic discourses of legitimacy surrounding the role of social actors within the school setting (las madres, administrators, teachers, and students) and in how they should perform within the dominant social order. The power relations that differentially positioned me in relation to las madres were unevenly dispersed through the social relations that gave shape to our subjective formations—women from different class positions, countries of origin, and of disparate educational backgrounds. The power that we carried with us—mothers and I as a non-childbearing woman from the proverbial middle class—produced and shaped our behavior with one another and within the school site. Las madres were on a journey of exorcising and exercising power that began to emerge from spaces that were identified with their own self-formation, and I had been on a journey of maintaining power that was dependent on rule-following. After la protesta ended, I made a deliberate effort to break from the normative and rule-oriented scripts of the social drama of Mirasur. Here, I am apprised of Turner's (1987) assessment of the performative roles that the self assumes in social dramas. As Turner (1987) notes, through performance the self also maintains the ability to break roles and declare to a given public that one has undergone a transformation of state and status, been saved or damned, elevated or released. I declared political allegiance to Jimenez and lasmadres and committed the rest of my pedagogical work to understanding the social drama of Mirasur from their embodied and mindful activity.

We invited each other into the social dramas, of which we formed two distinct parts—the social drama of Mirasur and our respective social dramas that marked our own personal journeys. I asked Jimenez to share my office space and supplied her with inside knowledge about school budgets, councils, and other processes that established norms, rules, and procedures within the social drama of Mirasur, and Jimenez invited me into her home and the spaces she shared with lasmadres. We breached social norms and examined the social and historical formation of our "selves" in our own contextually specific ways but maintained a shared vision to alter the relations and practices that we deemed unjust in our immediate surroundings. The social drama that we shared suspended the normative role-playing we had been accustomed to; we became reflexive of our roles and performances within the social drama of Mirasur.

SCHOOL IMPROVEMENT COORDINATORS VISIT

We were visited today by a new cohort of school improvement coordinators sent by the school district to help us get our "act together." The principal asked me to attend the meeting, since I officially formed part of the existing school improvement team. We sat around a large rectangular table, Mirasur staff on one side and school district coordinators on the other. The coordinators opened their legal-sized leather portfolios and began to ask us a series of questions enumerated on their checklists: are teachers aware of teaching and learning standards? Yes. Check. Are the standards visible in every classroom? Yes. Check. Do you offer teachers opportunities for professional development on a regular basis? Yes, every month. Check. Do you offer intersession classes for offtrack students? Yes. Check. Do you communicate with parents? Yes. The principal elaborated, "We have a bilingual newsletter that is sent home every week, and we are looking into a school marquee so that we can list our meetings and major school events. Communication with families is one of our top priorities."

I interrupted the conversation by asking the "improvement" team to consider the deeper and more fundamental issues of organizing interactions between the faculty, children, and community. I raised questions about the marginalization that many families experienced in the organizational structure of the school site and attempted to link standards for learning to meaningful teaching practices that made learning relevant to the children's lives and community. The principal interjected, "Ms. Jaramillo has been working very hard at initiating activities to integrate families in the school—we have a folklorico group, we celebrate Mexico's independence day, and all of those things are very nice, but what we need to do is get the test scores up, that is really where our efforts are at and we want to work with you to make sure we meet our benchmarks." The coordinators continued, "Do you have test-prep booklets?" Yes. Check.

I may have entered the social drama of Mirasur as an ivy-league-clad school administrator, a Harvard-certified prop that gave the school administration bragging rights at professional development meetings, but by the end of my tenure, the administration was, to put it bluntly, sick of me.

END OF THE YEAR

The school year was coming to an end, and I have less than four weeks left at the school site. I walked upstairs to check in with our savvy computer technician about the new website we were in the process of putting together. He said to me, "you know what Mr. Rodriguez said of you the other day?" No, I responded. "He told me you were a lame duck." I was not at all surprised by the principal's remark, since just a few days earlier he had asked me if, when my contract expired, I was going to join the unemployment line in downtown Los Angeles that ran several city blocks. And he had already indicated that many of the programs that I had initiated would not be funded the following year. I had grown accustomed to the principal's sense of "humor" over the years, but in every joke resides a bit of truth, and I could intuitively sense a growing separation from the school's administrative core.

My intent here is not to go into grave detail about the interactions that transpired between me and the school administration (actors who shared a similar rank and position within the school site) or to make these relations the centerpiece of the social drama of Mirasur that I have detailed in this chapter. I share these brief recollections from my diary accounts and field notes to illustrate the changes in role and position that I underwent over time within the social drama of Mirasur. What strikes me as worth noting are the overall *performative* characteristics of institutional settings themselves and the people who labor within them. Here, we appear to have two contradictory aspects of the laboring process. The act of labor itself comes with its own set of rules and guidelines that establish the governing framework in which people fulfill their duties and obligations. This sets up a person's subjective and objective *relation* to his/her work, whether it is manual or mental labor. This objective relation in capitalist society is predicated on the concept of organizing and conducting our work within the logic of profit maximization. The subjective relation is to create productive and law-abiding citizens who accept the free-market precepts of democracy upon which society is ostensibly built. The result of this contradictory relation produces a condition of alienation on the part of those who are obliged to perform this labor in the service of "democracy." In the case of teachers, administrators, consultants, and so on, alienation further results from increased mandates that limit the development and expression of an educator's capacities and methods for the purpose of generating "human capital." Human capital refers to the aptitudes and skills of the students that can be measured and quantified in terms of standards and test results. To be a successful school (read, administrator, teacher, successful student, and so forth) is to produce high levels (i.e., test scores) of human capital. Put simply, human beings are reduced to what can be measured numerically. In this case, all participants in a school setting are affected by this instrumental logic; the *performance* of the administration, teachers, and students is intimately connected to achieving preordained results. But what often goes unremarked when discussing the tragic results that often follow from the assigned institutional and pedagogical roles that teachers and students are forced to assume (high dropout rates among working-class students and students of color, etc.) are the dramaturgical principles that are constitutive of producing such roles. Erving Goffman has famously noted that the individual in ordinary work situations "presents himself and his activity to others, the ways in which he guides and controls the impression they form of him, and the kinds of things he may and may not do while sustaining his performance before them" (1959, xi). Conceivably, we all play various roles in managing the impressions that others have of us as we undertake the perfunctory duties assigned to us in the workplace. There is a difference, however, from playing a "part" with some level of awareness that it is indeed a part, and believing that we actually possess the attributes assigned to our roles. When I broke from the normative routines and guidelines in Mirasur and made an alliance with the mothers, my role was transformed from that of an outsider in the community to a *comadre*. Maria Jimenez allayed parents' fears when they approached me and she let them know that I was trustworthy; she called me her *comadre*. Trust among the mothers was determined by the level of commitment and transparency people demonstrated in attending to the needs and protecting the basic interests of the children. This change of status was not lost in the eyes of the administration. Rather, I surmise that at some level it signaled a form of betrayal. When I challenged the foundations upon which the administration claimed to have improved the learning process and outcomes of students and relationship to the community, I became an outsider to them. Such a break would necessarily cause anger and resentment, because it called into question the sacerdotal value of the "signs" (Goffman, 1959) already expressed as constitutive of an administration dutifully and successfully performing its work (or in Habermasian [1992] terms, a regime of signs that sanctified the "communicatively structured lifeworld" of the school).

Inner Theater: Social Drama as Shifting Consciousness

Before Jimenez rushed off to cafeteria duty after our family literacy class in the parent center, I apprehensively asked her to sit down with me for 15 minutes to talk about her life history. For the first time I had brought a tape recorder with me, eager to record the details of her life that I had failed to commit to memory or document in my field notes. Perhaps because of my familiarity with Jimenez, and her story, I did not think twice about the abruptness of my request. Jimenez quipped, "*Usted cree que en quince minutos voy a decir todo lo que tengo que decir?*/ Do you think that in fifteen minutes I am going to say everything that I have to say?" Jimenez speaks quickly and profoundly, and since we had some time to spare I thought we could at least begin. But as Jimenez reminded me, to talk about one's life's history would take much longer than a few minutes; the act of telling her story was a multilayered act, of recovering from scattered memory deposits the events, feelings, and dispositions connected to her consciousness. In the few minutes that she did spare, her facial expression transitioned from general happiness to tearful malaise, then to a cool look of detachment, and then to sober resignation. Her *inner theater* was replete with emotion and memories of the obstacles she faced as a girl who came from poverty and a woman who grew up in patriarchy's grip. The conversation that began that day in the parent center would take over six years to unpack, including hundreds of hours of conversation, at times continuous and at other times intermittent, recalling the subjugated memories that made up her story.

I was already partly familiar with aspects of Jimenez's upbringing and the difficulties she confronted. Jimenez had recounted several of her experiences during our long conversations over coffee at her kitchen table, sometimes before and sometimes after Jimenez picked the children up from school. If it was before, we could take advantage of the relatively quiet hum inside the home, with the exception of the sounds of a distant yelping dog that came through the open kitchen window, or of a *rancheras*-blaring car radio or chrome-spinning tires leaving their skid marks down the street in those rituals of machismo where burned rubber serves as an index of territorial presence and the fortitude of one's lowrider *ramfla*. And if it was after the children came home, then we would no longer enjoy the quiet of the home, but we would nevertheless experience a wide range of other emotions as siblings argued over the remote control, or laughed in the living room, or interrupted us with a request for cornflakes, cheetos, *leche*, or help putting a toy together that had just been slammed against the vinyl floor like the latest smackdown *luchador* taking on *el Mistico* or the *Gran Apache*. Jimenez shared her story not only with me but also with the women with whom she spoke—every morning, afternoon, and evening—on the street corner next to the vendor selling *champurrado* before the school bell rang, or while she guarded the side entrance gate as mothers, fathers, and older siblings escorted their young ones to class, or as *lasco madres* convened on the front steps that led to her home when the first hint of dusk broke through the clouds.

For Jimenez, the present is always accompanied by visitors from the past, sometimes fragments of fading memories, sometimes the scent of the agave plant that used to grow in her childhood *colonia/* colony, and sometimes a shadowy figure of a long-deceased relative standing in the wings of consciousness to bring solace and comfort in times of stress. In academic terminology, the present is, for Jimenez, always mediated by her past experiences and memories. All experiences have some kind of bodily or mental feeling attached to them, feelings that affect the "self" but that are not necessarily the "self" (Varela, Thompson, and Rosch, 1993). And while there are various competing theories and philosophies around the "self" in relation to one's experiences, emotions, perceptions, and developing consciousness, for Jimenez the relationship between memory, experience, thought, and being cannot be separated into isolated units or separate cognitive templates. As she says, "*Tal vez yo sea una persona que no puede vivir completamente en el presente, porque el pasado no se a borrado/*Perhaps I am a person who cannot completely live in the present, because the past has not been erased." Her ensuing activism and relationship to the community was always underwritten by an emotional link to the conditions of oppression that she identified in the social world. In this way, her embodiment of the past in the present served to unite the mothers in the community as a way of restructuring their relationship to the school for the betterment of their children. Can narrative work as a pedagogical tool of teaching/ learning and indeed rupturing the steady routines of institutional life? What about when the stories come from the struggles of women and mothers? Is there an essence, a particularity about the power of a woman's voice—a mother—that taps into the core of our structural unconsciousness and motivates people to act (or resist)? Sofia Villenas describes this as the "communal *mujer*," or "womanist-inspired spaces of teaching and learning where the power of mothers' biographies is exercised in the sharing of these stories." The intersections of resilience and resistance, what Villenas describes as "created from the tools of faith, spirituality and humor," can, perhaps, "resituate the dynamics of power and privilege" (2005).

Jimenez's story is textured and layered, and part of my role has been to understand the story within her story that she uses to articulate her experiences. The inner story of her personal narrative helps us to see beyond the singularity of her experience and understand how systems, institutions, metaphors, and *dramas* have evolved over time. The concrete, bodily, and gendered experiences that Jimenez narrates from the standpoint of a woman and mother are particular to her life history, but they also reveal the outer workings of societies marked by intense and systemic forms of exclusion and exploitation. Her story becomes a source from which to articulate localized and broad historical understandings of the dominant social structure of the school and society. Women philosophers have referred to this as "standpoint epistemology" and "situated knowledges," the learning in women's bodies that encompass various levels of seeing and analyzing the world from the particular settings and conditions in which life histories are formed. The act of narration allows for the objective structures of experience to be revealed. In other words, a person's ability to identify those structures that have informed her experiences is embedded within "situated" knowledges. The act of narration is, in part, a learning process, to the extent that speaking about our histories requires the ability to see what may have not been immediately present to us at the moment of the experience itself. In Donna Haraway's formulation, this kind of "vision" is connected to "self-knowledge." In turn, self-knowledge depends on a "semiotic-material technology" that connects social meanings with what is experienced in the body (1988). In this sense it is useful to consider the remarks made by cultural theorist Teresa Ebert, who refers to "abstract structures" as the social relations in which concrete actions acquire their meaning (2009). For Ebert, a focus on concrete conditions and a disregard for the abstract may display the complexity of everyday life but also make it hollow by cutting it off from the social relations in which experience generates its meaning. Meaning, she says, is not the correspondence of language to reality as realism implies, nor is it the endless play of the sign as linguistic theory suggests. Instead, she argues that meaning is a social relation, and the uncertainty of meaning and the existence of difference are not caused by the slippage of signs away from any fixed referent but by social change and contradictions. This represents a significant intervention in the rather complex debates over the relationship between language, action, and meaning. How we come to know power, authority, and our own position within various social settings is based on social relations. Meaning spawns from language, but ultimately it comes from interactions, from the active production and exchange of knowledge.

As the translator and interlocutor of Jimenez's narrative account, I am enmeshed in the telling of her story. As I listened to her story, I was inevitably caught up in a web of moral reasoning (Eckenwiler, 2001) as I made judgments about what she shared with me. I do not claim the position of impartiality in writing about Jimenez's life history, nor do I deny that my reading is shaped by the particular assumptions and commitments that I bring as a woman whose own subjectivity has been framed by a different, albeit related, set of social conditions. There is a dialectical praxis in play within the active process of telling and writing narrative accounts that moves beyond the merely discursive (whose voice is heard? why it is heard? and how loudly?) or beyond a democratization of oppression (trying to make everyone equally oppressed). In the social drama of Mirasur, neither the subject nor the object of a narrative account can be understood as separate from the material world she sees, hears, touches, feels, and labors in. And because one feels this connectedness to the world, one is obliged to work within it and against it. Change is not merely discursive but also extra-discursive; it resides simultaneously in the self and in social transformation. From this perspective, Jimenez's narrative account is directly connected to the living matter of her activity as a narrator. Therefore, a reading and telling of her story is not limited to describing the various identity markers that have been assigned to her, but, rather, to demystifying and denaturalizing the condition that she describes in her formation as "*la mujer sumisa*/the submissive woman."

LA MUJER SUMISA/THE SUBMISSIVE WOMAN

Yo nací en Jalisco, fuí la segunda hija del matrimonio de mi mama. Mi papá nos dejo al estar embarazada mi mama de mí. Tuvimos una vida como muchos en el abandono. Ella en ciertas ocasiones tuvo que separarse de nosotros para poder mantenernos. Porque en esos tiempos lo único que mi mamá hacía era trabajar en casa y en esos tiempos no debajan llevar hijos a trabajar a casa. No admitian a ninguna madre con hijos sin marido en una casa. Tuvimos tiempos separados. I was born in Jalisco, I was the second child of my mother's marriage. My father left us when my mother was pregnant with me. We had a life like many in abandonment. On certain occasion she had to separate herself from us to support us. Because in those times the only thing my mother did was work in home and in those times they didn't let women take their children to work in the homes. They wouldn't allow any woman with children and without a husband in the home. We were separated at times.

Jimenez's identity was partly forged through the engendering of exploitation and alienation in the laboring process and by submitting herself to the place and rank that she would occupy as a subaltern woman in a patriarchal capitalist society.

Mi hermano y yo nos llevábamos bien hasta los 10 años, porque siempre le teníamos que ayudar a mi mama. Siempre andaba vendiendo barritas, churros y yo corría atrás de él con la salsa. Llevábamos una vida bien. Ya cuando mi hermano tenía 13 años y yo 10 empezaron a cambiar las cosas entre mi hermano y yo. Mi mama empezó a marcar diferencias. Su hijo era el preferido. El podía ir a la escuela porque era el hombre de la casa. El tenia el derecho de pegarme o gritarme. En la cena el me decía, mire esta come como puerca. Yo lloraba. Yo era la burra, la tonta, yo no iba a la escuela. My brother and I always got along until we were about ten years old because we always had to help my mother. He was always selling bars, churros, and I would run after him with the salsa. We led a good life. Then when my brother was 13 and I 10 years old things started to change between us. My mother began to mark differences. Her son was the preferred one. He was able to go to school because he was the man of the house. He had the right to hit me or yell at me. During dinner he would tell me, look, this one eats like a pig. I cried. I was the mule, the idiot, I didn't go to school.

When I ask Jimenez to elaborate on the reasons for her not going to school, she responds:

> "*Yo siempre e vivido como humillada*/I have always been humiliated"
> *Miré, cuando mi mamá empezo a limpiar casas ella trabajaba horas muy largas. Ella me mandaba con mi hermano a la casa de unos amigos, donde me sentaban en una sillita en un pasillo largo. Nunca se me olvida ese pasillo, todo mocoso mugroso. Allí me sentaban por horas y yo jugaba con mi hermano. Yo no tuve la oportunidad de ir a la escuela.* Look, when my mother started cleaning houses she worked very long hours. She would send me and my brother to the home of some friends, where they would sit me in a chair in a long hallway. I will never forget that hallway, all nasty and dirty. There I would sit for hours and I would play with my brother. I didn't have the opportunity to go to school.

"*¿Cuando empezaste a trabajar?*/When did you start working,*"* Jimenez asks me. "*Cuando tenia quince años*/When I was fifteen years old," I responded. I told her about the ultimatum my mother gave me, that if I wanted to purchase more clothing or be able to drive a car when I turned 16 then I would need to find a job. I talked about my busy schedule between school and work, and the stench on my clothing from working in a restaurant. I shared stories about working as a hostess, and then as a food "runner," and I ended with the capstone of my teenage working days: I started cleaning the tables for better tips. I looked at Jimenez and expected some sort of empathetic wink or tap on the hand. "*Tuviste que limpiar casas*/Did you have to clean homes?" she asks. "No," I replied. "*Ponga atención*/Pay attention," Jimenez tells me.

> *Cuando yo tenía siete años yo empeze a trabajar con mi mamá. Ella limpiaba los cuartos del hotel donde iban muchos Americanos, muchos Americanos, entonces yo cuidaba los niños de las amigas de mi mamá. Cuando las cosas estaban mal, también trabajaba con mi hermano. Nosotros nos íbamos a los centros comercial y a los mercados como burros de cara donde llevabamos las bolsas de los ricos. Dependiendo del corazón de la persona nos daban 20 centavos o más o menos. Mi hermano y yo corríamos con el dinero para comprar café y azúcar para mi mamá.* When I was seven years old I started working with my mother. She cleaned the hotel rooms where there were many Americans, many Americans, so I took care of the children of my mother's friends. When things were really bad I also worked with my brother. We went to shopping centers and grocery stores with a donkey's face to carry the bags of the rich.

Depending on the heart of the person, they would give us 20 cents, more or less. My brother and I would then run with the money to buy coffee and sugar for my mother.

I watch Jimenez's eyes well up with tears as she talks about her mother. "*Mi mama nosa brazaba y era a llorar*/My mother would hug us and cry."

READING *LA MUJER SUMISA*

As the interlocutor of Jimenez' narrative account, it is necessary to read her words not just as a story of internal discord within the micro-cosm of her community or home, but as a reference point for the broader totality of colonization from whence her story was shaped. A failure to do so truncates her account to a sequence of isolated and bounded events without understanding the way in which the body, voice, and mind produce and consume meaning across historical time and space. Jimenez's words and memories connect to a historical lin-eage of colonization and oppression within her native land of Mexico, a dualistic land of many contradictions within contradictions that is suspended between what Guillermo Bonfil-Batalla (1996) refers to as *Mexico imaginario y Mexico profundo*. *Mexico imaginario* is the land of the conquerors, the Republic, the United States of Mexico, where the values of individualism, overwork, industrialism, and unlimited consumption prevail. *Mexico profundo* is the indigenous land shaped by traditions that defy easy conceptualization, stretching thousands of years into the past. Through violent force and a moral Christian crusade, *Mexico imaginario* has attempted to replace *Mexico profundo* for centuries, embedding a hierarchical grammar within the liminal fissure between colonization and resistance. Jimenez expresses these nuances and contradictions in her experiences as *la niña y mujer sum-isa*/the submissive girl and woman; they take form through insults and tongue-lashings, the self-reflective residue of colonization.

Insults affect the psyche all the way to the flesh and right through the bone. It penetrates even the most impermeable dimensions of mind and body; words of spite work as forms of social control, reify-ing social hierarchies of exploitation. Characterized by a language of deference, respect, and honor (Lipsett-Rivera, 1998), *Mexico imagi-nario* imposed scripts of subordination and indoctrination as sym-bols of social rank and hierarchy. High priests and officials inverted

the language of respect into the language of verbal and physical punishment (Lipsett-Rivera, 1998). Words and gestures secured corporeal and verbal humiliation and deference, bending the body into
a state of acquiescence. Horizontal relations of power were known
only among those who shared the same social class location, and even
there, women were expected to defer to the will of men. The lower-
ing of the head and the tip of the hat exploited power relations and
reinforced an awareness of one's social class membership and origins.
Inferior women in the social ladder were encouraged to keep their eyes
low and avoid gazing at others *fuera de la casa*/outside of the home;
moralists requested that they obey their husbands as much as their
Lord, "because the husband is the head of women as Christ is of the
Church." Words serving as insults did much the same, as a language
form meant to access power and exploit ambiguities among "others."
Puerco/Pig, *puta*/slut, *cabron*/asshole (literally, goat), *chismosa*/gos-
sip, *perros*/dogs, *cochinos*/filthy pigs are relics of Mexico's Spanish
colonial epoch. The configuration of a social order constituted by the
complex dynamics of class, language, gender, religion, and locality
(San Juan, 2006) is one that continues to keep in motion Mexico's
colonial legacy.

The language of power and exploitation has conditioned Jimenez
for as far back as she can remember. "*A mi me crearon ser una persona
malhecha*/I was raised to be a person ill formed." But her individual
story takes on added meaning to the extent that it symbolizes gener-
alizable experiences. Individual histories and experiences contain the
material substance of a collective past.[1] Hers is a past that goes back
for generations, a past of diaspora, colonization, culture, family, and
womanhood. In the parent center, in the company of madres who
had volunteered their time to help Jimenez with putting together
packages for graduating fifth-grade students, Jimenez shared the
following:

> *Nosotras no estamos preparadas, no podemos valernos. Cuando mi
> mama salió de embarazo de mi, ella dejó que se fuera mi papá, pero
> sólamente cuando ya había muerto mi abuela. Mi abuela le había dicho
> que se tenía que aguantar mi papá, no importaba lo abusivo que él era
> con ella.* We are not prepared, we don't value ourselves. When my
> mother was pregnant with me, she let my father leave, but only after
> my grandmother had already passed away. My grandmother had told
> her that she needed to put up with my father, didn't matter how abu-
> sive he was to her.

Miro mi historia, y veo que yo creci con el odio en la sangre. I look at my history and I recognize that I grew with hatred in my blood.

In recounting parts of her narrative account, Jimenez shares a common ground with all women who characterize themselves as la sumisa, because the very context in which women and men form their specific and unique identities has been foregrounded by a repeated history of colonization and oppression. The nepantlera as narrator is not merely engaged in a discursive act of dislodging memory and recasting life's events, she relives the material forms from which her body comes into being.

LA MUJER QUE NO VALIA/A WOMAN OF NO WORTH

Yo me veía como una mujer que no valía. Lo que lo acompleja a uno es que si no tienes estudio no vales, si no tienes dinero no vales. Cuando uno está trabajando siempre en las casas de los demás, a usted le marcan la diferencia. A mi me decían, este es tu plato del postre, tu cuchara, tu servilleta. La señora me llamaba, venga niñita, ven pa'ca, mire muchachita, esto es para ti. La comida que sobraba me decía que lo guardara para mañana. "No agarres de acá mas para hoy." Pero cuando yo separaba el tantito de mañana, yo me llevaba el resto para mi mamá y lo escondía bien. Hubo días que no tuvimos comida en casa. Nosotros no conocimos la leche, nos criamos tomando café. La leche nunca la probábamos. Pasamos días que comíamos solamente la tortilla, le echábamos limón y tantito sal. Le marcan a uno la diferencia, de que usted es de la clase baja, más baja. Y a las personas que tienen dinero siempre las tienes que tratar con respeto y aceptar cualquier humillación que te hagan. I saw myself as a woman of no worth. What causes you shame is that if you have no education you have no worth, if you have no money, you have no worth. When you work in the homes of others they always mark difference. They would tell me; this is your plate for cake, your spoon, your napkin. The woman would call me; come here little girl, come over here, this is for you. She would tell me that the leftover food was for me to eat tomorrow. "Do not grab from here more for today." But when I put aside the little bit for tomorrow, I would take the rest for my mother and me that evening. I hid it well. There were days we had no food in our home. We did not know what milk was. We were raised drinking coffee. We never tasted milk. Days would pass when we would eat only a *tortilla*, we added lemon and a bit of salt. So they mark differences onto you, that you are the low class, the lowest class. And the people with money are the ones you always have to treat with respect and accept whatever humiliation they make against you.

At the age of 11 Jimenez was taken to work in someone's home.

Mi tía me llevo a trabajar. Yo estuve secuestrada en esa casa, yo no podía tener comunicación con nadie. A las cinco de la mañana me tenía que despertar para empezar el quehacer. Medio dormida me paraba y salia al patio para hecharle agua.Tenía que trabajar hasta la medianoche. Me mandaban a dormir en una casita afuera. En ese cuarto solo cabía yo, la plancha y una mesita. Yo tenía que planchar la ropa antes de dormirme para que me los devolvieran al dia siguiente. Mi patrona era una señora como cualquier otra que buscaba una sirvienta. My aunt took me to work. I felt kidnapped in that home, I couldn't communicate with anyone. At five in the morning I had to wake up to start the house chores. Half asleep I would go to the patio to water it down. I had to work until midnight. They would send me to sleep in a shed outside. That room was big enough only for me, an iron, and a small table. I had to iron the clothes before I went to bed, only so that they could return the clothes to me the following day. My boss was a woman like any other who looked for a maid.

Occasionally, Jimenez's mother would visit and pick up her earnings.

SERVANTS: MATERIALIZING THE LANGUAGE OF THE BODY

The codes of poverty flow profusely through Jimenez' veins. Class relations between the oppressed and the ruling class shaped her physical, mental, and spiritual world as she distinguished her own otherness from what she perceived as the privileged and the powerful. In the process of her disassociation from individuals whom she deemed above her class position, Jimenez learned to be the woman of "no worth." Her teacher took the form of hunger, illiteracy, lack, and necessity. To the extent that words communicated relations between and within herself, others, and the social world, language assumed a specific meaning. Here Bakhtin's (see Volosinov, 1973) emphasis on the word as the expression of one in relation to the other takes significance as Jimenez recalls the exchanges that marked the tendons connecting mind and body to the existential self. She gave herself verbal shape according to others' points of view. The meanings that were generated occurred in an immediate and particular social situation but were informed by the broader social milieu in which she lived. "I saw myself as a woman of no worth. What causes you shame is that if you have no education you have no worth, if you have no money, you have no worth. When you work in the homes of others they always mark difference."

Discourse, the body, and material social relations of production together make the body visible to the self and others. The body "enfleshes" its labor, and labor in turn textualizes the body's reading (McLaren and Cruz, 2005). Enfleshment signals the "the mutually constitutive (enfolding) of social structure and desire; that is the dialectical relationship between the material organization of interiority and the cultural forms and modes of materiality we inhabit subjectively" (McLaren, 1995). Jimenez's narrative account reinitiates the dialectical meaning of her "interiority," of her laboring mind and body. Her enfleshment as the woman of no worth captures the motion between the formation of her "self" and the social relations that configured her gendered and laboring body. Jimenez's body—of no worth—reflects the cultural codes, forms, and practices that consume her. In discourse, her self-conception is reaffirmed, "*no agarres de acá mas para hoy/*do not grab more from here for today," "*esto no es para ti/*this is not for you;" in material (capitalist) social relations, her body is reified, "*Cuando tenia 11 años trabajaba en una casa. A las cinco de la mañana me despertaba al quehacer y me acostaba a las dos de la mañana planchando ropa/*When I was 11 years old I worked in a home. At five in the morning I would wake up to do the housework and I would go to bed at two in the morning ironing clothes." Through dominant cultural codes she is further reminded of her gendered value, "*a mi me llamaban lesbiana porque no tenía novios. Mi hermano se hizo sentir que era él que mandaba. Él podia fregar, molestar, tenía el derecho por ser hermano/*people would call me a lesbian because I didn't have boyfriends. My brother made himself to be the one who mandated. He could fuck around, bug me, he had these rights by being my brother." The body reproduces ideology insofar as the economies of power and domination are allowed to school the body. The body, to borrow a Foucaultian term, is a "social body" (Foucault, 1980). The living matter of the agentive body belongs to Jimenez, but its social form is negotiated in the broader world where power and domination are integrated into the economies of production, culture, the state, and so forth.

Social bodies are characterized by an inherently dual condition. On the one hand, social bodies are the sites of discursively inscribed experience and subjectivity, and on the other, social bodies are also formed extra-discursively as material sites of resistance and intervention. The social world outside Jimenez's body produced the knowledge that she internalized to define herself, but at the same time, her body as a site of mediation served as a site of tension from which she schooled the social world. In this way, Jimenez's body resembled Karen Barad's (2007) description of the piezoelectric crystal. It partakes of the dual functionality of both transmitter and receiver—a relationship that Barad calls, in philosophical terms, agential realism, an intertwining of the conceptual and physical, the making and remaking of boundaries, the "intra-actions" that always entail particular exclusions that foreclose the possibility of determinism, providing the condition for an open future (Barad, 2007).

Jimenez's body maintained an element of sovereign existence to the extent that she used her body subversively to survive and provide for her family.

> *La señora me llamaba, venga niñita, venpa'ca, mire muchachita, esto es para ti. La comida que sobraba me decía que lo guardara para mañana. "No agarres de acá mas para hoy." Pero cuando yo separaba el tantito de mañana, yo me llevaba el resto para mi mamá y lo escondía bien.* The woman would call me, come here little girl, come over here, this is for you. She would tell me that the leftover food was for me to eat tomorrow. "Do not grab from here more for today." But when I put aside the little bit for tomorrow, I would take the rest for my mother. I hid it well.

The daily performativity of her body, what Judith Butler describes as "the discursive mode by which ontological effects are installed," was interrupted by the way in which she used her body to survive, a process that gave rise to the emerging body to which she introduces us later in her story. In some respects, the social body is the medium of expression shaped by the social system, but this view gives us only one perspective from which to view the power of the body to resist, survive, defend, and transform those relations that constrain and encage the body. When the body travels, the mind travels with it (hence, we use the term body/mind), and memories prepare the self for encounters in differentially mediated border zones. The social body that emerges changes shape and form in response to the threats, both veiled and unveiled, of her environment. For Jimenez, this eventually led to disguising herself as a man, *el mojado*, and crossing into the Mexico–U.S. border.

> *Yo tenía 18 años. Me vine. Nos venimos mi hermano y yo. Batallamos por la pasada. Yo tuve que pasar como hombre. Estando en Tijuana nos*

siguió la policia, todos corrieron. Yo solamente buscaba a mi hermano.
Estuvimos en el cerro por un día. Tuvimos que correr por bastante tiempo.
Me disfrazaban con pantalón y cachucha. Con la lluvia, tuve que pasar
como una mojada. Para mi era un susto: La frontera era un lugar horri-
ble. Yo no pensaba en nada mejor más que trabajar en casa. Yo me vine a
trabajar en una casa cuidando niños. Llegué el 6 de enero. En Maywood.
A los dos días me fui a trabajar al este de Los Angeles cuidando dos niños.
Me pagaban 40 dólares la semana, pero yo allí comia, allí dormía. Allí
me trataron muy mal, a los dos meses conocí a mi esposo. Pero las personas
con quién yo trabajaba no querían que yo andubierá con él, querían
escogerme la pareja con quién yo andara. Entonces casi iba repitiendo la
misma cosa...tenía que ver alguién quién te gobernara. I was 18 years
old. I came. My brother and I came. We struggled crossing. I had to
cross over as a man. When we were in Tijuana the police chased us, we
all ran. I only looked for my brother. We were in the desert for one day.
We had to run for long periods of time. They disguised me with pants
and a cap. With the rain I had to pass like a wetback. For me it was
scary. The border was a horrible place. I did not think of doing anything more than working in a home. I came to work in a home taking
care of children. I arrived on January 6. In Maywood. Two days later I
left to work in East Los Angeles, taking care of two children. They paid
me 40 dollars a week, but I ate there and slept there. I arrived there
and they treated me badly. Two months later I met my husband. But
the people who I stayed with didn't want me to spend time with him;
they wanted to choose the partner who I would be with. So there it was
almost as if everything was being repeated...there had to be someone
to govern me.

The Body of Submission and Submissiveness

La mujer sumisa assumes multiple roles to protect herself and her family. In the act of submission lies the quality of submissiveness, but
both are not necessarily complimentary in form. Rather, they are frequently in contradiction with one another. In relation to the structures
that mediate submission—economic, cultural, and institutional—
submissiveness invokes an opposite distinction. Submission is the relation that generates the appearance of submissiveness. Submissiveness
is the performative register that temporarily displaces the relation of
submission. In other words, it has a dimension of resistance. Through
submissiveness, *la mujer sumisa* travels into an unknown border; she
is the chameleon who abandons the mirror image of her body and
assumes the masculine form that will increase her chances of acquiring
power in the world. As a man, she could move with a certain sense of

security through an insecure zone, the drapings on her body conceal-ing her vulnerability as a sexual object in a militarized borderland.

Those who patrol the borderland, official and vigilante, read her body as the sign of a feminized nation. The female body has been written all over with signs of weakness, savagery, and submissiveness. But the submissive woman will not submit to the relations of submis-sion. She is sometimes the trickster; in submissiveness (when Jimenez crossed the border as a man) she resists, contests, and challenges the coloniality of power. Her body jolts between fight and flight as she confronts the authoritative grasp of the "undaunted vigilant protec-tors" of the U.S. border. She is an agent on a course of change. She submits her gendered border-crossing body to the unknown, but she refuses to remain submissive to the colonial authority that would jeop-ardize the economic well-being of her family.

In border crossing *la mujer sumisa* meets her familial obligations. "*Yo no me queria venir, me vine por obligada. Mi hermano ya estaba aquí por un año. Él nos abandonó. Cuando regresó le dije en broma: yo me voy contigo. Pues porque pensamos llegar y trabajar, nuestra ilusión era comprarle una casa a mi mamá*/I didn't want to come, I came out of obligation. My brother was already here for one year he abandoned us. When he returned I told my brother in a joke that I would go with him. Well we thought we would arrive and work, our illusion was to buy our mother a home." Jimenez chooses to leave but does so out of a sense of obligation to the clutches of a social order where status prevails. Choice is an operative word that must be understood in conjunction with the relations of submission that reconfigure opportunities for her in the social world. In making the decision to choose to stay in Mexico or to leave to provide for her family, Jimenez is thrust into another site of liminality, where she must negotiate the dominative social relations that limit and constrain her actions. Jimenez is in a constant state of negotiation with relations of power that attempt to define her.

EL MATRIMONIO/MARRIAGE

His name is Abel and he calls Jimenez *la Leona*/the Lion.

Yo estaba en una situación fea. Cuando mi esposo me pidio matrimo-nio le dije si. No dije que si para salirme. No era como una tabla de salvación como decia mi mamá. Yo lo quize desde el primer dia que lo conoci lo quize. Yo realmente estaba enamorada de él/I was in a bad situation. When my husband asked me to marry him, I said yes. I didn't say yes to escape. He wasn't my table of salvation as my mom said. I loved him since the first day I met him, I loved him. I was really in love with him.

*Mi vida fue de obecer y no de protestar. Si protestaba sí que me iba mal. Y con el era lo mismo. De novios fue una cosa de casados era algo distinto. Él me hizo pasar humillaciones feas. Tal vez yo sea una persona que no puede vivir el presente, porque el pasado no se ha borrado. Él me marcó en muchas cosas y fui infeliz. Siempre tuve el problemita, porque yo le pedía permiso para salir y el se daba el gusto de decirme que no podía salir. Entonces empecé a pensar que esto no es vida. Yo me dejé, porque sentí que él era mas. Yo pensé, pues cómo es que un muchacho tan guapo se fijó en mí, pues le debo de darlas gracias. Pero nunca me ha maltratado física ni verbalmente. Nunca. Levantarme la mano, tampoco/*My life was about obeying and not protesting. If I protested, I knew that things wouldn't go my way. And with him it was the same. When we were dating it was one thing, but once we married, it was something else. He made me go through some ugly embarrassments. Maybe I am someone who cannot live in the present, because the past has not been erased. He marked in me many things and I was unhappy. But always with the little problem because I would ask him for permission and he would please himself in telling me that I could not go out. And so I began to think that it was not life. I began to think that this isn't life. I let myself think this because I felt that he was more. I thought, well how is it that a young man so good looking will notice me, well, I should give him thanks. But he never mistreated me physically or verbally. He never raised his hand at me.

Jimenez's account of the oppression she underwent in her marriage is not an atypical formulation of heteronormative male-female relations in the broader social order of capitalist society. Women's household productive relations reproduce the alienated form of capitalist social relations as people are increasingly prohibited from developing the creative capacities of their species-being. Power becomes inscribed in the biological differences between men and women, thereby naturalizing the execution of power over women's bodies—women who do not receive a wage for their household labor. The social relations that govern the binary elements of "male" and "female" within the social division of labor reproduce the relations of alienation in the workplace to those between the sexes. For Jimenez, the division between her, as a mother and wife, and her wage-earning husband established an alienating condition that restricted her creative capacities for full personhood.

Ser ama de casa para mí es esclavitud. Una mujer que tiene que vigilar que esté la ropa limpia, la ropa planchada que vigila que se bañen los niños que hagan la tarrea es la misma rutina diaria. Esta es la carrera de ama de casa. Si yo hubiera sacado mis uñas antes, si yo hubiera dicho quiero estudiar. El matrimonio no es seguro entonces yo haya hecho algo, haya sido alguien. Pero uno se detiene por el miedo de lo que va decir la gente, verte sola sin estudio sin saber trabajar, en apenas saber como limpiar casa. Ya es un pocotarde, son 26 o 27 años perdidos. Si hubiera dicho: yo soy yo y yo quiero hacer esto para mi. Si yo misma no me hubiera atacado tanto. Si no me hubiera dicho, no, no vas a salir, no te pongas esa ropa, es la cultura. La mujer esta para obedecer. To be a housewife for me is slavery. It is to be a mother who needs to make sure that the clothes are clean, that the clothes are ironed, that has to make sure that children bathe, that they do their homework, it's the same routine every day to be a housewife. If I would have taken my nails out sooner then I would have said that I wanted to study. Marriage is not secure, so I would have done something, I would have been somebody. Now it's a bit late, 26 or 27 years lost, if I would have said I am, I am who I am and I want to do something for myself, and if I hadn't attacked myself so much, telling myself that I wasn't going to go out, to not put on certain clothes, it's the culture. The woman exists to obey.

Jimenez's experiences as a laboring wife and the sentiments that she reveals,—"to be a housewife for me is slavery," "my life was about obeying and not protesting,"—reflect the normative conditions of patriarchal capitalist society in both (so-called) "first" and "third-world" nations. Capitalist patriarchy travels from city to city, country to country, and continent to continent. It moves beyond territorial and cultural borders and becomes part of the "natural" fabric of social life in late capitalist societies. Women have been writing and sharing their narratives about living within transnational capitalist patriarchal systems for quite some time. Certain commonplaces have been talked about, time and time again—the international division of sexual labor, cultural machismo, sexual oppression—and Jimenez's narrative account reveals those commonplaces once again from the contextually specific class position that she inhabits. Jimenez's narrative account about marriage and wifedom is as much about gender/sexual alienation and oppression as it is about her class consciousness. In other words, Jimenez's awareness about the perceived limitations of being a married woman—"marriage is not secure, so I would have done something, I would have been somebody"—and about the value she ascribed to her personhood in relation to a man's view of her—"how is it that a young man so good looking will notice me, well, I should give him thanks"—are expressions of a class-patriarchal self-consciousness that she has developed since she began identifying as *la mujer sumisa*. The added dimension of class consciousness transforms the concept of patriarchy altogether, becoming more akin with what the feminist theologian Maria Pilar Aquino refers to as "kyriarchal reason." As opposed to the rule of the Father associated with patriarchal knowledge, kyriarchal reason references the rule of the master. In patriarchy, the father is given a sacrosanct status, of the all-knowing and all powerful figurehead over the identity and life choices of women. Kyriarchal reason breaks[2] from the primordial attribute of man as oppressor within patriarchal knowledge, into "multiplicative intersecting structures of domination" (Aquino, 2007, p. 25). The rule of the master or the rule of the owner is not specific to women, but rather to women and men who find themselves in the intersecting dynamics and transnational economy of masculine and female enactment and representation. Here, the enactment of male and female roles is supported by the cultural apparatuses attached to the sexual division of labor (i.e., marriage) as well as the historical teachings surrounding male and female unions passed from one generation to the next. In the case of Jimenez, it is family that passes on this informal understanding of womanhood, while for others it may be the authority given to religion or biblical text. Jimenez's narrative foregrounds the systemic and intersecting dynamics of engendering womanhood as articulated by Kyriarchal reasoning.

NARRATORS

The retelling of Jimenez's formation as a laboring woman, wife, mother, immigrant, and Mexicana is not an abstract exercise. On the contrary, Jimenez's narrative account is a purposeful analysis of the living material and discursive conditions that shaped her personal thinking and the impact that such thinking had in her agential "becomingness" that eventually led to the community that she formed with lasmadres of Mirasur. From the real and lived expressions of her life, Jimenez invites us to analyze the social relations out of which she comes to understand the social world. As Jimenez tells her story, she not only rediscovers the condition of her life in recollecting a contingent reiteration of events, but she begins a process of retelling and enacting a new narrative that reflects an opposition to her previous narrative account. The social world is reflected and refracted in the way she embodies knowledge, and her body in turn reflects and refracts the surrounding social world. With time the body matures into a written text marked by the social world; it enfleshes the materiality of everyday life.

The telling and retelling of life histories allows us to learn how the symbolic world represents our world, and mediates thought and place, in representations of reality (Bruner, 1991). The return of a memory takes place in the context of becoming an image—in the case of Jimenez, the image of being a woman, a submissive woman, a married woman, and an enslaved woman. At the point of articulating our social lives, we engage in a process of constructing new knowledge about ourselves and the social world and actively use it to rewrite our position in it.

In giving testimony of her *autohistoria*/autobiographic history, Jimenez creates a relief for self-reflection, a physical, material, and spiritual place where memory and experience merge to form a type of personal-practical knowledge that helps her navigate the terrain of her children's education *a la gringolandia*. Jimenez grew distant from her sense of otherness and started to reflect on the outside world from an insider's position. She became an outsider from the inside and an insider from the outside.

For Jimenez, the activation of her "self-knowledge" was accompanied by her involvement in the institutional drama of Mirasur as a protagonist. The simultaneity of actions and dramas (institutional and personal) revealed a concomitant change in her external presence and internal self-knowledge. It so follows that Jimenez's narrative account affords us a better appreciation of the social drama of Mirasur. The historical registers of how Jimenez and the women had come to know themselves and their relation to others set the backdrop for the visions they expressed to improve the lives of their children. Life histories, in this respect, served to establish emotional bonds among the mothers, a deep understanding based on identifying common experiences and relationships. In this respect, the mothers of Mirasur are not very different from the mothers in other mother-activist groups around the world who come together around an issue of injustice or violence against their children and community. "Mother-activists" in the northern states of Mexico have wielded the power of testimonial speech to mobilize the public against the abject disappearance and killing of their daughters (Wright, 2009). The femicide of Juarez dates back to the early 1990s, when hundreds of working-class women employed by the maquiladora industry disappeared, some only to be found raped and tortured days, months, or years later. As the mothers began to put names to the faces of the disappeared women and as they began to tell stories about the nights when their daughters did not return home, their "testimonies" became a form of activism against femicide both in northern Mexico and worldwide (Wright, 2009).

5

ANTISTRUCTURE: COUNTERPOINTS TO PEDAGOGY OF THE BURRO

Like me you may be tired of making a tragedy of our lives. *A abandoner ese autocanibalismo: coraje, tristeza, miedo* (let's abandon this autocannibalism: rage, sadness, fear).

Gloria Anzaldúa, 1983

Today's liminality is tomorrow's centrality…Silence is not the answer…silence is our problem. We are provoked by silence, negativity, liminality, ambiguity, into efforts of extended comprehension.

Victor Turner, 1975, 33

Following their ritual performance of protest, another transition was about to take place as las madres quieted their voices and returned to their daily routines. The school community shifted uneasily to a less stable state, neither "here" nor "there," as the mothers introduced their new "selves" to administrators, staff, and the families. Prior to the protest the Mirasur community could be understood as having a relatively stable cultural appearance. The mechanisms for framing the school experience came from above—district, state, and federal authorities—and operated within the ideological horizon of neoliberal economic and social policy that slowly chiseled away at communitarian or participatory relations of governance within the school site. The standardization of curriculum, high-stakes testing, punitive accountability systems, and English-only policies clearly affected the cultural "essence" of the school site. The value given to each child and family depended upon their performance on the measures of prescribed academic success. In this way, social hierarchies become more exacerbated, as success on these measures of academic achievement are largely mitigated by children's class location and the ways in which they are classified as either part of the acceptable archetype associated with U.S. citizenship or subalternized on the social fringes. Binary oppositions, such as immigrant versus citizen, male versus female, savage versus civilized, rich versus poor, and literate versus illiterate, stabilized the "social body" and were reflected in the value systems of Mirasur and the broader community. Presumably, then, a change in the institutional culture would depend upon the mothers' shift in self perception and their continued efforts to be seen by the administration as active participants in Mirasur.

Prior to the protest, las madres had become unwilling accomplices in their own subjugation, or what Anzaldúa refers to as "autocannibalism," the slow eating away of self and agency that accompanies the subjective feelings of victimhood. They had come to view themselves as victims of poverty, patriarchy, racism, and simple acts of exploitation. After the protest they were better positioned to express dimensions of protagonistic agency that they had only recently begun to recognize. They had experienced an individual and collective awakening marked by the power of voice and body. And yet the feelings of rage, sadness, and fear that had tempered the mothers' previous actions were still very much a part of their social consciousness. Mirasur had become both a reflection of everything the mothers no longer wanted to be and a space of multiple possibilities for everything they *could* be. In fact, their agency and ensuing activism partly depended upon the daily misgivings of the school staff and administration, those small acts of contempt that gave rise to a complaint or grievance by a child or family member. But their activism also depended upon the bonds that they formed as mothers and women who had come to recognize the power of collective protest and a shift in their consciousness. They were invigorated, enraged, and emboldened. Inner and outer borders had been crossed, and slowly, over time, the mothers adjusted to their new "selves" in their daily performance of subversion and resistance.

PEDAGOGY OF THE BURRO: ANTISTRUCTURE AND COMMUNITAS

While the protest forced administrators and staff to examine the legality of their policies and practices, the question remained as to whether or not the underlying ideology of the school-community relationship had changed. In other words, could the mothers manage to adapt to the "structure" of the school site, given Mirasur's preexisting views of the community? Or would the mothers develop spaces outside

Mirasur's structure to enact new visions and practices of possibility within the community? This question cannot be fully answered with an either/or response. Everyday life and activity carries the seeds of its own negation, and such was the case in Mirasur. But the very act of negation remains connected to the structure that is being negated. Las madres were in an interesting paradox following the turmoil and triumph that they associated with the protest. They had negated their subjective placement as working mules/*burras*, and they were still connected to that same institutional setting that would inform their future activity.

It is in this sense that Turner's anthropological look in the formation of antistructure and communitas is particularly insightful. As Graham St. John notes, academics often labeled Turner as a Western post-functionalist who examined status-role performance in the reproduction of culture (i.e., ritual and rites of passage, St. John, 2008). St. John, however, perceives Turner's work to be more in line with "structural processualism" (4), a framework that examines the interstices of a society in composition, as both structure and antistructure collide and merge in the process of collective becoming. In Turner's view, antistructure reveals those spaces of cultural experience outside, in-between, and below structure, or what could be simply understood as stemming from positions of marginality and inferiority (St. John, 2008, 4). In other words, Turner was concerned with the thresholds of cultural experience through which the sociocultural order is reconstituted (St. John, 2008). Such thresholds occur in relation to the "structure" that conveys to individuals their status, role, and subjunctive mood as people immersed in preexisting structural conditions (and rites of passage) tackle the meaning and order ascribed to the organization of social life. A heuristic device, antistructure as a transitional space exposes the gaps, omissions, and contradictions in society's structural apparatuses. It is a place of marginality and inferiority where a different ethos serves to unite various peoples across difference, suspending space and time to enact alternative visions of human sociability. This shift in ethos was defined by Turner as "communitas," a collective sense of well-being, solidarity, and affectual relationships with others who have undergone or have experienced and a personal transformation.[1] As described by St. John (2008), communitas "designates a feeling of immediate community, and may involve the sharing of special knowledge and understanding" (7). Communitas has been regarded as an experience that "liberates from conformity to general norms" (Turner, 1974, 52). Communitas challenges normative cultural frameworks that invalidate the "extraordinary"; as a research category it calls into question that which does not fit snugly into a strict empirical analysis or verification. While not speaking directly about communitas, Anzaldúa invoked a similar sentiment in her various writing on activism and what she referred to as "la tarea de alianzas." Drawing on the work of Gregory Bateson and his theory of metacommunication,[2] Anzaldúa wrote about the communicative characteristics of "alliance work" (143).

Echoing Turner's conception of antistructure, Anzaldúa conceived of alliance work as occurring both inside the community and outside ordinary life. Alliance work, in other words, stands outside an existing role or structure. For Anzaldúa, activists in alliance work are engaged in an element of role playing, "as if one were someone else" (143). This "someone else" is not a deceitful projection; rather, Anzaldúa was referring to that role model or self-image that activists aspire to be. In bringing together Turner's conception of antistructure with Anzaldúa's alliance work, an important distinction is revealed. In her writings, Anzaldúa brings into critical relief the contradictions inherent in cultural paradigms, what she defines as "the entire baggage of beliefs, values, and techniques shared by the community" (144). These cultural paradigms add another layer of complexity to antistructure and communitas. For instance, while a group may share an affinity and bond (religious, spiritual, political, or otherwise), and express it in the actions of antistructure, such groups are never fully released from the confines of their cultural history and memory, which continues to "structure" their actions and activities. There is always an "excess" of structure, almost as if structure could never be fully overcome. Its traces are always there, erased perhaps from clear visibility but underlying the text of cultural exchange and experience, like a palimpsest. This reveals a double bind in discussing the formation of antistructure and communitas from the margins. Anzaldúa's words expose the difficulties of social transformation and change when the action that is required challenges deep roots and profound cognitive schemas that easily reproduce themselves in society's dominant institutional settings.

In the excerpts that follow, I present a series of recollections from the time that I spent with Jimenez and las madres following la protesta. These field notes collectively point to what I call the antistructure of the pedagogy of the burro; they do not follow a linear sequence in time nor establish a clear pattern of how las madres organized their acts of defiance. On the contrary, these notes are in line with what Turner referred to as "spontaneous communitas," the immediate and direct relationships that transpire among women in transition who interact with openness and honesty. Collectively, these excerpts suggest that certain social experiences can be conceived as communitas, those moments when personal bonds are exercised spontaneously in the struggle for a good that exceeds the immediate desires of the self. I am oftentimes a participant in these instances of communitas, at times suspending my role of "ethnographer" in the text and situating myself as a woman and friend who shared Jimenez and las madres' concern for what was taking place in the Mirasur community. These excerpts also point toward the challenges of institutional and collective change. In their entirety, they represent a vision and an understanding of the kinds of spaces, contradictions, and relationships that emerge when social actors attempt to transcend the confines of their own subjugation. In the case of Maria Jimenez and the mothers of Mirasur, such spaces were fomented by an entrance gate in the (mobile) parent center, and, on some occasions, in Jimenez's home. These "spaces" were "portals"—entrances and exits—for transformative understandings and actions. Liminality is a volatile site that cannot be reversed, as you never know its outcome. The spontaneity of cultural experiences in communitas can lead to a variety of resolutions and reintegrations in the structural setting. But as the following excerpts make clear, the processes of self, collective, and institutional change are wrought with contradictions, deserving of our attention and focus as the vision of a socially just human sociability exceeds the limits of time and space reflected in antistructure.

THE SIDE GATE

Jimenez joined the paid staff. Instead of becoming a school volunteer, she has officially become a school worker. Her hours are early in the morning and late in the afternoon. She works in two-hour to three-hour shifts. Every morning from approximately 5:30 to 8:00 she guards the side entrance. Mothers, fathers, older siblings, aunts, and uncles bring the children to the school as early as six in the morning. A majority of these children qualify for a warm breakfast in the cafeteria, while many others simply need a place to go while their families begin their early shifts at work. Jimenez has the responsibility of making sure that no adult walks past the gate and onto the school grounds. Five days a week Jimenez can be found at the side gate, typically with a cup of coffee in hand.

La Lucha de la Raza/Struggle of the People

Jimenez appeared apprehensive when I greeted her at the gate this morning. What's wrong with you, I asked. With a frustrating grunt she described the race riot at the local high school just a mile down the road. Helicopters swarmed the skies. Ten black-and-white squad cars arrived on the scene. Fifteen people were arrested. Schools in the area were shut down for over two hours. She then quickly placed a newspaper with an image of police vehicles circling the high school in front of my face, presumably in case I remained in doubt.

"*Mire aqui Jaramillo, lea, ah no, tu no sabes leer en Español/*Look here, Jaramillo, read, oh right, you don't know how to read in Spanish."

The riot quickly became the topic of conversation this morning. As I sat next to Jimenez and listened to her description of the events, it seemed as though mother after mother approached us eagerly to discuss the riot. The mothers with high school–aged children were particularly agitated. "Riots in Mexico take place in the prison, not the school," a woman exhorted. From the distance I could see Señora Valencia anxiously approaching the fence. Upon arrival she queried, "*¿Ya oyeren esta bola de noticias/*Have you heard about the mess in the news?"

Within minutes, Señora Alvarez joined the small group of women coiling by the fence, and a discussion on race and ethnicity ensued.

> Alvarez: *Mi hija estaba en la cafeteria almorazondo cuando una niña cayo encima de su comida. Estaba todo sangroso la oreja, y que casi se le sale su ojo/*My daughter was eating lunch in the cafeteria when a young girl fell on top of her food. Her ear was all bloody, and her eye almost popped out.

Admittedly, I responded with a ghastly look of disbelief.

> Alvarez: *Hay que hacer algo/*Something needs to be done.
> Valencia: *Si amiguita, yo estoy contigo, pero solamente con los padres que quieren hacer algo para la comunidad. La mayoría de los padres llegan y dicen, yo solamente estoy aquí por mi hijo, entonces con ellos no me pongo/*Yes friend I am with you but only with the parents who want to do something for the community. A majority of parents arrive and say, I am only here for my child, so I do not align myself with them.

Alvarez: *Mi hijo dijo que todos sabian que iba ver una pelea, desde la mañana se soplaban/*My son said that everyone knew that there was going to be a fight, in the morning they started whispering to each other.

Valencia: *La escuela no hace nada. Los morenos se cuidan ellos mismos, los Latinos también.* The school does nothing. The blacks take care of themselves and the Latinos do too.

Alvarez: *Que se puede hacer, tener una escuela solamente para los morenos y otra por los Hispanos?* What can be done, have only one school for blacks and another for Hispanics?

MEAL TRAFFICKING AND THE POLITICS OF THE CAFETERIA

A six-year-old, a seven-year-old, and an eight-year-old approach Jimenez simultaneously and ask: *Tienes un lunch ticket/*Do you have a lunch ticket?

Jimenez: *Si, mijo, vente pa'ca aqui esta/*Yes children, come over here, they are here.

She walks over to her bag and pulls three tickets out, the kind that I associate with county and school fairs or a raffle. The children grab the tickets quickly and put them in their pockets. What are they going to do with those tickets, I ask Jimenez. They need those tickets to eat a full lunch, she responds. If they forget their tickets, they will only receive a slice of bread and cheese. *"Es un castigo por no traer ese maldito ticket/*It's a punishment for not bringing their damn tickets."

Where do you find the extra tickets? Do you buy them at a store? How do you know which color they will be during a given month?

*No, Jaramillo, no es haci/*No Jaramillo, it is not like that. Some mothers, when the children are offtrack, won't need their lunch tickets. So, they bring me their tickets. I keep some with me and give others to the mothers who supervise the lunch line. If someone doesn't have a ticket we'll give them one. I don't care if the cafeteria manager sees me. She can fire me. I'm not going to let the children go without food.

DISCIPLINING THE CAFETERIA

Jimenez greeted me with another story this morning. "I spoke with the principal today about discipline in the cafeteria. You know the kids are scared of the administrator in the cafeteria. She doesn't let them speak. I have to communicate with the children like a gangster throwing signs at them because I can't speak to them. She separates the children into two sections. The ones who come in talking, she'll grab them and punish them, and the ones who enter *quietly* (Jimenez purses her lips and presses her index finger against them, mocking the school administrator) will be sent to eat on one side of the cafeteria. The other day two children came in talking and the vice principal made them stand against the wall holding their plates of food. They couldn't eat like that. And another time she scolded a child, ordered him to sit down, and then tossed his plate on the table. The food ricocheted."

Señora Alvarez is standing next to us while we are having this exchange. She adds:

> "I took my son to the cafeteria line because he forgot his ticket. I went to buy him another one. I was standing behind him when all of [a] sudden the worker threw his plate of food down, like he was a little animal. I told her that my son had paid for his food and that she didn't need to throw it at him like he was a dog. Although I think that animals receive better treatment. We show dogs more care. We open their cans and set the food down gently. Can you imagine if they did that with me present, what they do when we are not there?"

A few minutes pass and Alvarez starts talking about her eldest son's deportation to Iraq. She talked about her fear, sleepless nights, and the joy she hopes for to have him back home.

CUIDANDO LA ENTRADA/GUARDING THE GATE

Jimenez has a stack of flyers on the table at the side entrance of the school. Mothers huddle around her as she distributes the papers. Have you registered your child for tutoring classes? Has a computer been delivered to your home? We have a family literacy class next week, would you like to come? *Hechale ganas/*Give it your effort.

WALK OUT/CHALK OUT

I arrived in the morning to an anxious Jimenez waiting for me. She had just rung my cell phone to make sure I was on my way. She greeted me with "*tengo una idea madrista/*I have an idea for mother empowerment." Leticia was there and she started laughing, adding "*a madre que/*a mother what?" to which I responded, "*es que tenemos una palabra nueva, madrisimo/*we have thought of a new word, madrisimo."

Jimenez added, "*si, en el poder de la mujer y de la madre/*yes, in the power of woman and mother."

The conversation quickly shifted to the protests against the Sensenbrenner bill, otherwise known as The Border Protection, Antiterrorism, and Illegal Immigration Control Act of 2005 (H.R. 4437), which would make it a felony to be in the United States illegally, will impose new penalties on employers who hire undocumented workers, and result in the erection of fences along one-third of the Mexico-U.S. border. The Sensenbrenner bill had passed the House and was being debated in the Senate.

"*Todos los estudiantes van a salirsen de la escuela hoy/*All of the students are going to walk out of school today," Jimenez reported.

"*Este fin de semana yo vi la pelicula chalk out, como es, algo out, su madre/*Over the weekend I watched the movie chalk out, what is it, something out." She continued, "*de los Chicanos que tuvieron una gran manifestación/*of the Chicanos that had a great protest." Yes, I responded, it is called *Walkout.*

"I watched the movie with my children over the weekend. They asked me questions about why people were treated that way. *Es triste/*It is sad. What is it that is happening, Jaramillo? What did we talk about the other day? What is the purpose of all the people who have protested, who have been injured and beaten in protest? What was the purpose of Cesar Chavez's hunger strike? Everything stays the same. Nothing changes. *Se mueren los lideres y la gente no sigue no hacen nada. De que sirve todo esto entonces/*Leaders die and the people don't do anything. What is the purpose of our activism, then?"

I ask Jimenez: What are you going to say to the students, that they should not protest because it will eventually be meaningless?

ORGANIZING WORKERS

The school has cut the supervision aides' hours. This is the first round of cuts to be implemented following California's dwindling state budget. As auxiliary and noninstructional staff, the mothers are the first to experience reductions in their work hours. Jimenez had one hour cut; Chepita, two; Gonzalez, three; and Rodriguez, none. After convening at the side gate to discuss their work hours, they moved the conversation to the classroom in one of the outlying bungalows designated as the parent center.

Figure 5.1   Side gate entrance, photograph courtesy of Carmen Jimenez.

Jimenez: *¿Que vamos hacer con el corte de horas?*/What are we going to do, our hours have been cut.

Gonzalez: *Pues no se, no esta justo que le corten a unas mas que otras*/Well I don't know, it's not fair that they cut more hours for some than others.

Jimenez: *¿Pues que hacemos? ¿Escribimos una carta? ¿Nos ponemos en huelga?*/Well what do we do? Do we write a letter? Do we go on strike?

Chepita: *Si nos ponemos en huelga!*/Yes, let's go on strike!

Jimenez: *Lo que pasa es que no estamos preparadas, no podemos valernos. Haci nos crearon, imaginate, esto viene en la sangre. Como mi mama, quizo dejar a mi papa porque el era abusivo con ella pero mi abuela no la dejaba*/What happens is that we're not prepared, we don't value ourselves. That's how we were raised, imagine, this comes in our blood. Like my mother, she wanted to leave my father because he was abusive with her, but my grandmother wouldn't let her.

Rodriguez: *Dicen que te tienes que aguantar, que es tu cruz. La mujer aguanta porque cree que no puede salir para adelante*/They say that you have to hold it in, that it's your cross to bear. The woman holds out because she doesn't think she can raise herself up.

Jimenez: *Las mujeres ponen de pretexto los hijos, que los hijos van a querer un padre. Yo tuve suerte con mi viejo, él nunca ni me dice una mala palabra. Y eso es que mi padre le dio la bendición a él. Cuando conoció a Abel, le dijo "póngale una bola de chingasos."/* The women put as pretext the children, that the children want a father. I was lucky with my old man, he never even says a bad word to me. And that is the case even after my father gave him a blessing. When my father met Abel he told him, "give her a good beating."

Gonzalez: *Pues una vez que peleé con mi esposo, él hizo como si me fuera a tirar una silla. Tírala le dije, tírala, yo a usted no le tengo miedo. Hágalo y vas a ver cómo te va caer la policia. Desde ese entonces él no me ha hecho nada/* Well, one time I fought with my husband and he motioned like he was going to throw a chair at me. Throw it I said, throw it, I'm not scared of you. Do it and see how the police are going to come. Well, since then he hasn't done anything.

Rodriguez: *Oye Jaramillo, ¿usted cuando se va encargar un chiquillo para que lo cuidemos?/* Hey Jaramillo, when are you going to get pregnant so we can take care of the baby?

MEETING THE DIRECTOR

Every end of a school year marks a point of transition. For children in the fifth grade it signals a movement from the relatively safe and guarded environment they have come to know and understand in elementary school—prepared school lunches, limited class sizes, and familiar childhood friends—to the more chaotic lifeworld of early adolescence marked by sundry degrees of stratification. The girls and boys have no choice but to follow the rhythms of their changing bodies and environments, and in a brief period of time the notion of "childhood" will become a distant and seemingly irrelevant memory. Many of the mothers and fathers of the children recognize that "graduation" from elementary school is much more than a change in grade level alone. In many ways it signals a change in parenting. The families prepare themselves for their new roles as their children begin the journey toward adulthood. For some children and families, the changes will be more dramatic and unsolicited than for others. Given these reasons and more, the mothers of Mirasur and the graduating children and their teachers approach the final month of school with excitement and a relaxed attitude toward *enjoying* themselves. They also protect their privileges and endorse the commemorating activities. And yet, the governing body of pleasure and punishment—the school—will ultimately decide who can transition with comfort and ease during this final stage of elementary development.

Families of graduating fifth graders received a notice in the mail yesterday. Ms. Jimenez read it to me over the phone. It stated the following:

Dear Parents:

Fifth-grade culmination is right around the corner. We have many activities planned for the students: a beach trip, pizza party, and distribution of signature books. These activities are privileges. School discipline continues to be a problem. In preparation for these events, please let your children know that they need to behave. All students have been assigned 50 points. Teachers can take away points when students misbehave. Students who do not behave will lose their privileges. The total amount of points that children have at the end of the year will determine what privileges they lose:

40 points: no signature book
35 points: no pizza party
20 points: no beach trip
10 points or less: will not be allowed to participate in culmination ceremonies

Thank you,
School principal

Jimenez's daughter had an argument with a student on the playground and she had ten points taken away. Jimenez wanted to meet with the school principal but hesitated.

> *Jimenez*: *Ellos van a decir que allí voy buscando privilegios*/They are going to say that there I go looking for privileges. *Si hablo, malo, si no hablo, malo. Yo digo, ¿Cuál privilegio tengo? ¿Que golpean mi hija y yo no hacer nada?*/If I say something, bad, if I don't say something, bad. I ask, what kind of privilege do I have? For my daughter to be hit and for me not to do anything? *Yo le pregunte al director, ¿Cuando me voy a quejar a su oficina? ¿Cuando me meto en los salones?*/I asked the principal, when do I go and complain in your office? When do I go into the classrooms?

Jimenez recalls the principal telling her: *No señora Jimenez el dijo, usted es muy buena persona*/No Mrs. Jimenez he said, you are a very good person.

Jimenez continued, *No me dijo nada mas, me di la vuelta y me fui*/ He said nothing more, I turned around and left.

I suggested that she meet with him again and discuss the school discipline policy.

> *Jaramillo*: *Ponte las pilas Jimenez, tu sabes que te tienes que defender/*Get
> on the ball Jimenez, you know that you have to defend yourself.
> *Jimenez*: *O si, tan facil verdad Jaramillo/*Oh yea, so easy right
> Jaramillo.
> *Jimenez*: *Y usted que hizo cuando el maestro de quinto grado trato de
> agarrarte, y usted que hizo cuando el director te humillaba. Nada,
> verdad. Tu sabes que no es tan facil/*And what did you do when the
> male fifth-grade teacher tried to grab you, and what did you do
> when the principal would insult you. Nothing, right? You know it's
> not that easy.

PARENT COUNCIL MEETING

A woman from the district addressed parents in the council meeting. The topic of the day was school discipline. She talked to parents about discipline in the home and instructed them not to spank their children. "The police can arrest you." Jimenez waited until she finished and then asked for the microphone. She addressed the 30 or so parents in the room:

> *Aqui para cambiar se empieza como cuando un árbol esta podrido. Ese*
> *árbol hay que cortarlo desde la raíz. Y si queremos que las cosas cam-*
> *bien tenemos que empezar desde abajo. Los problemas en la escuela es*
> *de años. Es de todos.Entonces cuando el niño creció rebelde, el papá es el*
> *que tiene miedo. El muchacho se hizo ladrón, pandillero. ¿Quien tiene*
> *la culpa? Los padres. No, es la culpa del gobierno. Y nosotros con papeles*
> *o sin papeles por creer que nos están dando algo en la educación. Ustedes*
> *consumen aquí. Están pagando por estos servicios del bolsillo de nosotros.*
> *No nos estan haciendo un favor/*For things to change here we begin
> like when a tree is spoiled. That tree we need to cut it at the root. And
> if we want things to change here, we need to start from the bottom.
> The problems in the school are years old. It's everybody's problem.
> So, when the children grow up and are rebellious, the parent is the
> one who has fear. The child becomes a thief or a gangster and whose
> fault is it? The parents. No, it's the government's fault. And our fault,
> even if we are immigrants with or without papers, for thinking that
> something is being given to us in the school. You are all consumers
> here. The school pays for these services from our pockets. No one is
> doing us a favor.

SLUMLORDS, COCKROACHES, AND EVICTIONS

Five mothers and I are working in the parent center. The mothers decided to clean and tidy the room. The previous night Jimenez had phoned me and asked if I knew anything about tenant rights. I told her I would bring any information I could find.

At least an hour had passed before two women entered the room. Jimenez escorts one of them to me. "She needs advice about housing." "*Hablale*/Speak," she says to her. "*Jaramillo es de confianza/* Jaramillo is trustworthy." We sat down, and I listened to the mother speak and cry for a while.

Her story went something like this:

> For twelve years she had occupied a small apartment with her husband and children. She was approximately six months pregnant. The family paid six hundred dollars in monthly rent, never missed a payment, but was now facing eviction. Her landlord was a police sheriff. They were undocumented. The sheriff had appeared at her apartment, in uniform, when she was alone to serve the family eviction papers. She asked the sheriff to return when her husband was home. She felt intimidated. The entire family was afraid, she said. Her husband and eldest daughter feared getting behind the wheel because the sheriff might call the police and cite them for driving without a license.

I ask her to explain to me why she was being evicted. "I don't know," she responds. "My apartment is the only one without cockroaches and rats. I am clean. My house is clean. I spend hours cleaning. I don't leave food in the kitchen."

A few weeks earlier, the sheriff sent a worker to each apartment to clean and fumigate. "When he walked into my apartment, he said there was not anything to do, that it was very clean."

"Why am I being evicted? Where are we going to go? It is not easy to move without papers."

VOTING IN

Jimenez approached me and said that a parents' organization was formed several years ago. It was called *Padres Unidos*, Parents United. She told me the vice principal had all of the information, since he was one of the persons who helped form the group when he was responsible for Title I programs. After approaching Mr. Ramos we set a date to formally elect a cabinet: President, Treasurer, and Secretary. Jimenez approached the school district's community liaison and she agreed to attend the election and to clarify the roles and responsibilities of the parent group. That morning we met in the cafeteria. Roughly 100 mothers and a few fathers were in attendance. We asked if everyone in the room spoke Spanish, or if anyone needed English translation. One woman raised her hand requesting translation. We explained the voting procedure, which would be done anonymously. The mothers and fathers were to indicate their choices on a blank piece of paper.

Several of the mothers began to nominate members of the community. One by one, the women rose to their feet and expressed their voting selection. *Yo voto por Maria para presidenta, porque ella se preocupa por la comunidad y los niños. Yo voto por Delia para presidenta porque ella tiene mas experiencia con el distrito/*I vote for Maria for president because she cares about the community and the children. I vote for Delia for president because she has more experience working with the school district. Within minutes it was clear that Jimenez would compete against another mother whose children had graduated from the elementary school. Both women were given the opportunity to make a case for their selection. Jimenez stood and said, "*Yo accepto la nominación. Ustedes quienes me conocen saben que yo quiero lo mejor para los niños, para ustedes. A mi me gusta trabajar en la escuela. Yo no voy a cerrarle la puerta a nadie. Todos somos iguales. Yo puedo hablar mas, ustedes saben que me gusta hablar. Pero no quiero decir mucho ahora. Apenas que sepan, que todos podemos ser padres unidos/*I accept the nomination. Those of you who know me, know that I want what is best for the children, for all of you. I like working in the school. I will never close the door to any of you. We are all the same. I can speak more, you know that I like to talk. But I'm not going to say much right now. I only want you to know that all of us can be parents united." Delia also rose and accepted her nomination. "*Pues yo era presidenta de padres unidos hace muchos años. Todos mis hijos han venido a esta escuela y yo tengo la experiencia para ser presidenta otra vez. Yo conozco las reglas del distrito, y si me dan la oportunidad de representarlos, hare un buen trabajo/*Well, I was the president of Parents United many years ago. All of my children have come to this school and I have the experience to be president again. I know the school district's rules, and if you give me the opportunity to represent you, then I will do a good job." Mr. Ramos translated the women's speeches into English.

The women began chanting for their respective favorites. Maria! Maria! Delia! Delia!

Mr. Ramos brought a baseball cap to collect the votes. The mothers and fathers dropped their pieces of paper into it. Some had tightly folded them to the size of a penny. Others didn't bother to fold them. Some stayed and served themselves a cup of coffee. The mothers always made coffee in the thermos they had purchased for large meetings. Next to the coffee was a tray of sweet bread from the local bakery. Other women and men left promptly. Mr. Ramos, the district liaison, and I counted the votes. Maria Jimenez won the vote. Ms. Valencia demanded that she witness the count to make sure that we did not interfere with the result. We smiled and responded, "of course."

NO CHICKEN

The Title I coordinator had arranged a luncheon at the end of the school year to thank the mother volunteers, which Jimenez did not attend. Chepita approached Jimenez one morning and asked her why she did not attend. "Only five parents went, Maria." "Why didn't you call the volunteers and ask them to go?" Chepita continued. Jimenez quipped, "Why would I call the parents? I was told by the Title I coordinator that she was in charge of the volunteers and that I did not have a role in the luncheon. I'm in charge of the parent center and that has nothing to do with the volunteers. Why would I call mothers? So they could go fight amongst themselves for a piece of chicken that was going to be given to them?"

DITCH PARTY

Jimenez once asked me to visit her home in the evening, saying it was an emergency. When I entered the room at her home, I saw three mothers seated in the living room, two of whom I recognized, but there was one I had never seen before. The woman I did not recognize held a tissue in her hand and was crying. Just a few days prior, her sixth-grade daughter jumped the school fence in the morning and went to a "ditch party," the name students give to parties when they take place during the school day. The guys at the party handed her an uncapped beer bottle. She drank, and several hours later she awakened on a thorny mattress in a cold and stale apartment, her uniform skirt pulled down to her ankles. The mother had taken her daughter to the hospital that evening, and they gave her a physical exam. As the mother recalled these events she sobbed uncontrollably. It felt like hours had passed, and we simply sat and attempted to offer her some consolation. But all of us were crying. The mother had phoned the school and asked them why she wasn't informed that her daughter was missing during the school day. She asked them what they were going to do about her daughter being raped during school hours. And she asked why they didn't monitor the side gate more closely if they were aware of ditch parties. She said the school responded with silence. *"Porque no son responsables si yo deje mi hija en cargo de la escuela durante las horas escolar? Porque si ellos saben que este es un gran problema en la escuela? Porque no me dicen nada?/*Why aren't they responsible if I left my daughter in their care during school hours? Why if they know that these are big problems happening in the school? Why don't they say anything to me?" We talked for hours. At the end of the evening, lasmadres decided to organize a walkout in protest of school violence. *"Marchamos contra la violencia/*We will protest against the violence"

Ten days passed. I phoned Jimenez and asked about the march. "It is tomorrow," she replied. "We notified the police department and the school. We are going to march against violence with our children." And they did carry it out.

I Didn't Steal the Granola Bar

Jimenez' daughter ate a granola bar that belonged to her teacher. The teacher called her a thief for eating the crunchy snack. She had reserved the granola bars for children on testing day, to make sure they had full bellies the morning of the exam. Jimenez's daughter apparently didn't think twice about eating the granola bar. Jimenez told her, "Look, if you have enough food to eat at home, then why would you grab one of the teacher's granola bars?" Jimenez met with the principal and teacher. She apologized for her daughter but asked for respect. "I teach my children to respect others but also to demand respect. She shouldn't be called a thief." The principal defended the teacher's actions. No more granola bars.

No *Chilaquiles*

Teacher's day was fast approaching and the school administration had offered to cook lunch for the teachers. The principal approached the mothers at their spot in the main entrance and asked if he could borrow the coffee thermos for the luncheon. The mothers asked if they were going to be invited; the year prior they had collaborated with the administration and brought dishes from home. The mothers thought of it as a time to show their appreciation to the faculty and to share a positive experience. But this year was different. The previous week Jimenez and the principal were engaged in a heated debate about discipline in the cafeteria, and relations between them were tense. The principal indicated that the administration decided to organize the luncheon without the assistance of the mothers. In effect, the mothers were not allowed to show their appreciation to the faculty. The mothers lent them the thermos, regardless.

PARENT CENTER MOVES AGAIN

We had ordered lunch from a local hamburger joint, Tam's. We had also decided to meet in the parent center to continue organizing the room after the administration had again designated a new place for the parents. In fact, it was the third time the parent center was moved. The parents were first allocated a room in a building near the main entrance, a convenient location for the mothers who arrived with their infants in strollers. They were then moved to one of the temporary bungalows just outside the main building. And they were moved again, this time into one of the farthest bungalows on the school grounds. It takes approximately five minutes to make it there from the school entrance. I walked in and saw Jimenez, Chepita, Gonzalez, Leticia, and Laura in the parent center. The center looked beautiful. The mothers had been working on remodeling the room for the past two weeks. On one table they displayed a number of handouts that covered health, domestic violence, and understanding school standards. They had just finished putting together a bulletin board with images and text about Benito Juarez, Cesar Chavez, and Martin Luther King. Jimenez wanted to make sure that "las dos culturas/the two cultures" would be represented in the room.

RAPE: AGAIN

A mother raced toward Jimenez at the side gate. She told her that she had just witnessed the rape of a young girl. She gave a physical description of the girl, and based on the information she provided, Jimenez thinks the child is either in first grade or kindergarten. They walked toward the school patio where the children played in the morning, but they did not see her. They went to the administration and the police were called. After the mother described where the rape took place, the police discovered camera footage of the crime. The girl had been assaulted in an alleyway adjacent to an apartment complex. The police returned to the school later that week and allowed Jimenez to view the tape, hoping that she could identify the girl and/or the assailant. Jimenez knows almost everyone in the community. She described the scene: "The old man walks past the girl and he turns to her and says something. It looked like the girl had a kindergarten folder draped around her neck. It got dark on the screen and then we saw the girl pulling her pants up as she walked away. The old man never looked at the camera. We couldn't find the girl, because the image was fuzzy. But the police have the technical means to do it. These things can't stay this way. I told the administration that they should send letters home about the rape." A few days later, they found the girl. They also found the man. He was arrested.

PROFICIENT . . . HOORAY!

The school principal addressed a group of roughly 20 parents who attended the monthly Title I council meeting. He informed the parents of a new program that was recently developed to celebrate the students' successes. After every testing cycle the principal arranged an awards ceremony for those students who tested "proficient" on standardized tests. The idea, he told parents, was to motivate the students who were not being rewarded. He explained the logic behind the awards: "When the students witness the success of their peers, they will want to work harder." The principal encouraged the mothers and fathers to support the program. How will you feel when your child comes home and says I am proficient! Won't it feel good to know that your child is learning in school? The majority of parents nod in agreement. That is why we send our children to school, a mother exclaims. The principal leaves the meeting. When it was Jimenez's turn to speak, she addressed the question of testing. Do you know what I would say to my child if she came home with a bad test result? *Que no vale madre!*/That it was not important! I tell her that she will go to college, regardless. Our children are tested too much. Why don't we focus on the things that do matter, like the quality of teachers, or safety in our school? Why don't we focus on encouraging our children to go to college?

Closing(s) and Opening(s)

In the above scenarios, I have tried to demonstrate the breadth and scope that characterize Jimenez's and las madres' ongoing struggles within the school site. Here, we can take notice of the fact that las madres' activity at times takes a subversive form, or one that we could call overtly protagonistic. In either case, Jimenez and lasmadres continue to identify practices that they deem unjust in the school setting and seek pathways to "redress" these practices in the evolving social dramas of Mirasur. Las madres are neither submissive within the school site nor adamantly opposed to it. They recognize that the school site is the place where they must be present because it is the source of education for their children and community. They are in a social drama of antistructure, a liminal phase of social drama insofar that las madres assume "functional" activity—they have assumed a special duty in the course of the school's social practices, but they often reverse or invert social practices to compensate for the rigidities or unfairness of the normative structure.

In antistructure, las madres liberate their capacities and creative energies from the normative constraints incumbent upon engaging a sequence of social statuses (as reflected in the pedagogy of the burro), enacting a multiplicity of social roles (Turner, 1987), as well as them being aware and conscious of their membership to women in the community. As Jimenez and las madres convene at the side gate every morning, they engage the conditions of their community critically. This is not to suggest that on every occasion las madres are able to come up with redressive action; their work is difficult, especially when they are attempting to transform and alter structural relations that are historically situated and embedded within state power. In the case of las madres, the school site reproduces broader dominative relations and follows the directives handed down from the state to the school district and then to the school site. Such is the case with the example of meal ticket distribution to students who qualify for free or reduced-price lunch. The state requires strict reporting mechanisms to ensure that no child undeserving of a free lunch receives one; the school district designs a clumsy accounting procedure; in the face of district pressure, the cafeteria manager initiates an unforgiving food distribution system; and in light of all of this, las madres see what is most immediately visible to them: that children are denied the right to eat and that they are treated like "animals." All of these relations are interconnected—entangled—and these are well beyond the scope of this discussion or of las madres' stated ability to contest these over-lapping hierarchical processes (which one could, in turn, speak of in terms of social dramas). Las madres are continuously responding to and contesting unjust practices and issues in the community—whether it is the rape of a ten-year-old, unjust disciplining practices, or punitive procedures against those children who forget their "lunch tickets." In a school with a population of close to 2,000 students, it is clear how one policy, or even one individual's actions, can impact a great majority. Las madres see it because they are there, always vigilant and concerned for *el bienestar* of their community. Their awareness stems from the cracks and fissures of their own developing sociopolitical consciousness and activity. Las madres are border dwellers in multiple senses of the word. They occupy the geographical space of the "bor-der" in a community that is continuously shaped and renegotiated, given the politics of a school population that primarily originates from south of the U.S. border, and the governing policies and ideologies that shape how these "southerners" are incorporated and excluded from the dominant register of citizenship in Mirasur.

FROM LIMINAL TO LIMINOID

While the work of Jimenez and las madres created spaces of liminal-ity and communitas—as a way of separating them from the norma-tive relationships of the pedagogy of Mirasur and thus enabling the community of las madres to consider its own history and the his-tory of women more critically—the overall function of their evolv-ing critical agency was what Turner (1977) referred to as a "liminoid event." Turner coined the term *liminoid* to refer to experiences that have characteristics of liminal experiences (creating spaces of betwixt and between and feelings of communitas), but they don't involve a resolution of a personal or collective crisis. The liminal (while seem-ingly anarchistic and providing a temporary rupture from the domi-nant social norms) is functional for the reproduction of society and depends upon the structures of ritual (as an aspect of social or reli-gious ritual that functions to reintegrate the actor back into society and its norms), while the liminoid (which has more to do with indus-trial societies) is a break from society, part of play designed to disor-der the orderly and to subvert the already established. Unlike liminal events, liminoid events are not intended to return social actors to the same unjust, unequal, and hierarchical world that they left. Liminoid events are meant to transform the world by challenging the wider social structure by means of social critique. Whereas liminal events are integral to the functioning of society by returning social actors to the rules and structures of the official social hierarchy and space, that is, by reenacting and reanimating the main principles of the social order, liminoid events (while clearly isomorphic with liminal events but more secularized) are plural, fragmentary, free-form, risky, and subversive of the social order. They can lead to civil disobedience and even revolution.

Reading the activity of las madres through the heuristic lenses offered by Turner and Anzaldúa creates a relief for understanding evolving social action among women immigrants—the outliers of a community. These liminoid spaces of activity and evolving consciousness offer the ordinary observer a discomforting look into how the seemingly mundane and "innocent" acts of school life ripple through the substratum of a school community, impacting not only the immediate sense of "worth" that families encounter as they are incorporated in the school site but also ultimately the life choices and opportunities that our future generations will have at their disposal. The ways in which a school administration, faculty, and staff perceive and act upon a community shape that community. Patterns of dominance and subordination (here I am borrowing the concept of dominance from Louis Althusser, 1969) in social relations imply an "internal hierarchy" that is lived out through the specific conditions of any given epoch or locality. And how people negotiate processes of structural dominance is as equally contingent as the historical, cultural, and social conditions that leave their mark on aggrieved groups. These structural understandings, prejudices, and beliefs both foster and negate growth. From the anthropology of experience perspective, this has been revealed in understanding the role of ritual and processes of cultural cohesion and change. And from the interstices of cultural and literary criticism, the necessity of developing "other" epistemic frameworks and activist paradigms that can endure the historical legacy of the "structures" that shape our interactions in society is central for moving toward liberatory conceptions and acts in the future.

The idea here is that society is an ensemble of competing social dramas, some of which are horizontal, that is, existing on a plane of relative political equality (in the realm of education, these would refer to struggles over issues of course material, getting supplies, organizing the curriculum, and the school schedule), and those that are vertical, that is, existing on a plane of inequality (struggles over standardized testing, unequal distribution of students in special education or behavioral classes, etc.). The social drama of las madres, nested with the larger social drama of Mirasur, was a vertical struggle, and kept under control (that is, allowed to continue but under controlled situations that would render their protest largely symbolic), it would not threaten the social drama of Mirasur (the way Mirasur is reproduced as a "structure in dominance"). But the social drama of las madres, under the leadership of Jimenez, which began as a symbolic struggle, eventually developed into what I call a full-blown "revolutionary social drama," one that was carried out by means of contesting and resisting what I have named "the pedagogy of the burro." It was a vertical social drama that directly posed challenges to create a rift or major schism within the larger social drama of Mirasur that represented the dominant social, economic, and pedagogical interests of the larger society.

6

REVOLUTIONARY SOCIAL DRAMA:
DECOLONIAL PEDAGOGICAL PROCESSES

Jimenez and I remain close friends and *comadres*. We speak on the phone regularly, see each other less, but continue to debate and contemplate our ongoing social dramas, whose conditions—most of them, at least—have not been of our own making. Shortly after a new principal was hired in 2009, Jimenez was abruptly removed from many of her parent-organizing functions. *Padres Unidos/Parents United* was dismantled and the parents were told that they could apply for official organizational status through the Parents and Teachers Association (PTA). Jimenez continued to serve on various governance committees (e.g.,Title I) and she advised the women and men who approached her to settle any grievances with the school while she maintained her job as a supervision aide. She intuitively *felt*, however, that the new school administration had deliberately stripped her of authority. *"Ese boboso es peor que el primero. Eran buenos amigos, todo aqui se conoce. Seguro le dijeron que yo causo problemas/*That moron is worse than the first principal. They were good friends, everything here is known. I'm sure they told him (new principal) that I cause problems." Jimenez survived various rounds of budget cuts in the Los Angeles school district and remained on the official payroll of mother workers until July 2011. The new principal fired the mother workers following the most recent "trimming" of the school budget. Jimenez was one of eleven mothers given a pink slip and asked to reapply. Only six were rehired and she did not make the cut. In the words of the school principal, the women who demonstrated that the children were their priority were given their jobs back. According to Jimenez, the principal was attempting to restrict her from providing advice and support to the families. Following the principal's encouragement, the new school workers and volunteers began to offer "valet" services to families who drive their children to school, thus limiting the direct interaction that parents have with the mothers who used to greet them at the school entrance. For the most part, these changes severely impacted Jimenez's outreach efforts and she felt slighted, to say the least. Her grandchildren have moved to another neighborhood, and without a remaining family member at the school site, the administration has told her that she no longer has any role to play. *Usted ya no tiene nada que hacer aquí/*You no longer have anything to do here, they told her. Several families have stepped forward and offered to circulate a petition for rehiring Jimenez. *El apoyo de las familias/*the support of the families means everything to Jimenez and has inspired her to find new pathways to keep her connection with the community alive. In spite of the administration's efforts to block Jimenez from participating in the school's governance committees, the families have reinstated her as the community representative for the school site council. She feels invigorated, "*Lo que no se da cuenta el director es que con mas que me trate de humillar, mas energía me da para estar presente y representar las familias/*The principal does not recognize that the more he tries to humiliate me, the more energy he gives me to participate and represent the families."

Jimenez's children and grandchildren continue to anchor her day's work, "*me levanto a las cinco para arreglar estos chiquillos y me acuesto a la media noche después de que hayan hecho la tarea y e podido planchar la ropa/*I wake up at five to get the kids ready and I go to bed at midnight after I've made sure that they have finished their homework and after I've had time to iron their clothes." Her family is steadfastly moving along educational and worker ranks. Her youngest son, el Prieto, and her grandson, Jorge, attend a charter middle school where Jimenez believes they will have better chances of receiving a quality education outside the neighborhood of South Central Los Angeles. Her eldest daughter, Betty, is the first university graduate in the family, despite the challenges she faced as a single mother of three. Tiffany attends high school; Carmen has graduated with her associate's degree from community college and plans to continue with a career in law enforcement; and Anuar, the eldest son, works alongside his father in the electricity trade. Jimenez continues to assume the weight of her children's futures on her shoulders:

Me siento con el trabajo que estaba haciendo antes cuando me importaba que la casa brillara como un espejo limpio como tiempo perdido. Perdido porque el quehacer de la casa me puede esperar. El quehacer podria esperarme todo el tiempo que quisiera. El quehacer no se iva ir pero la educación de mis hijos seguia caminando. Lo que no pude hacer antes por mis tres grandes hijos ya no lo puedo hacer. Ahora se siente uno mas feo cuando alguno de sus hijos de los mas grandes me incrimina. Anuar me pregunta, "¿Porque no hiciste conmigo lo que estas haciendo ahora con mis hermanos?. Usted nunca menciono el colegio. Usted nunca me ayudo. Si me hubieras ayudado yo hubiera podido superarme." Cuando a uno le hacen esos reproches tus hijos si duele y uno se da cuenta pues que la casa, la limpieza de la casa no importaba como deberia de haber importado la educación de sus hijos. I feel that the work I was doing before, when I cared about my house sparkling like a clean mirror, like time lost. Lost because the housework could have waited for me. Housework could have waited for me all the time that I wanted. Housework wasn't going to go anywhere, but the education of my children kept moving along. What I was not able to do before for my three oldest children I cannot do now. Now it feels bad when one of my children, one of the oldest, incriminates me. Anuar will ask me, "Why didn't you do with me what you are now doing with my siblings? You never mentioned college. You never helped me. If you would have helped me I would have been able to help myself." When one of your children reproaches you that way it hurts and, well, you notice that the house, the cleanliness of the house, did not matter in the same way that the education of my children should have mattered.

The extended corpus of knowledge and meaning, the *conocimiento*, which Jimenez has generated over the years, provides her with a solid basis from which she is able to continue her efforts to resist and contest relations of injustice in a manner similar to her actions during *la protesta de las mujeres sumisas*. Conocimiento, "that aspect of consciousness urging you to act" (Anzaldúa, 2002, 542), serves as the recursively constituted and enduring guidepost for Jimenez's political activism. Critical consciousness is not something that can be taken away; it is a reservoir linked to memories associated with the body-self, a type of felt experience activated in the presence of injustice. Jimenez "embodies" conocimiento as a form of protagonistic agency that accommodates to the social relations in which she finds herself. She is a gift giver, an improviser, and a trickster guarding the crossroads who keeps conocimiento flowing in the contextually specific location of her community, a *"mulier abscondita/*hidden woman" who represents the shadowy presence behind the mask of servitude, the latent revolutionary power of the oppressed.

Jimenez's protagonistic agency has taken up permanent residence in the liminal spaces of conocimiento (nepantla), but this time, as part of her revolutionary praxis, she negotiates the social relations that mediate her laboring body (as a housewife and mother). She inserts herself into the community and school in an ongoing effort to encourage political consciousness and redress relations of domination and exploitation that she witnesses. Here, her liminal presence (she stands both within and outside of the ascribed and proscribed cultural/political boundaries of the immigrant mother) affords her a unique vantage point in redressing the injustices of the school site as she reincorporates herself into the social order *on her own terms* as a social activist, a nepantlera. In this way she has moved through Turner's stages of social drama, but with a difference. This difference is what I call "revolutionary social drama."

REVOLUTIONARY SOCIAL DRAMA

The copresence of all the social, political, and economic elements of Mirasur, their specific affectivities and the relations of domination and subordination that obtained between them, enables the dominant ideology and mainstream pedagogical practices to reproduce themselves, but always within unstable sites of contradiction. In other words, the social drama of Mirasur is a fluid and processual drama that reproduces asymmetrical relations of power and privilege, but always in the context of forces that resist such reproduction. I discussed these forces in the context of the "pedagogy of the burro," demonstrating how actors within the social drama of Mirasur enacted and reproduced (consciously and unconsciously) relations and performative registers that positioned las madres as low-wage "burritas" and others as "burrito managers." While the social drama of Mirasur plays itself out in a relatively continuous form that is coincident with the broader social relations that shape schooling practices within the United States (especially in relation to immigrant communities), Jimenez and las madres participate in a social drama of their own making: the internal drama of nepantleras.

For Jimenez and las madres, the inner theatre of nepantla has pushed forward a new conception of their "selves" in the social world, and as a result they continuously jolt the pedagogy of the burro out of place. "Breach," "crisis," "redress," and "reintegration" are mobile stages that characterize social dramas in general; but in the case of Mirasur, Jimenez and las madres have effectively destabilized the seemingly predictable pattern of addressing and resolving conflict situations. The social drama of las madres and Jimenez (and one in which I also participated) could be considered social dramas *from below* and are nested within the larger social drama of Mirasur, which is a social drama *from above*. It is the coming together of these two social dramas—one from above and one from below—that give meaning to revolutionary social drama. Revolutionary social drama begins with change from below and with change from within. It then seeks to transform dramas from above, and it does so in spite of the conditions that limit change from taking place. Revolutionary social drama is the drama of nepantleras who are in constant pursuit of the "zone of possibility" that can give new shape and form to their and others' participation in the world. It is a zone produced through the dialectical transcendence of seemingly insurmountable contradictions (of patriarchy-kyriarchy and racism in "democracy," of "labor" and "capital," of "family" and "culture"). The concept of time in revolutionary drama can be considered in terms of *Messianic time*, "when history through which the memory of the past is interpreted will now reveal itself through the struggles of the oppressed" (Kona, 2010). When time is brought together with space, we have movement, and in the case of revolutionary social drama it is a two-fold movement: from inner consciousness to outer action and from outer consciousness to inner action, effectively annulling the boundary between thought and intentionality. Thought, in other words, is always populated with the intention of confronting and challenging social injustice. Social drama works through what Judith Butler calls "performative reiteration" (1993), a reiterative or ritual practice that we use to separate out people in everyday life (via gender, race, immigrant status, etc.), producing what looks like what has always been there but what is essentially an ideological construction created by one group or class of people. Revolutionary social drama sheds critical light on the nature of the performative reiteration, which has acquired the status of an independent existence and has negated or obscured the process of its own formation. Revolutionary social drama as a heuristic device can serve as a dialectical means for examining the constitutive nature of personal identity, individuality, consciousness, and the structural conditions of everyday life. In this sense, it references Anzaldúa's nepantla state as one of dialogue between "my Self and el espiritu del mundo. I change myself, I change the world." Anzaldúa writes:

> I think that identity is relational, that it exists in relation to some Other. And so it's always in this in-between zone, the nepantla or the borderlands. And that in being in this in-between zone it's saying your fixed

categories are permeable. There are aspects that overlap, that break down the categories, through osmosis or through some kind of very elusive, being-in-two-or-three-places-at-once kind of metaphor. And that the same thing happens with the laws of language, that the laws of language say "this is reality, this is possible, this is not possible, up has to have a down." etcetera....And that being in between, overlapping spaces is very much my metaphor for the shape-shifter shaman, which I'm now using instead of using the word "protean," I'm using the word "nahual." Which is shaman, a different kind of shaman from maybe some of the Native American shaman or Siberian-Russian shaman, or Japanese-Korean shaman, but it's basically that ability to travel through worlds, to jump from one locale to the other or one particular identity to the other...(Reuman and Anzaldúa, 2000, 12)

In Nahuatl terms, life is inconceivable without the element that defines it: movement (Leon-Portilla, 1963). While Anzaldúa's nepantla state is admittedly a very mystical conception, there are aspects to it that bear a resemblance to what Michael Lebowitz (2005) has identified as Karl Marx's concept of "revolutionary praxis." Like Anzaldúa, Marx recognized the gap between what is and what *ought* to be. According to Lebowitz (2005),

> Implicit [in the concept of revolutionary practice] is the recognition that the full development of our creative potential is not occurring but that it is *possible*. In other words, what we observe now in the capacities of human beings is not *all* that is possible, what we observe now is a fraction of what we can be. It is a clear recognition that human development is not fixed and that we do not know its boundaries. It is a political statement—because it implies that there is an alternative.

Marx defined revolutionary practice as "the coincidence of the changing of circumstances and of human activity or self-change" (cited in Lebowitz, 2005). In other words, we develop our capacities and capabilities through our activity, and as a consequence of self-change we change the circumstances in which we live and labor. That is, we change ourselves through our activity. It is clear that both Anzaldúa and Marx are emphasizing the dialectical interaction between subjectivity and acting in and on the material world. Marx's emphasis on the relation between subjectivity and acting in and on the world is perhaps best captured by Antonio Machado's well-known verse, "*Caminante no hay camino, se hace el camino al andar*/Voyager there is no path, one makes the path by walking." Anzaldúa's concern for understanding subjectivity in all its heteronomous nature compels her to articulate a slightly modified version of Machado's prose. She writes, *"Caminante no hay puentes, se hace puentes al andar/*Voyager there are no bridges, one builds them as one walks" (Anzaldúa, 2002). For Anzaldúa, bridges are the "thresholds to other realities, archetypal, primal symbols of shifting consciousness. They are passageways, conduits, and connectors that connote transitioning, crossing borders, and changing perspectives" (2002, 1). Anzaldúa is interested in revolutionary practice to change the world, but for Anzaldúa this stipulates changing the self in multiple dimensions, some of these directly linked to the spiritual. This does not imply that she was not interested in changing material reality in the interests of the oppressed. But Anzaldúa sees the process of becoming a revolutionary as becoming, first and foremost, a nepantlera, a spiritual being, a being that uses images and archetypes to release her creative capacities so that the world can be created anew, but with a much more inclusive vision of what those social relations between people might be. Bridging the material world with the subjective pathways toward becoming is what essentially characterizes revolutionary social drama. In Turner's terminology, it is much more of a "liminoid" act than a "liminal" one.

In working through revolutionary social drama with Jimenez and las madres, a certain *sentido/*sense of spiritual activism transpired among us. Spiritual activism results from spiritual inquiry, the conocimiento reached through "creative engagements" where you "embed your experiences in a larger frame of reference, connecting your personal struggles with those of other beings on the planet, with the struggles of the Earth itself" (Anzaldúa, 2002, 542). Anzaldúa writes of spirituality as a "devalued form of knowledge" where attempts are made to "understand the greater reality that lies behind your personal perceptions, (and where you view) these struggles as spiritual undertakings" (2002, 542). Spiritual activism may begin with one individual; but in the practice of nepantla, activism moves outward to the public realm as nepantleras begin to challenge the broader continent of social relations found in the public spheres. Nepantla is fundamentally a collective space, what Keating calls a "radical interconnectedness" that "encourages spiritual activists to look for commonalities among differently situated social actors" (2006, 246). Such a quest is essentially a configuration of spaces of resistance and transformation, where hegemonic forms of knowledge are taken into custody and where subaltern epistemologies that speak from spaces of colonial difference are given pride of place. Spaces of colonial difference are spaces of latent power, of the power to make the invisibility of the oppressed visible to the world. Comandante Ana Maria of the Zapatistas captures this aspect of colonial difference when she remarks:

> The voice that arms itself to make itself heard. The face that hides itself to show itself. The name that is silent in order to be named. The red star that calls to people and to the world that they should listen, that they should see, that they should name. The tomorrow that is harvested in the yesterday. Behind our black face. Behind our armed voice. Behind our unnameable name. Behind the us that you see. Behind are the we that are you. (cited in Holloway, 2010, 214)

While my focus in this book has been to examine the dramaturgical aspects of institutional life and of changing consciousness, the revolutionary social drama of Jimenez and the mothers also provides us an insight into the machinations of reproducing and transcending the historical legacy of coloniality within the pedagogical processes of shifting consciousness. Coloniality (as opposed to "colonialism") is an ideological formation that is manifested according to an overlapping system of racial, ethnic, gendered, economic, sexual, and cultural hierarchies (or what Ramon Grosfoguel terms "heterarchies"). Decolonial thinkers provide a more nuanced way of critiquing the political economy—in terms of the epistemological foundations that give rise to concepts such as race, gender, and sexuality—than do postcolonial thinkers. The conquest and colonization that tragically marked the so-called founding of the Americas was attached to an evolving economic system of differentiation between those who claimed ownership of land and resources and those who were subjected to extracting resources from the land in order to generate profits for the plantocracy. But these economic relations were "entangled" in a structure that shaped power relations within and across other metrics of social identity and identification. The decolonial philosopher Anibal Quijano refers to this "entanglement" as the "coloniality of power" (2000). Quijano's notion of the "coloniality of power" affirms "that there is no overarching capitalist accumulation logic that can instrumentalize ethnic/racial divisions and that precedes the formation of a global colonial, eurocentric culture" (Grosfoguel, 2008). Quijano's notion that racism is constitutive and entangled with the international division of labor and capitalist accumulation at a world-scale suggests that multiple forms of labor coexist within a single historical process and that, according to Grosfoguel (2008), "free" forms of labor were assigned to the core or European origin populations and "coerced" forms of labor assigned to the periphery or non-European populations according to the racist Eurocentric rationality of the "coloniality of power." Grosfoguel identifies those elements that give the coloniality of power its appearance as multiple, intersecting, and entangled hierarchies that include race/ethnicity, sexuality, spirituality, language, epistemology, an interstate system of political-military organizations controlled by European males, an international division of labor of core and periphery, and a particular global class formation that situates nation-states geopolitically. Within this framework, coloniality is understood as constitutive of modernity and not derivative of or accidental to it. The notion of coloniality of power is central in linking the subjective dimensions of coloniality to the material relations of exploitation in that it attempts to "integrate as part of a heterogeneous structural process the multiple relations in which cultural, political and economic processes are entangled in capitalism as a historical system" (Grosfoguel, 2008). With respect to questions of gender and sexuality, decolonial feminists have critiqued and extended concepts of coloniality to address the "processes by which the colonial invention of gender operated"[1] (Maese-Cohen, 2009, 11). Altogether, decolonial thinkers and pedagogues examine the fundamental organization of society through a historical lens that addresses how and under which conditions the concepts of "race," "gender," and "sexuality" (among others) came into being in the process of conquest and colonization of the Americas. Moreover, decolonial theories of liberation demonstrate that the struggle for humanization needs to be waged on multiple fronts, which includes an interrogation of the dominant worldviews that shape how we come to know ourselves, our relationships to one another, to the nation, and to the global community in general. The point here is to understand how lived oppression becomes a way of life within the colonial matrix of power—a matrix that is constitutive of capitalist society—and to engage in a multipronged effort to contest the economic, political, and social injustices that are waged against the dispossessed. While schools are necessary but insufficient sites in bringing about the kinds of transformation sought by decolonial scholars, activists, and pedagogues, schools remain important arenas of contestation and possibility.

The rendering of my account of Jimenez and las madres tells a story about how these women embodied these colonial processes as

laboring immigrant women in Mirasur, yet at the same time participated in revolutionary acts of transformation that became more self-
conscious over time. Their actions both in securing the hegemony of
the social order through their consent to relations of coloniality and
their resistance to and transformation of such relations were all part of
the processual dimensions of the social drama of Mirasur. In analyzing this social drama, I have tried to demonstrate the ways in which
the coloniality of power can be challenged by small acts of collective
protest. The "undoing" of coloniality is simultaneously the undoing
of self-incarceration and has important pedagogical dimensions—for
various settings and multiple purposes—which I refer to *in toto* as
decolonial pedagogy.

DECOLONIAL PEDAGOGY, ENTANGLEMENT, AND CONSCIENTIZAO

> Self-education requires that we open all of our senses, not just our
> minds, and allow ourselves to be changed by the books and perspec-
> tives of other people.
>
> Anzaldúa, 2009

The United States has a complex (and complicated) history in relation
to its immigrant populations, and the multifarious ways in which the
social drama of Mirasur enacted this history could be glimpsed through
the various means by which a primarily immigrant community was
incorporated into the social, cultural, and epistemological universe of
the school site. In many ways, Mirasur and its attendant social practices and relations with the community can be understood through
the trope of neocoloniality, where educational practices (including the
school's relationship to families) represent the continuity of colonial
relations between groups consisting of asymmetrical relations of power
and privilege grounded in class exploitation, racism, kyriarchal reason,
and patriarchy. Mirasur as a neocolonial institution practices education
as a way to transmit "American" culture and to fashion youth according to the dominant discourses and practices of an evolving concept of
U.S. citizenship. Clearly, educational institutions do function as sites of
cultural transmission, but not all can be considered as "neocolonial."[2]
What gave Mirasur its particular neocolonial characteristics were the
ways that the dominant tropes surrounding families and children and
their relationship to the state were produced in the social relations that

transpired in the school site: mothers conceived as burras, free laborers, and gossipy troublemakers; children brutally silenced, ignored, and violated. These relationships between the dominant strata of the school site (administrators, faculty, and staff) and the inferior strata of community are neocolonial in character; they reference deeply rooted practices and histories about the social location of peoples from south of the U.S. border. Neocoloniality references the manner in which the "other" is inscribed into dominant discursive systems and a set of practices—an ideology—involving human relationships among opposing cultural groups. I am employing the concept of neocoloniality epistemically, as a reference point for understanding systems of intelligibility, the frames of knowledge, practices, and beliefs that shape the educational encounter. This implies a bidirectional understanding of school-community relationships insofar as the mothers and community were often complicit in their own subjugation, a position that further establishes the legacy of coloniality in the sense of how people reproduce asymmetrical relations of power given the geopolitics and body-politics of knowledge at work in any given cultural encounter. Grosfoguel notes an important distinction between social location and locus of enunciation. He argues that "the fact that one is socially located in the oppressed side of power relations does not automatically mean that he/she is epistemically thinking from a subaltern epistemic location" (2008, 3). Here, the focus is on the ways that the "modern/colonial world-system" has functioned to make subjects that are "socially located on the oppressed side of the colonial difference think epistemically like the ones in dominant positions" (2008, 3). This is a sentiment echoed by the Brazilian educator Paulo Freire when he illustrates how dehumanization marks "not only those whose humanity has been stolen, but also (though in a different way) those who have stolen it" (1998, 26). Neocoloniality, understood as dehumanization, is connected in Freirian terms to an "unjust order" (1998, 26) that conditions the structure of thought of both dominant and subordinate social groups.

Decolonial pedagogy stems from an awareness of the enduring logic of neocoloniality in our schools, including the legislative measures and social relations between "teachers" and "learners." It applies not only to the "subaltern" groups struggling assiduously for citizenship (and therefore, human) rights but to groups in all school settings who find themselves in the throes of cultivating future generations of youth in a society increasingly marked by intolerance, violence among and between groups, hyper-nativism/nationalism, and a widening disparity between the rich and the poor. To put it bluntly and perhaps even rhetorically, decolonial pedagogy is not an "additive" approach to an already existing curriculum or pedagogy—it should be a foundational approach for all educators. Its character is utopian in vision, and if we do not claim utopia in our thinking about the possibilities of education contributing to a socially just and humane future, then to where will we carry our imaginations? It is not only our imaginations that need movement, however, the utopian vision of decolonial pedagogy has its anchors in the objective and concrete reality of the current historical moment. That is, the ways in which public schooling have been hijacked by neoliberal economic and social policy (that dates back to the Ronald Reagan administration of the 1980s, and its practices of privatization, standardization, and heightened accountability systems) offer educators an opportunity to interrogate and challenge such odious policy developments on the premise that these very ideological shifts are part of a colonial matrix of power and privilege. These shifts in educational practice have over the past several decades increasingly parceled the fundamental organization of school life into a mixed pattern of success or failure based on the capitalist marketplace and the logic of consumption: winners and losers, good citizen and intransigent deviants, capable and at-risk. The colonial matrix of schooling shapes the rank order applied to the student population, to teachers, and to the production of knowledge itself. It so follows that in decolonial pedagogy, the concrete practice of schooling is understood as linked to the broader imperatives of capitalist commodification in which education is subjected to the logic of the "market" for extracting profit at the expense of intellectual inquiry. And importantly, we discern from the processes of commodification the structure in which subjectivities and knowledges are formed and entangled.

The entanglement of social hierarchies was clearly evident in the social drama of Mirasur. Entanglement is a category that can help us move away from the dualisms that shape educational practices and relationships to a more robust and dialectical understanding of how social actors—and their social location—shape the "culture" (and structure) associated with school sites. Entanglement binds individuals into an indivisible whole. This is not just an epistemic proposition; it is grounded in a scientific understanding of the properties that bind organisms—including people—together in the physical realm. To quote the *Scientific American*, "A classical system is always divisible, at least in principle; whatever collective properties it has arise from components that themselves have certain properties. But an entangled system cannot be broken down in this way. Entanglement has strange consequences. Even when the entangled particles are far apart, they still behave as a single entity, leading to what Einstein famously called 'spooky action at a distance'" (Vedral, 2011, 41). In other words, entanglement—a term derived from quantum physics—is an observable phenomenon that offers explanatory power for how it is that social systems (and organisms) are organically interdependent. Understanding this phenomenon has concerned physical scientists for millennia, and philosophers have contemplated the "unity" (or disunity) of social life equally as long. Breaking down organisms into "particles" or social life into measurable "variables" is connected to an effort to understand how meaning is generated in the social totality. More often than not, however, interconnections are obscured from social analysis, which then allows the system to behave "classically." If, for example, we do not contemplate the relationship between coloniality and schooling, then the deprivation that children and families experience in the school site can be easily subsumed as a question of "individual circumstance," "culture," or just a plain inability to integrate into the social order. One-half of the equation is left outside the purview of analysis, and this is simply not how social institutions function.

It so follows that decolonial pedagogy stems from a recognition of the entangled web of social, political, economic, historical, or cultural relations that shape educational practices, relations that are not nested in traditional hierarchies of power but rather that constitute heterarchies. It is a processual way of addressing latent contradictions between and among communities. Decolonial pedagogy encourages educators to question the leitmotifs that organize the schooling encounter, the epistemic provisions that shape curriculum and teaching, and the social relations that inform relationships between social actors. In decolonial pedagogy, educators are attuned to the "rituals" that frame integration into the school site, as well as those sites/ events of rupture that open other understandings and conceptions of how people relate to the dominant institutional setting. Taking their cues from this relational awareness of how people cohere and disassemble, decolonial pedagogues foster participatory and dialogic governance structures that can keep educational practices addressing the concrete concerns of communities and developing responses that foster mutual growth and recognition. Central to decolonial pedagogy is the link between learning and consciousness, as it relates to the historical conditions and context in which communities are epistemically and socially located. On this note, I am reminded of the work of Paulo Freire (1998, 2005, 2008) and the contributions that he made to what is commonly referred to as "critical pedagogy." For the purposes of decolonial pedagogy, it is instrumental to examine Freire's writings on education, and in particular the role of conscientizao.

Freire insisted that education was an inherently political act that either reproduced or ruptured relations of domination and oppression. Freire (1998) writes, "Education either functions as an instrument which is used to facilitate integration of the younger generation into the logic of the present system and bring about conformity or it becomes the practice of freedom, the means by which men and women deal critically and creatively with reality and discover how to participate in the transformation of their world." The relation between education, society, and political economy influenced Freire's writings on teaching, learning, and literacy practices, which he came to refer to as "reading the word and reading the world" for the development of a critical consciousness (conscientization). Freire maintained the idea of syncretism in his theorizing by mixing diverse voices together while demonstrating the strength of dialogical thinking. As Freire puts it:

> We must know, or at least we must make clear here, we are not falling into an idealistic position where consciousness changes inside of itself through an intellectual game in a seminar...Liberating education can change our understanding of reality. But this is not the same thing as changing reality itself. No. Only political action in society can make social transformation. (Shor and Freire, 1987, 175)

In this sense, Freire emphasizes the *active* and *actionable* component of liberating education and, by extension, of liberating forms of reading the word and the world critically (Scatamburlo-D'Annibale, Suoranta, McLaren, and Jaramillo, 2005). The basic characteristic of Freire's account of the dialogical process of reading the word and world is dialogue as a process that is internal to the formation of a revolutionary class—in fact it is the crucial mode of organization of this class against oppression, and against the oppressors (DeLissovoy, 2005). For Freire, the relation between the self and the counter-self that emerges from the radical dialogic encounter is a recognition that the reciprocal process of developing the "whole and authentic being" has to be "undertaken against an organization of social relationships that systematically violates and precludes it" (DeLissovoy, 2005). As elaborated by McLaren (2000), "Freire understood that the subjectivities of the oppressed are to be considered heterogeneous and ideologically pertuse" (158). bell hooks further elaborates on Freire's contributions to the relations between the "self"—consciousness—and political activity when she writes about Freire's global understanding of liberation struggles as "the important initial stage of transformation—that historical moment when one begins to think critically about the self and identity in relation to one's political circumstances" (1994, 47). hooks writes, "again and again Freire has had to remind readers that he never spoke of conscientization as an end itself, but always as it is joined by meaningful praxis" (1994, 47). In an attempt to understand the dialectical relationship between subjectivity and objectivity, the "promise and limitations" of conscientization, Freire turned himself into a "tramp of the obvious, becoming the tramp of demystifying conscientization" (Freire, 1985). As the tramp of the obvious, Freire moves beyond a simplification of everyday life and looks at the importance of the "obvious" as the object of critical reflection.

The teacher-student relation for Freire was a dialectical one where each occupied the position of the other throughout the critical learning/teaching encounter. Freire notes, "there is no teaching without learning" (2005, 31). He elaborates, "Only insofar as learners become thinking subjects, and recognize that they are as much thinking subjects as are the teachers, is it possible for the learners to become productive subjects of the meaning or knowledge of the object. It is in this dialectic movement that teaching and learning become knowing and reknowing. The learners gradually know what they did not yet know, and the educators reknow what they knew before" (2005). In his later works, Freire expanded on the role of the "teacher" in terms of "cultural workers," people who find themselves working in the schools but who move beyond the practice and technique of teaching to inquire about schools as sites of indoctrination, socialization, and also places that promote the "capacities of students and the transformation of them" (2005). Generating knowledge for its own sake did not, in Freire's architectonic, constitute a fundamental part of the critical pedagogical encounter. The pursuit of knowledge and the need to learn to read and to write marked, for Freire, a "presence" in the world as a revolutionary act of transcending oppressive social conditions and relations. Freire invited cultural workers to examine themselves as persons living and producing in a given society who needed to become sensitive to the actual historical, social, and cultural conditions that contribute to forms of knowledge in the classroom (Freire and Macedo, 1987). Further, Freire exhorted women and men to acknowledge that they are the makers of culture and that culture does not inexorably make them in some deterministic fashion. Teachers as cultural workers unpack the relations that constitute their subjective locations in the social world—their corporal existence and experiences—as a form of giving testimony through announcing and denouncing, eventually producing a "coherent and permanent discourse" (2005, 97) about their profession and pedagogical practices.

In the Freirian sense, activity that begins in educational settings has to be related to the wider social order that frames student experience. It so follows that the social totality is understood as entangled human activity within the wider social order that cannot be isolated into fragments or autonomous parts; our social existence is unequivocally interconnected, a world of reality based on the activity of humankind to realize truth, a world in which truth is not given but one in which truth "happens" (Kosik, 1976, 7). For Karel Kosik, understanding how truth can be aided by the concrete cognition of reality is derived from the processes of *concretization*. In Kosik's assessment, concretization implies a process that proceeds from the whole of social life to its parts and from the parts to the whole (1976, 23). This "spiral" movement in our thinking of, in, and about the social world can be found in Freire's own dialogical propositions, from his frequently cited preoccupation with generative themes to his discussion of codification/decodification as processes that function as a way to apprehend reality as "interacting constituent elements" of the "whole." Only in understanding the fragmented aspects that characterize individual experience (i.e., as a gendered-ethnic-racialized body) in relation to the totality of social relations in which such experience is embedded does Freire suggest that one can "truly know that reality" (1998 104). As Freire maintains, knowledge of the totality must occur before one can separate and isolate its constituent elements as part of the total vision of concrete reality.

Decolonial pedagogy through the writings of Anzaldúa builds upon and extends the insights outlined above in the work of Paulo Freire (1998). While Freire speaks of conscientization as a process of engaging with social actors in "generative themes," which Freire identifies as "iconic representations that have a powerful emotional impact in the daily lives of learners," Anzaldúa talks about entering the state of "Coatlicue." For Freire, conscientization is a process of moving out of the "culture of silence," in which the socially dispossessed internalize the negative images of themselves created and propagated by the oppressor in situations of extreme poverty, and moving toward a critical consciousness. Anzaldúa speaks of Coatlicue as moving into a psychic state, a way of being in, with, and against the world simultaneously. It involves conjuring an archetype in the Jungian sense. According to Anzaldúa:

> *Coatlicue* is one of the powerful images, or "archtypes," that inhabits, or passes through my psyche. For me, *la Coatlicue* is the consuming internal whirlwind, the symbol of the underground aspects of the psyche. *Coatlicue* is the mountain, the Earth Mother who conceived all celestial beings out of her cavernous womb. Goddess of birth and death, *Coatlicue* gives and takes away life; she is the incarnation of cosmic processes. (1987, 68)

Decolonial pedagogy is philosophically grounded in examining the connections between the psyche and the material world. Philosophically, decolonial pedagogy does not set forward orthodox "materialist" readings of the self and the social world; rather, it pursues the liminal, transcendental, and spiritual spaces of knowledge construction in light of the material relations that shape subjectivities. Decolonial pedagogy maintains Freire's insistence on transforming oppressive political, economic, and social conditions as part of developing critical consciousness, and it points to the spontaneous forms of developing pedagogical practices that educate against and work at abolishing exploitative and alienating social conditions and relations. Educators resist mainstream pedagogical approaches with their imposition of a hierarchical relation of leader and the led. Decolonial pedagogy stipulates that critical consciousness and practical activity must be developed through an active interchange between concepts dealing with sexism, patriarchy, kyriarchy, and capitalism that emerge from an encounter in which those who "teach" and those who "learn" remain united. Thus, in decolonial pedagogy, the vertical or hierarchical relation in traditional pedagogical environments is replaced by a dialogic or horizontal relation.

Decolonial pedagogy requires that we undergo a systematic and profound process of coming to know the social world and the ways in which we are implicated in it. This is not a simple task; it requires that we simultaneously step within and outside the immediacy of the local environment that shapes our subjectivities. From within, we can identify that which brings an uncanny sense of comfort and awareness in what we come to know as focalist approaches to knowledge, or the "local experience." We can parcel experience into its tangible elements, but doing so will only give us a narrow view or different nook from which to examine the totality of that experience. Once we step outside local frames of references, then we call into question the deeper antagonisms of political consensus, exclusion, and alliance-building. In decolonial pedagogy we must be able to recognize and respond to those antagonisms that prevent the self and the collective "we" from seeing its interconnectedness to the larger horizon against which culture is contested and struggles for justice are pursued. In the dramaturgical processes of developing critical consciousness, this means that we examine positions of marginality within the margin, of the oppressed within oppression, and that we expose and work through the contradictions of autonomous or isolated movements of social change in relation to the global totality of human relations. This marks a shift from what Freire termed *semi-intransitivity* of consciousness to naïve transitivity, and then to critical transitivity. In semi-intransitivity, the sphere of perception is limited, impermeable to change, representing a near disengagement between people and their social environment. In other words, social phenomena are naturalized, fixed, and closed to critical engagement. Consciousness in this stage is framed by a quiet acquiescence to general norms and prescriptions. In naïve transitivity, people recognize the problems present in the social sphere, but such problems are "oversimplified," resulting in emotional polemics as opposed to critical dialogue around the questions and contradictions that plague the historical moment. Critical transitivity epitomizes Freire's overarching *oeuvre*. Freire writes,

> The critically transitive consciousness I characterized by depth in the interpretation of problems; by the substitution of causal principles for magical explanation...by rejecting passive positions; by soundness of argumentation; by the practice of dialogue rather than polemics; by receptivity to the new for reasons beyond mere novelty and by the good sense not to reject the old just because it is old—by accepting what is valid in both old and new. (14)

The point here is not to assume that Freire saw the development of consciousness in a strictly linear progression, or that these conceptual categories do not offer a more nuanced understanding of the cognitive processes associated with critical reflexivity. For decolonial pedagogy, what these conceptual categories offer is a way of addressing "habits of mind" that are socially and epistemically located in particular social contexts, inscribed by unique historical antecedents. Teachers, students, researchers, and cultural workers labor within and against various settings, linked to the coloniality of power and to the potentiality of change. Critical transitive consciousness is not so much an endpoint or "objective" in decolonial pedagogy as much as it is a starting point for meaningful learning and action to take place. Learning in this sense is directed, active, and amenable to change.

FINAL COMMENTS

The revolutionary social drama of Jimenez and las madres destabilized the "traditional" processes of social inquiry of actors who exercise a monopoly on truth and knowledge production. In this social drama, each subject breaks from the dramas that she engages in (via Turner) as well as from the inner drama that has shaped her subjective formation (Anzaldúa, 2002). In other words, revolutionary social drama, as a form of social inquiry and action, takes place in the overlapping spheres of self and institutional dramas. My own effort as a critical educator-ethnographer—activist in the writing of the social drama of Mirasur has been to facilitate the disruption of conventional understandings of the school and community relationship and its, and structures and relations of governance, in an effort to develop a more nuanced understanding of the social world and way to transform it. In the writing of this text, nothing stood benign or outside the realm of critique: not the nation, state, culture, religion, family, or community. My understanding and analysis of immigration and the challenge to education were intrinsically scripted by my own positioning as a child of immigrants. Growing up, I had the opportunity to live—in many ways—between cultures and nations. I never felt fully anchored in any one place, nor did I give allegiance to any one particular nation. This detachment enables me to move across borders more fluidly, but it also occasions me to peer more deeply into the reasoning behind others' actions. Jimenez and the actors in the social drama of Mirasur revealed to me different perceptions of the social totality; they demonstrated truth in other ways of looking at the world. I have tried to demonstrate through the open veins of this

Figure 6.1   Future pathways, photograph courtesy of Carmen Jimenez.

analysis my respect for Jimenez and las madres' own truth and not my efforts to absorb it into my own. On the notion of "truth," Philip Kain (2005) writes,

> We want the other to remain other for itself, with its own integrity, dignity, and access to the truth. And we want this for ourselves. I am not suggesting that the value of this other truth is simply the use it has for us. I do not want to set up yet another hierarchy with our culture at the top. I am suggesting that other cultures, because they have access to truth, are ends in themselves...

These "truths" materialize when we attempt to recuperate those aspects that have denied our full presence in the social world. Truth emerges from within and moves outward; the object of truth is not to reproduce existing hierarchies, but to dismantle them and to put in motion new forms of generating and producing knowledge for the betterment of the self and society. Jimenez words are apposite:

> *Si yo hubiera tenido la oportunidad de hacer algo con mi vida, yo me hubiera visto como politica. Como una persona siguendo, si hubiera, se*

da cuenta del poder de la palabra: hubiera. Hubiera estado yo a la par de César Chávez me hubiera visto luchando con el. Pues a mi me hubiera gustado ser como César Chávez, Martin Luther King, Madre Teresa de Calcutta, o como Rigoberta Menchú. A lo mejor no hubiera hecho nada porque ese el problema, de lideres esta lleno el cemeterio. Y sus causas han quedo perdidas como los heroes de Mexico, Benito Juárez, Miguel Hidalgo. Los años pasan y sigue el racismo, la exclavitud, sigue el abuso. Que ha pasado con su causa. If I would have had the opportunity to do something with my life, I would have seen myself like a politician. As a person whowould have had, see the power of the phrase, "if I would have." I would have been next to César Chávez, I would have seen myself struggling with him. Well, I would have liked to be like César Chávez, Martin Luther King, Mother Teresa of Calcutta, Rigoberta Menchú. Or maybe I wouldn't have done anything because that is the problem, the cemetery is full of leaders. And their cause has been lost, like the heroes of Mexico, Benito Juárez and Miguel Hidalgo. Years pass and racism continues, slavery and abuse continue. What has happened with their cause?

Jimenez and I speak often about our desire to continue on a path of change and transcendence. We are often overcome by pessimism about the possibility of change, but we always hold out a sense of hope for the future. We may feel doubt when we recall the lessons that history has taught us, but we remain committed to working for the betterment of our community. We ask ourselves why so many struggles for justice have been forgotten and why certain efforts have brought about their opposite results. As we pursue answers to such questions, we begin to travel into different spaces and places—those that reside in our imagination, in our memory, and in our historical repertoires. We never know where a conversation, an idea, or an effort to alter and transcend the oppressive relations and practices that we confront day in and day out will take us. Spaces of change are always in transition. We too are in transition, like shape-shifters moving from one crevice to another and trying to maintain the energy that keeps us in movement. We have been a source of energy for each other over the past several years, but we know we are on different life courses and that we will always occupy distant geographical spaces. Jimenez tells me that everything will end, and that we will no longer work together. I tell her no, that it is not true. As I write this closing paragraph I feel an unlimited connection with Jimenez and with the work that has circumscribed my identity—my philosophy of praxis—as a researcher, scholar, and activist over the years. Perhaps I feel this way because I see *our* revolutionary social drama, *our* drama from below, as one without an ending. Revolutionary social drama is in dialectical motion with the overarching drama of society. In fact, if a revolutionary social drama arrives at an endpoint, then it ceases to be revolutionary. It will then have become a different type of drama: maybe liberating, maybe oppressive, or maybe somewhere in-between.

NOTES

PRELIMS

1. The National Conference of State Legislatures reports that 1538 immigration bills were introduced in 50 states and Puerto Rico during the first quarter of 2011. This is an increase from the 1180 introduced during the same period in 2010. In addition, the National Conference reports that a majority of immigration bills in state legislatures deal with questions of employment, identification, and law enforcement. Since the health reform act, health has also emerged as a top contender of immigration reform. In addition, copycat bills of Arizona's SB1070 that have passed in 2010–2011 include Utah's HB497, Georgia's HB87, and Indiana's SB590. Alabama's house has passed HB56, which would make it a crime for undocumented persons to live in Alabama. HB56's sponsor, Representative Micky Hammon, upheld it as attacking "every aspect of an illegal alien's life." Hammon further declared, "This bill is designed to make it difficult for them to live here so they will deport themselves" (as cited in Chandler, K. (2011), *The Birmingham News*, April 5). According to the National Conference of State Legislatures, more immigration bills are expected to be introduced. A majority of these bills are being spearheaded by the anti-immigrant extremist, Kris Kobach, a constitutional lawyer and Kansas' secretary of state.

2. I discuss kyriarchal reason in greater length in chapter 4. Simply stated, it refers to the rule of the master as opposed to the rule of the father (patriarchy).

3. Roxanne Doty defines societal security as "a group's concern about threats to their identity and survival as an entity."

4. In 2011, similar reports of detainee abuse on the U.S. side of the border have emerged. According to a report released by the Arizona organization No More Deaths, between fall 2008 and spring 2011, 30,000 incidents of human rights abuses against undocumented immigrants were reported (Fernández, 2011). Many of these incidents, as defined by the United Nations Convention against Torture, classify as human torture. They include "threatening detainees with death while in custody, and verbal and physical abuse" (Fernández, 2011).

5. On a related note, it is also worth mentioning that Arizona is currently under federal investigation for possible civil rights violation for the State Department of Education's "accent police" (Lacey, 2011). For almost

a decade, Arizona has sent state-authorized monitors to classrooms to check on non-native English-speaking-teachers' articulation.

6. For further discussion of the link between nativism and racism, see Galindo, R. and Vigil, J. (2006), "Are anti-immigrant statements racist or nativist? What difference does it make?" *Latino Studies*, 4: 419–447.

7. In 2011, an independent watchdog group released a report indicating that no evidence was found to demonstrate that Ruben Salazar was intentionally targeted. Lopez, R. (2011), "No Evidence Ruben Salazar was Targeted in Killing, Report Say," *Los Angeles Times*, February 19.

1   SETTING THE STAGE: THE SCHOOL-COMMUNITY BORDERLAND

1. The idea of a pedagogical unconscious is not meant to signal a Lacanian psychoanalytic turn in addressing the teacher-student, administration-teacher, or faculty-community relationship. Rather, I am apprised here of Richard Lichtman's classic work, *The Production of Desire* (1982), in which he discusses how the bourgeois worldview conflates individuals with individualism. Each individual, as noted by Lichtman, is "an experiencing nodule or terminus of the ensemble of relations that constitutes the social system" (220). Individualism, on the contrary, is a by-product of capitalist society that claims that individual self-realization can be achieved outside of society. The salient point here is that the educational encounter appears and is often treated as a practice in support of individualism—each individual can realize his/her potential outside of society's constraints vis-à-vis curriculum delivery, etc. The pedagogical unconscious references the ways in which individuals—understood as sensuous human beings who embody social relations in society—constitute and are constituted by educational interactions, aspirations, etc., in a dialectical engagement.

2   THE PEDAGOGY OF THE BURRO

1. Special thanks to Alicia Gaspar de Alba for suggesting the pedagogy of the burro as a subtitle.

4   INNER THEATER: SOCIAL DRAMA AS SHIFTING CONSCIOUSNESS

1. Here I am especially grateful for the insights presented in Walter Benjamin's article, "The Storyteller." Benjamin, W. (1968). *Illuminations*. New York: Harcourt Brace and World.

2. Aquino citing the work of Elisabethe Schussler Fiorenza (2001), in which she defines kyriarchy as a "socio-political system of domination in which elite educated propertied men hold power over wo/men and other men."

5   ANTISTRUCTURE: COUNTERPOINTS TO PEDAGOGY OF THE BURRO

1. Communitas can also occur in moments of extreme violence. In a recent interview with James Zwerg, the famous Freedom Rider whose beaten face shocked the nation in the 1960s when he and others were attacked by a mob at the bus station in Alabama, Zwerg describes feelings that come close to what Turner describes as communitas. As noted in John Blake's book, *Children of the Movement* (2004): In the midst of the savagery, Zwerg says he had the most beautiful experience in his life. "I bowed my head," he says. "I asked God to give me the strength to remain nonviolent and to forgive the people for what they might do. It was very brief, but in that instant, I felt an overwhelming presence. I don't know how else to describe it. A peace came over me. I knew that no matter what happened to me, it was going to be OK. Whether I lived or whether I died, I felt this incredible calm." This peace was coupled with what Zwerg described as the bond of strength that he shared with other Freedom Riders during this time. Blake further documents: "He never found the bond he experienced with the other Freedom Riders. 'Each of us was stronger because of those we were with,'" he says. "If I was being beaten, I knew I wasn't alone. I could endure more because I knew everybody there was giving me their strength. Even as someone else was being beaten, I would give them my strength." Those bonds across social difference (Zwerg as a white man participating in a black struggle) that seemingly suspend social norms and roles are what Turner referred to in communitas.

2. Bateson defined metacommunication as taking place when "the subject of discourse is the relationship between speakers" (1972). Put simply, it refers to communication about communication, those cues and elements that are exchanged in the act of communication. Such cues, according to Bateson, are largely dependent on the relationship between speakers and listeners. It is the framing and signaling that take place within and beyond language.

6   REVOLUTIONARY SOCIAL DRAMA: DECOLONIAL PEDAGOGICAL PROCESSES

1. Maese-Cohen's article, "Toward Planetary Decolonial Feminism," offers a series of critiques to Quijano's conception of the coloniality of power that provides various important theoretical insights into the coloniality of power from a decolonial feminist perspective.

2. Here I am appreciative of the insights offered by Luis Antonio Bigott (2010) *El Educador Neocolonizado*. Caracas, Venezuela: Fondo Editorial Ipasme.

BIBLIOGRAPHY

Aljoe, N. (2004). "Caribbean Slave Narratives: Creole in Form and Genre." *Anthurium* 2(1). Found at: http://scholar.library.miami.edu /anthurium.

Althusser, L. (1969). *For Marx.* Ben Brewster, trans. London: Penguin Books.

Alvarez, R. (1986). "The Lemon Grove Incident." *San Diego Historical Society Quarterly* 32(2) (Spring).

Alvarez, R. (1995). "The Mexican-US Border: The Making of an Anthropology of Borderlands." *Annual Review of Anthropology* 24: 447–470.

Anzaldúa, G. (1983). Foreword to the 2nd edition. *This Bridge Called My Back.* Cherríe Moraga and Gloria Anzaldúa (eds.). New York: Kitchen Table, Women of Color Press.

Anzaldúa, G. (1987). *Borderlands.* San Francisco: Aunt Lute Books.

Anzaldúa, G. (1990). "Haciendo Caras, una entrada." In G. Anzaldúa (ed.), *Making Face, Making Soul.* San Francisco: Aunt Lute Books. xv–xxvii.

Anzaldúa, G. (2001). "La prieta." In G. Anzaldúa and C. Moraga (eds.), *This Bridge Called My Back.* San Francisco: Third Women Press.

Anzaldúa, G. (2002). "Now Let Us Shift . . . the Path of conocimiento . . . Inner Work, Public Acts." In G. Anzaldúa and A. Keating (eds.), *This Bridge We Call Home.* New York: Routledge. 540–578.

Anzaldúa, G. (2009). Transforming American Studies, 2001 Bode-Pearson Acceptance Speech. In Ana Louise Keating (ed), *The Gloria Anzaldúa Reader.* Durham: Duke University Press. 239–241.

Aquino, M. P. (2007). "Feminist Intercultural Theology, Toward a Shared Future of Justice." In Maria Pilar Aquino and Maria José Rosado-Nunes (eds.), *Feminist Intercultural Theology.* Maryknoll, New York: Orbis Books. 9–28.

Arendt, H. (1954). *Between Past and Future.* New York: Penguin Books.

Arendt, H. (1958). *The Human Condition.* 2nd edition. Chicago: University of Chicago Press.

Avant-Mier and Hasian, M. (2008). "Communicating 'truth': Testimonio, Vernacular Voices, and the Rigoberta Menchú Controversy." *The Communication Review* 11: 323–345.

Banks, J. (2004). "Teaching for Social Justice, Diversity and Citizenship in a Global World." *Educational Forum* 68: 289–298.

Barad, K. (2007). *Meeting the Universe Halfway*. Durham and London: Duke University Press.

Bateson, G. (1972). *Steps to an Ecology of Mind*. New York: Balantine.

Bell, E. (2006). "Social Dramas and Cultural Performances: All the President's Women." *Liminalities* 2(1).

Berezin, M. (2009). *Illiberal Politics in Neoliberal Times: Culture, Security and Populism in the New Europe*. New York: Cambridge University Press.

Beverley, J. (2004). *Testimonio*. Minneapolis: University of Minnesota Press.

Bickford, S. (1997). "Anti-identity Politics." *Hypatia* 12(4): 111–131.

Blake, J. (2004). *Children of the Movement*. Chicago: Lawrence Hill Books.

Blake, J. (2011). "Are Whites Racially Oppressed? Editorial." *CNN* (March 4). Found at http://edition.cnn.com/2010/US/12/21/white.persecution /index.html.

Bledsoe, C. (2004). "Reproduction at the Margins: Migration and Legitimacy in the New Europe." *Demographic Research*. Special Collection 3(4): 87–116.

Boje, D. (2003). "Victor Turner's Postmodern Theory of Social Drama: Implications for Organization Studies." Found at http://business.nmsu .edu/~dboje/theatrics/7/victor_turner.htm.

Bonfil-Batalla, G. (1996). *Mexico Profundo*. Austin: University of Texas Press.

Bourdieu, P. (1989). "Social Space and Symbolic Power." *Sociological Theory* 7(1): 14–25.

Brandes, S. (1984). "Animal Metaphors and Social Control in Tzintzuntzan." *Ethnology* 23: 207–215.

Bruner, J. (1991). "The Narrative Construction of Reality." *Critical Inquiry* 18 (Autumn).

Bullock, P. (2010). "Arms Merchants of South Central." *LA Weekly* 32(37).

Butler, J. (1993). *Bodies That Matter: On the Discursive Limits of Sex*. New York: Routledge.

Chang, H. (1985a). "Dialectics of Racial Categories." In P. Liem and Montagure, E. (eds.), *Towards a Marxist Theory of Racism: Two Essays by Harry Chang. Review of Radical Political Economics* 17(3): 34–45.

Chang, H. (1985b). "Race and Class." In P. Liem and Montagure, E. (eds.), *Towards a Marxist Theory of Racism: Two Essays by Harry Chang. Review of Radical Political Economics* 17(3): 34–45.

Da Silva, T. and McLaren, P. (1993). "Knowledge Under Siege: The Brazilian Debate." In Peter McLaren and Peter Leonard (eds), *Paulo Freire, A Critical Encounter*. New York: Routledge.

DeLissovoy, N. (2005). "Oppression, Liberation and Education: Problems and Possibilities in Social Justice Approaches to Pedagogy and Curriculum." Doctoral dissertation, University of California Los Angeles.

Deloria, V. (1991). "Foreword." In P. Nabokov (Author), *Native American Testimony*. New York: Penguin Books. xvii–xix.

Detention Watch Network. (2011). "The Influence of the Private Prison Industry in Immigration Detention. A report by Detention Watch Network." Found at: http://www.detentionwatchnetwork.org /privateprisons

Dorsey, J. (1996). "Women Without History: Slavery, Jurisprudence, and the International Politics of partus sequitur ventrem in the Spanish Caribbean." *Journal of Caribbean History* 28(2).

Doty, R. (2010). "The Anti-Immigrant Movement and the Politics of Exceptionalism." *Perspectives*, The Immigration Policy Center.

Dussel, E. (1985). *Philosophy of Liberation*. New York: Orbis Books.

Dussel, E. (1995). *Invention of the Americas*. Michel D. Barber (trans.). New York: Continuum.

Dwyer, D. (2011). "Decline in U.S. Illegal Immigrant Population Stalls, Study Finds." ABCnews. February, 1.

Ebert, T. (2009). *The Task of Cultural Critique*. Chicago: University of Illinois Press.

Eckenwiler, L. (2001). "Moral Reasoning and the Review of Research Involving Human Subjects." *Kennedy Institute of Ethics Journal* 11(1): 37–69.

Eyerman, R. (2008). *The Assassination of Theo Van Gogh*. Durham: Duke University Press.

Fanon, F. (1967). *Black Skin, White Masks*. New York: Grove Press.

Felman, S. and Laub, D. (1992). *Testimony*. New York: Routledge.

Fernández, V. (2011). "Report: Border Patrol Abuses on the Rise." *Truthout*, (September 24).

Foucault, M. (1980). *Power/Knowledge: Selected Interviews and Other Writings 1972–1977*. New York: Pantheon Books.

Freire, P. (1998). *Pedagogy of the Oppressed*. M. B. Ramos (trans.). New York: Continuum.

Freire, P. (2005). *Teachers as Cultural Workers*. Boulder, CO: Westview Press.

Freire, P. (2008). *Education for Critical Consciousness*. New York: Continuum.

Freire, P. and Macedo, D. (1987). *Reading the Word and the World*. Massachusetts: Bergin & Garvey Publishers.

Geiger, S. (1986). "Women's Life Histories: Method and Content." *Signs: Journal of Women in Culture and Society* 11(2): 334–351.

Giroux, H. (2005). *Border Crossings*. 2nd edition. New York: Routledge.

Goffman, E. (1959). *The Presentation of Self in Everyday Life*. New York: Doubleday Anchor Books.

Gonzalez, M. (2004). "Postmodernism, Historical Materialism and Chicana/o Cultural Studies." *Science and Society* 68(2): 161–186.

Gordon, L. (2008). "Not Always Enslaved, Yet Not Quite Free: Philosophical Challenges from the Underside of the New World." *Philosophia* 36(2): 151–166.

Grosfoguel, R. (2008). "Decolonizing Political Economy and Post-colonial Studies: Transmodernity, Border Thinking, and Global Community." Eurozine. Found at: http://www.eurozine.com/articles/2008-07-04 -grosfoguel-en.html

Gross, A. (2007). "The Caucasian Cloak: Mexican Americans and the Politics of Whiteness in the Twentieth-Century Southwest." *Georgetown Law Journal* 95(2): 337–392.

Guillaumin, C. (1995). *Racism, Sexism, Power and Ideology.* New York: Routledge.

Habermas, J. (1992). *The Theory of Communicative Action: Reason and the Rationalization of Society.* Boston: Beacon Press.

Haraway, D. (1988). "Situated Knowledges: The Science Question in Feminism and the Privilege of Partial Perspective." *Feminist Studies,* 14(3): 575–599.

Harding, S. (2004). "Rethinking Standpoint Epistemology: What is 'Strong Objectivity'?" In S. Harding (ed.), *The Feminist Standpoint Reader.* New York: Routledge.

Hartsock, N. (2004). "The Feminist Standpoint: Developing the Ground for a Specifically Feminist Historical Materialism." In S. Harding (ed.), *The Feminist Standpoint Reader.* New York: Routledge.

Harvey, D. (1989). *The Urban Experience.* Baltimore: Johns Hopkins University Press.

Hernandez, K. L. (2006). "The Crimes and Consequences of Illegal Immigration: A Cross-Border Examination of Operation Wetback, 1943–1954." *The Western Historical Quarterly* 37(40): 421–444.

Hill Collins, P. (1999). "Reflections on the Outsider Within." *Journal of Career Development* 26(1): 85–88.

Hise, G. (2004). "Border City: Race and Social Distance in Los Angeles." *American Quarterly* 56(3): 545–558.

Holloway, J. (2010). *Crack Capitalism.* New York: Pluto Press.

hooks, bell. (1994). *Teaching to Transgress: Education as the Practice of Freedom.* New York: Routledge.

Huang, P. (2010). "Anchor Babies, Over-Breeders, and the Population Bomb: The Reemergence of Nativism and Population Control in Anti-Immigration Policies." *Harvard Law and Policy Review* (2): 385–406.

Jacoby, K. (2008). "The Broad Platform of Extermination: Nature and Violence in the Nineteenth Century North American Borderlands." *Journal of Genocide Research* 10(2): 249–267.

Joyce, S. (2001). "The Creation of Bent Knowledge: How Lesbian, Gay, and Bisexual Youth Negotiate and Reconfigure Homophobic and Heterosexist Discourse." *Information Research* 6(2).

Kane, N. (2007). "Frantz Fanon's Theory of Racialization." *Human Architecture: Journal of the Sociology of Self-Knowledge*, v, (Summer): 353–362.

Keating, A. (2006). "From Borderlands and New Mestizas to Nepantla and Nepantleras: Anzaldúan Theories for Social Change." *Human Architecture*, iv (Summer): 5–16.

Kirmayer, L. (1993). "Healing and the Invention of Metaphor: The Effectiveness of Symbols Revisited." *Culture, Medicine and Psychiatry*, 17: 161–195.

Kosík, K. (1976). *Dialectics of the Concrete: A Study on Problems of Man and World*. Boston Studies in the Philosophy of Science. New York: Springer.

Kozol, J. (1991). *Savage Inequalities*. New York: Harper Press.

Lacey, M. (2011). "In Arizona, Complaints That an Accent Can Hinder a Teacher's Career." *Truthout*, (September 25).

Lebowitz, M. A. (2005). "The Knowledge of a Better World." *Monthly Review* 57(3): 62–69.

Leiman, M. (2007). "DeSaussere's and Bakhtin's Semiotic Conceptions." Paper. Found at http://evans-experientialism.freewebspace.com/leiman.htm.

León-Portilla, M. (1963). *Aztec Thought and Culture: A Study of the Ancient Náhuatl Mind*. Jack Emory Davis (trans.) Norman: University of Oklahoma Press.

Levine, A. (2005). "Champion of the Spirit: Anzaldúa's Critique of Rationalist Epistemology." In A. Keating (ed.), *EntreMundos/Among Worlds: New Perspectives on Gloria Anzaldúa*. New York: Palgrave Macmillan.

Lichtman, R. (1982). *The Production of Desire*. New York: The Free Press.

Lipsett-Rivera, S. (1998). "De obra y palabra: Patterns of Insults in Mexico, 1750–1886." *The Americas* 54(4): 511–539.

Lipsitz, G. (1990). *Time Passages*. Minneapolis: University of Minnesota Press.

Lugones, M. (2005). "From Within Germinative Stasis: Creating Active Subjectivity, Resistant Agency." In Ana Louise Keating (ed.), *Entre Mundos/Among Worlds*. New York: Palgrave-MacMillan.

Lyons, J. (2007). "In Mexico, Wal-mart is Defying Its Critics." *Wall Street Journal*, March 5.

Machado, D. (2007). "Voices from Nepantla, Latinas in U.S. Religious History." In Maria Pilar Aquino and Maria José Rosado-Nunes (eds.), *Feminist Intercultural Theology*. Maryknoll, New York: Orbis Books. 89–108.

Maese-Cohen, M. (2009). "Toward Planetary Decolonial Femisms." *Qui Parle* 18 (2):3–27.

Maldonado-Torres, N. (2007). "On the Coloniality of Being." *Cultural Studies* 21(2–3): 240–270.

Martinot, S. (2010). "The Duality of Class Systems in US Capitalism." Manuscript. Found at: http://www.ocf.berkeley.edu/~marto/ClassDuality.htm

McGreal, C. (2010). "Republicans Move to Block US Citizenship for Children of Illegal Aliens." *The Guardian*, August 3.

McLaren, P. (1982). *Schooling as a Ritual Performance*. London: Routledge.

McLaren, P. (1995). *Critical Pedagogy and Predatory Culture*. New York: Routledge.

McLaren, P. (2000). *Che Guevara, Paulo Freire and the Pedagogy of Revolution*. New York: Rowman and Littlefield.

McLaren, P. and Cruz, C. (2005). "Queer Bodies and Configurations: Toward a Critical Pedagogy of the Body." In P. McLaren (ed.), *Red Seminars*. Crasskill, NJ: Hampton Press.

McLaren, P. and Pinkey-Pastrana, J. (2005). "The Search for the Complicit Native: Epistemic Violence, Historical Amnesia, and the Anthropologist as Ideologue." In P. McLaren (ed.), *Red Seminars*. Crasskill, NJ: Hampton Press.

Medina, J. (2011). "Arriving as Pregnant Tourists, Leaving With American Babies." *The New York Times*. March, 28.

Medrano, L. (2010). "Ethnic Studies Classes Illegal in Arizona Public Schools as of Jan. 1." *The Christian Science Monitor*, December 31.

Memmi, A. (2005). *Decolonization and the Decolonized*. Minneapolis: University of Minnesota Press.

Mignolo, W. (2005). "Prophets Facing Sidewise: The Geopolitics of Knowledge and the Colonial Difference." *Social Epistemology* 19(1): 111–122.

Mora, P. (2008). *Nepantla: Essays from the Land in the Middle*, 2nd edition. Albuquerque: University of New Mexico Press.

Moraga, C. (2000). *Loving in the War Years*. Cambridge: South End Press.

Newton, J. (2007). "Realist with Passion." *Los Angeles Times*, August 19.

Nolacea-Harris, A. (2005). "La Malinche and Post-Movement Feminism." In R. Romero and A. Nolacea-Harris (eds.), *Feminism, Nation and Myth: La Malinche*. Houston: Arte Público Press.

Ollman, B. (2006). "A Model of Activist Research: How to Study Class Consciousness and Why We Should." Retrieved from http://www.nyu.edu/projects/ollman/docs/class_consciousness.php.

Pease, D. (2001). "Border Laws/Frontera Justice: Orson Welles's Touch of Evil Working Papers in Cultural Studies Department of Comparative American Cultures." Washington State University Pullman, Washington.

Prakash, K. (2010). "Notes Towards a Definition of Resistance." *The Hobgoblin*. Found at: http://www.thehobgoblin.co.uk/2010_prakash_kona.htm

Pratt, M. L. (1999). "Arts of the Contact Zone." In D. Bartholomae and A. Petroksky (eds.), *Ways of Reading*, 5th edition. New York: Bedford/St. Martin's.

Prince, G. (1982). *Narratology: The Form and Functioning of Narrative*. New York: Mouston.

Quijano, A. (2000). "Coloniality of Power, Ethnocentrism, and Latin America." *Nepantla* 1(3): 533–580.

Rancière, J. (2010). "Racism, a Top-Down Passion." *Truthout*. Found at http://www.archive.truthout.org:81/racism-a-top-down-passion64392.

Reuman, A. and Anzaldúa, G. (2000). "Coming Into Play: An Interview with Gloria Anzaldúa." *MELUS*, 25 (2): 3–45.

Ridgeway, J. (2011). "The Threat of America's Nativist Far Right." *The Guardian*, March 24, www. Guardian.co.uk.

Robbins, T. (2011). "A Year Later, Arizona Still Split Over Immigration." National Public Radio. Found at: http://www.npr.org/2011/04/20/135574803/arizonas-strict-immigration-law-one-year-later.

Rosaldo, R. (1993). *Culture and Truth*. Boston: Beacon Press.

Saldivar, J. D. (1997). *Border Matters: Remapping American Cultural Studies*. Berkeley: University of California Press.

Sanchez, G. (1993). *Becoming Mexican American*. New York: Oxford University Press.

Sanchez, G. (1997). "Face the Nation: Immigration and the Rise of Nativism in Late Twentieth Century America." *International Migration Review* 31(4): 1009–1030.

San Juan, E. (2006). "Ethnic Identity and Popular Sovereignty: Notes on the Moro Struggle in the Philippines." *Ethnicities* 6(3): 391–422.

Scatamburlo-D'Annibale, V., Suoranta, J., McLaren, P., and Jaramillo, N. (2005). "Farewell to the 'Bewildered Herd': Paulo Freire's Revolutionary Dialogical Communication in the Age of Corporate Globalization." *Journal for Critical Education Policy Studies* 4(2). Found at http://www.jceps.com/?pageID=article&articleID=65.

Schulman, D. (2010). "Rep. Louie Gohmert's Terror Baby Meltdown." *Mother Jones*, August 13. Found at http://www.motherjones.com/mojo/2010/08/rep-louie-gohmerts-terror-baby-meltdown.

Schweninger, L. (2009). "Slave Women, County Courts and the Law in the United States South: A Comparative Perspective." *European Review of History* 16(3): 383–399.

Segura, L. (2010). "Tourists Seek Out Mexico's Darker Side." *Reuters*. August, 24.

Shor, I. and Freire, P. (1987). *A Pedagogy for Liberation: Dialogues on Transforming Education*. Massachusetts: Bergin and Garvey.

Smith, D. (1974). "Women's Perspective as a Radical Critique of Sociology." *Sociological Inquiry* 44: 1–13.

Spivak, G. (1998). "Can the Subaltern Speak?" In C. Nelson and L. Grossberg (eds.), *Marxism and the Interpretation of Culture*. Chicago: University of Illinois Press.

Stephens, G. (2008). "Interpenetration in the Borderlands: Recovering Memory and Rewriting Scripts in Fuentes' Old Gringo." *Journal of Borderland Studies* 1(1), (Spring).

Stetsenko, A. (2008). "Collaboration and Cogenerativity: On Bridging the Gaps Separating Theory-Practice and Cognition-Emotion." *Cultural Studies of Science Education* 3: 521–533.

Stoll, D. (1999). *Rigoberta Menchú and the Story of All Poor Guatemalans.* Boulder, CO: Westview Press.

St. John, G. (2008). *Victor Turner and Contemporary Cultural Performance. An Introduction.* New York: Berghahn Books.

Su, R. (2010). "The Overlooked Significance of Arizona's New Immigration Law108." *Michigan Law Review First Impressions*, 76. Found at http://www.michiganlawreview.org/assets/fi/108/su.pdf.

Turner, V. (1967). *The Ritual Process: Structure and Anti-Structure.* Chicago: Aldine.

Turner, V. (1974). *Dramas, Fields, and Metaphors: Symbolic Action in Human Society.* Ithaca/London: Cornell University Press.

Turner, V. (1977). *Performance in Postmodern Culture.* Madison, WI: Cota Press.

Turner, V. (1980). "Social dramas and stories about them." *Critical Inquiry* 7: 141–168.

Turner, V. (1986). *On the Edge of the Bush: Anthropology as Experience.* Phoenix: University of Arizona Press.

Turner, V. (1987). *The Anthropology of Performance.* New York: PAJ Publications.

Varela, F., Thompson, E., and Rosch, E. (1993). *The Embodied Mind.* Cambridge, MA: The MIT Press.

Varsanyi, M. (2010). "Neoliberalism and Nativism: Local Anti-Immigrant Policy Activism and an Emerging Politics of Scale." *International Journal of Urban and Regional Research* 35(2): 295–311.

Vedral, V. (2011). "Living in a Quantum World." *Scientific American*, (June): 38–47.

Villenas, S. (2005). "Latina Literacies in Convivencia: Communal Spaces of Teaching and Learning." *Anthropology and Education Quarterly* 36(3): 273–277.

Volosinov, V. N. (1973). *Marxism and the Philosophy of Language.* Cambridge, MA: Harvard University Press.

White, H. (1981). "The Narrativization of Real Events." *Critical Inquiry* 7(4): 793–798.

Williams, R. (1977). *Marxism and Literature, Marxist Introductions Series.* London and New York: Oxford University Press.

Wilson, T. D. (2008). "Research Note: Issues of Production vs. Reproduction/Maintenance Revisited: Towards an Understanding of Arizona's Immigration Policies." *Anthropological Quarterly* 81(3) (Summer): 713–718.

Woo, E. (2009). "Marian Wagstaff Dies at 97; Teacher Integrated Compton School's Faculty in 1940s." *Los Angeles Times*, May 24.

Wright, M. (2009). "Justice and the Geographies of Moral Protest: Reflections from Mexico." *Environment and Planning D: Society and Space*, 27: 216–233.

Wynter, S. (2003). "Unsettling the Coloniality of Being/Power/Truth/Freedom: Towards the Human, After Man, Its Overrepresentation." *The New Centennial Review* 3(3), (Fall): 257–337.

Zavarzadeh, Mas'ud. (2003). "The Pedagogy of Totality." *Journal of Advanced Composition* 23(1): 1–52.

Index

actors in social drama, 21, 44, 57, 69, 72–3, 101, 117–18, 127, 132–3, 136
Afghanistan, xvii
alliance work, 100
Althusser, Louis, 118
"anchor babies," xv–xvii
antistructure, 43, 45, 55, 97–101, 116
Anzaldúa, Gloria, xxvii–xxviii, xxx, 12, 43–6, 63–4, 66–8, 97–8, 100, 118, 125–8, 130, 136–7
Aquino, Maria Pilar, 95, 144n2
Arpaio, Joe, xxii
Aubry, Larry, xxv
autocannibalism, 97–8

baby boomlet, xvii
Bakhtin, M., 88
Banks, James, xx
Barad, Karen, 90
Bateson, Gregory, 100, 145n2
Bell, Elizabeth, 39
Benjamin, Walter, 144n1
Bigott, Luis Antonio, 145n2
binary oppositions, 44, 93, 98
Blake, John, 145n1
Boje, D., 38
Bonfil-Batalla, Guillermo, 85
Borderlands (Anzaldúa), 12
Botach Tactical, 6
Bracero program, xix, 7
Brown v. Board of Education, xxv
burro, pedagogy of the, 31–2, 37–45, 57, 69, 98–101, 116, 119, 124
Butler, Judith, 90, 125

Catholic Church, 41
Chavez, Cesar, xxv, 105, 114, 141
childcare, 23–5, 32, 70–1

Children of the Movement (Blake), 145n1
class consciousness, 94–5
Coatlicue, 66, 137
coloniality of power, 27, 92, 128–33, 139, 145n1. *See also* neocoloniality
communitas, 97–101, 117, 145n1
concretization, 136
conscientization, 42, 134–7
consciousness, stages of, 66–7
Cortés, Hernán, 8
cultural racism, 9
cultural workers, 66, 135–6, 139

decolonial pedagogy, 128–39
Delay, Tom, xvii
Demme, Jonathan, xvi
detainee abuse, xix, 144n6
dominance, 38, 118–19, 124
donkey. *see* burro, pedagogy of the
Doty, Roxanne, xviii, 143n3
Duran, Fray Diego, xxviii

Ebert, Teresa, 82
enfleshment, 89, 95
entanglement, 116, 128–33
ethnic revitalization, xx
Eurocentrism, 44, 128–9
"Euroskepticism," xx–xxi
Eyerman, Ron, xiii, 39

Felman, S., 67, 68
Frankenheimer, John, xvi
Freedom Riders, 145n1
Freire, Paulo, 131, 134–9
Fuentes, Carlos, 12

Gigante, Inc., 7
Gohmert, Louie, xvi

Gordon, Lewis, xiii
Great Depression, 9
Gringo Viejo (Fuentes), 12
Grosfoguel, Ramon, 128–9, 131
Gross, Ariel, 8–9

Habermas, J., 77
Hammon, Mickey, 143n1
Haraway, Donna, 81
Hernandez, Kelly, xix
Heston, Charlton, xxiv
Hidalgo, Miguel, 141
hooks, bell, 135
Huang, Priscilla, xvii
Huerta, Dolores, xxv

immigration legislation, xiv–xv,
    8–9, 143n1
inner theater, 79–96, 124
Iraq, xvii, 104

Jacoby, Karl, 41–2
Japanese-American internment, xvi
Juárez, Benito, 114, 141

Kain, Philip, 140
Keating, A., 127
King, Jr., Martin Luther, xxv,
    114, 141
King, Rodney, xii
Kiwanis club, 35–6
knowing, stages of, 66–9
Kobach, Kris, 143n1
Kosik, Karel, 136, 144n1
Kozol, Jonathon, 20–1
kyriarchal reason, 95, 125, 130, 137,
    143n2

La mujer que no valia (A Woman of No
    Worth), 87–8
La mujer sumisa (the submissive
    woman), 60, 66, 68, 83–7, 91–2
Laub, D., 67, 68
Lebowitz, Michael, 126
Lemon Grove incident, 9–10
Levine, Amala, 44
Lichtman, Richard, 144n1
limen, 56
liminoid event, 117–19, 127
looking south, xi–xiii

Machado, Antonio, 126–7
Machado, Daisy, xx
Maese-Cohen, M., 145n1
Malinche, La, 8
Manchurian Candidate, The, xvi
marriage, 92–5
Martinot, Steven, xxiv
Marx, Karl, 64, 126
McLaren, 55, 135
Menchú, Rigoberta, 141
metacommunication, 100, 145n2
Mexico imaginario y Mexico profundo
    (Bonfil-Batalla), 85–6
Mignolo, Walter, xxviii–xxix

narrators, 95–6
nativism, xx–xxiii, 132
neocoloniality, 130–1
nepantla, 43–5, 63, 66–7, 123–7
North American Free Trade Alliance
    (NAFTA), 6

Obama, Barack, xvii, xxii
Operation Wetback, xix–xx

Padres Unidos (Parents United),
    110–12, 121
Parents and Teachers Association
    (PTA), 121
Parks, Rosa, xxv
patriarchy, 63, 69, 79, 83, 94–5, 98,
    125, 130, 137, 143n2
Pease, Donald, xxiv
pedagogical unconscious, 22, 144n1
pedagogy of the burro, 37–45, 57, 69,
    98–101, 116, 119, 124
politics of discomfort, 63
Pratt, Mary Louise, xxix
Production of Desire, The (Lichtman),
    144n1
Proposition 227 (California), xiv–xv
protest of las madres, 47–77

Quijano, Anibal, 128, 145n1

racism, 9, 59, 62, 98, 125,
    128–30, 141
Rancière, Jacques, xxi
rape, 96, 112–15, 117
Reagan, Ronald, xv, 132

Romancing the Stone (film), 8
Ronstadt, Linda, xxii

Salazar, Ruben, xxv, 144n7
Sanchez, George, xx
Savage Inequalities (Kozol), 20–1
SB1070 (Arizona bill), xiv, 143n1
school-community borderland, 11–22, 39, 45, 69, 98, 131
school improvement coordinators, 74–5
Schussler Fiorenza, Elisabeth, 144n2
segregation, 5, 9–10, 56
September 11, 2001, attacks of, xvii
Shakespeare, William: *The Tempest*, xiii
situated knowledges, 81
Sleepy Lagoon case, xxiii
social drama, xi–xiii, xxiv–xxxi
   actors in, 21, 44, 57, 69, 72–3, 101, 117–18, 127, 132–3, 136
   antistructure and, 43, 45, 55, 97–101, 116
   bestialization in, 40–2
   breach stage, 39, 42–3, 47–54, 57–8, 63, 67, 69–75, 124
   crisis stage, 39, 51–8, 124
   four acts of, 39
   liminal phase of, 116
   as meta-theatre, 57
   pedagogy of the burro and, 37–45, 57, 69, 98–101, 116, 119, 124
   redress stage, 39, 52, 57–8, 116, 124
   reflecting on from within, 69-70
   reintegration stage, 39, 58, 117, 124
   revolutionary, 124–42
   vertical, 119

societal security, 143n3
staff development, 32–3
stages of knowing, 66–9
standpoint epistemology, 81
state racism, xxi
St. John, Graham, 99
structural processualism, 99
submission, 64, 91–2. See also *la mujer sumisa* (the submissive woman)

Tea Party movement, xvi
Teresa of Calcutta, Mother, 141
testimony, 67, 68, 96, 136
Title I, 16, 19, 32, 35, 110, 112, 115, 121
torture, 144n6
Touch of Evil, xxiii–xxiv
Treaty of Guadalupe Hidalgo, 7–9
Turner, Victor, xxvii, xxix, 37–47, 52, 56, 72–3, 97, 99–101, 117–18, 124, 127, 139, 145n1

United States Constitution, 14th Amendment to, xvi

Vietnam War, xxv
Villenas, Sofia, 81

Wagstaff, Marian, xxv
Wal-Mart, 7
Watts riots of 1965, 5
Welles, Orson, xxiii–xxiv
Wilson, Pete, xiv–xv
womb-politics, xiv–xx
World War II, xvi, xxiv

Zwerg, James, 145n1